CATHOLIC LABOR PRIESTS

IN THE UNITED STATES:

A 20ᵀᴴ CENTURY STORY OF SOLIDARITY

Volume 1.

Five Giants in the Bishops' Social Action Department

Among More Than 400 U.S. Catholic Labor Priests

Rev. Patrick J. Sullivan, C.S.C.

Pacem in Terris Press Series on Religion & Labor

Produced in Cooperation with
CATHOLIC SCHOLARS FOR WORKER JUSTICE
www.catholicscholarsforworkerjustice.org

PACEM IN TERRIS PRESS
Washington, D.C
www.paceminterris.net

PACEM IN TERRIS PRESS

is the publishing service of

PAX ROMANA

CATHOLIC MOVEMENT FOR INTELLECTUAL & CULTURAL AFFAIRS

USA

Washington DC

ISBN-13: 978-1502709752

ISBN-10: 1502709759

`With gratitude to *The Catholic Worker* for the cover print
"Christ of the Breadlines" by Fritz Eichenberg*

This book is published with gratitude to
REV. THEODORE M. HESBURGH, C.S.C., S.T.D.
President Emeritus of the University of Notre Dame
ever the Growing and Encouraging
Friend and Mentor of Academics and Activists
and Counselor and Confidant of Leaders
in Education, Business, and Politics

About the Author

Rev. Patrick J. Sullivan, C.S.C., is a Catholic labor-priest, a university professor, and member of the Congregation of the Holy Cross. He holds a B.A. in philosophy from the University of Notre Dame, a M.A. in sociology from Fordham University, and a Ph.D. in sociology from the Catholic University of America.

Father Sullivan has served as: Professor of Sociology and an administrator at Kings College in Wilkes-Barre, Pennsylvania; Catholic liaison to the J.P. Stevens union organizing campaign; adjunct professor and associate director of the Higgins Labor Center at the University of Notre Dame; and executive director of the Catholic Labor Guild in the Archdiocese of Boston. He is a currently member of the Steering Committee of Catholic Scholars for Worker Justice.

In addition, Fr. Sullivan has written several earlier books, including *Catholic Church Involvement in Labor–Management Controversies: 1950–1980* and *Catholic Institutions and Labor–Management Relations: 1950–1980*. He has also published articles in *America, Emmanuel, Sojourners,* and *U.S. Catholic.*

This new book by Fr. Sullivan is the first of multiple volumes by him on Catholic Labor priests. Part of Pacem in Terris Press Series on Religion and Labor, the volumes to come are tentatively titled: *Labor Priests and the Unions; Labor Priests, Labor Schools, and Institutes of Industrial Relations; Labor Priests on Economics and Politics;* and *Labor Priests' Vignettes.*

Table of Contents

Glossary

AACD	American Academy of Christian Democracy
ADA	Americans for Democratic Action
ACTU	Association of Catholic Trade Unionists
ACWU	Amalgamated Clothing Workers Union
AFL	American Federation of Labor
ALI	Archdiocesan Labor Institute (Detroit)
APA	American Protestant Association
AWA	Agricultural Workers Association
AWOC	Agricultural Workers Organizing Committee
CCC	Civilian Conservation Corps
CCD	Confraternity of Christian Doctrine
CCIP	Catholic Conference on Industrial Problems
C.P.P.S.	Society of the Precious Blood
CCUM	Catholic Committee on Urban Ministry
CIO	Congress of Industrial Organizations
CORE	Congress of Racial Equality
C.S.C.	Congregation of Holy Cross
C.S.S.R.	Congregation of the Most Holy Redeemer (Redemptorists)
CSU	Conference of Studio Unions
FEPC	Fair employment practices
FLSA	Fair labor standards
FSC	Fellowship of Southern Churchmen
HUAC	House Un-American Activities Committee
IATSE	International Association of Theater and Stage Employees
IIR	Institute for Industrial Relations
ILA	International Longshoremen's Association
ILGWU	International Ladies' Garment Workers Union
ILO	International Labor Organization
ILWU	International Longshore and Warehouse Union
ISO	Institute of Social Order
ISS	Institute of Social Sciences
M.M.	Maryknoll Missionary
NAACP	National Association for the Advancement of Colored People

1

NASAC	National Association of Social Action Conference
NAWU	National Agricultural Workers Union
NCCB	National Conference of Catholic Bishops
NCCC	National Conference of Catholic Charities
NCCM	National Council of Catholic Men
NCCW	National Council of Catholic Women
NCRLC	National Catholic Rural Life Conference
NCSAC	National Catholic Social Action Conference
NCWC	National Catholic Welfare Conference
NFWA	National Farm Workers Association
NIRA	National Industrial Relations Act
NLRA	National Labor Relations Act
NMU	National Maritime Union
NRA	National Recovery Administration
O.F.M. Cap.	Order of Friars Minor Capuchin
O.M.I.	Missionary Oblates of Mary Immaculate
O.P.	Order of Preachers (Dominicans)
O.S.B.	Order of St. Benedict
PAC	Political Action Committee
RLB	Rural Life Bureau
RTW	Right to work
S.J.	Society of Jesus
S.S.	Society of Saint-Sulpice
SAD	Social Action Department
SEIU	Service Employees International Union
SMHA	Southern Mutual Help Association
SODEPAX	Committee on Society, Development and Peace
SWOC	Steel Workers Organizing Committee
TWOC	Textile Workers Organizing Committee
TWU	Transport Workers Union
UAW	United Auto Workers
UFWA	United Farm Workers Association
USCC	U.S. Catholic Conference
WFTU	World Federation of Trade Unions
WPA	Works Progress Administration
YCS	Young Christian Students
YCW	Young Christian Workers

PREFACE

Joseph J. Fahey

Joe Fahey is Co-founder and Chair of Catholic Scholars for Worker Justice.
He is also Professor of Religious Studies and founder of the B.A.
in Labor Studies at Manhattan College.

When Joe Holland, Mary Priniski, O.P. and I founded Catholic Scholars for Worker Justice (CSWJ) in 2008, one of the very first people we invited to join us as a charter-member was Fr. Pat Sullivan, C.S.C.

Pat's teaching and research on labor issues at Notre Dame and King's College were already matters of legend, but he is also a priest and an academic who "walked the walk" and is a labor priest in his own right. He worked with the J.P. Stephens campaign along with another labor priest and CSWJ charter-member, Glenmary Fr. Les Schmidt and Sister Mary.

Throughout his long career Pat never forgot his New York Irish working class roots and has consistently championed working men and women from textile worker to farm worker, and from teacher to civil servant. Pat walked picket lines, challenged employers (including a former Bishop of Scranton!), and fought for the poorest and weakest among us. He still does even now in his 80s.

In one of our first conversations at CSWJ, Pat told Mary, Joe and me about the research he was doing on the hundreds of labor priests during the 20th century. We knew, of course, about the labor priests and the large number of Catholic labor schools that were spread throughout the U.S. from the early part of the twentieth century to today. (Sadly, however, there is only one left, but it is thriving: The Labor Guild of the Archdiocese of Boston.)

This book represents a monumental task and you are about the read the first volume of several in this series that examines this wonderful period in U.S. Catholic Church history. When we learned about Pat's research, we immediately told him that we would like to help him to publish this important work. Catholic Scholars for Worker Justice is now delighted to see this book published as a part of the Pacem in Terris Press's Religion & Labor Series.

You are in for a real treat when you read this book. This is a story of courage, solidarity, and faith. You will meet scholars and activists, parish priests and professors, diocesan priests and members of religious orders (many of them Jesuits). You will find that these men were sometimes unpopular with members of the hierarchy, and some were hated by the employers and capitalists to whom they spoke truth to power. But they always stood with the workers and even, at times, had to be critical of some of labor unions that misrepresented the workers. This is a story of 20th century priestly struggle, of men who left the pulpit and got into the trenches with the workers.

In the movie *On the Waterfront* one of the longshoremen shouts to Karl Malden (who played the real life Fr. Pete Corriden, S.J.), "Go back to your Church, Father." Malden, deep in the hold of a ship and standing over a dead man, replies, "Boys, this is my Church. If you don't think Christ is here on the waterfront, you got another guess coming." Those were labor priest Pete Corriden's actual words.

This book is the story of those priests on the waterfront, at the factories, in the mines, on the farms, and, in the words of Mother Jones, "wherever the worker is in trouble." Fortunately, the labor priests have not left us.

A new generation of labor priests is now being networked and supported by labor priest Fr. Clete Kiley of UNITE/HERE, with assistance from Interfaith Worker Justice and Catholic Scholars for Worker Justice. These new priests – representing now greater ethnic and cultural diversity than before (for example, many are Latinos) – continue the courageous ministry of those on whose shoulders they stand.

Despite the inspiring story of the labor priests, however, we must soberly realize that today there few pro-labor Catholic institutions. Practically all of the Catholic labor schools have vanished, now replaced by Catholic business schools. And the trustees of many Catholic institutions currently oppose unions. The labor priests of the 20th century correctly criticized capitalism for its injustice to workers, but they probably never dreamed that so many Catholic institutions would turn anti-union. If you think this fight is going to go away soon, I have a bridge in Brooklyn that I want to sell you.

For that reason We in Catholic Scholars for Worker Justice believe that one of the best ways to continue the great tradition of the labor priests is to establish academic programs in Labor Studies at our Catholic colleges and universities. Degree granting programs have a way of surviving their founders and of ensuring institutional support for rigorous academic training and scholarly research that will form leaders for the long haul.

So let the inspiration of these priests now motivate all of us, people of faith and of no-faith, to continue the great treasure of Catholic Social Teaching on workers' rights through degree-granting programs that will form professionals to "fight the good fight" begun by the labor priests of the 20th century.

Finally, a word must be said about Fr. Pat himself. "Sully," as he is known to his friends, is one of the nicest, warmest people I know. He is also a feisty "Irishman" who has made an enemy or two because of his relentless pursuit of justice for workers, which is central to his dedication to the Gospel and which remains his singular mission in life.

Sully has a wonderful sense of humor, so be prepared for a joke or two when you meet him. And then watch him grow angry at the injustice done to workers. Listen to him as he tells you a story on one or another worker whom he met on the picket line yesterday, or last year, or thirty years ago. One cannot fail but to be inspired by this great man, this great labor priest.

And now on to Pat's wonderful book!

INTRODUCTION

Across the world, religious leaders of the Abrahamic religions—ministers, priests, and rabbis—have often been and still are involved in labor–management issues.

This study analyzes the persons and activities of Catholic priests, bishops, and Brothers involved with workers and their unions—all referred to here under the category of "labor priests"— within the context of the Roman Catholic Church in the United States, during what might be called the peak years of labor priests. The story begins with Msgr. John A. Ryan (1869–1945), whose 1906 doctoral dissertation, later published as the widely acclaimed book *A Living Wage*, may be taken to mark the beginning of these peak years.

Amid the struggle of workers from the end of the nineteenth century until the 1970s, labor priests were inspired by the challenge of Pope Leo XIII's landmark 1891 social encyclical *Rerum Novarum* (often called the "Magna Carta" of modern Catholic Social Teaching) and by Pius XI's fortieth-anniversary commemoration of the encyclical in his own powerful 1941 social encyclical *Quadragesimo Anno*. These priests were also challenged by the 1919 social statement of the U.S. Catholic bishops and by subsequent pastoral letters.

In addition, they were initially assisted by the Social Action Department (SAD) of what was then called the National Catholic Welfare Conference (NCWC), based in Washington, D.C., and by Catholic colleges and universities in regular contact with the SAD.

These labor priests contributed in many ways to labor–management relations. Some were activists, administrators, arbitrators, mediators, educators, or organizers, often playing many roles. Some worked on their own initiative, while others were agents of national or diocesan agencies. Some were members of college or university Labor Schools and Institutes of Industrial Relations. A few were bishops or religious Brothers, but most were diocesan or religious priests.

Some labor priests assisted union locals or internationals of the American Federation of Labor (AFL) and of the Congress of Industrial Organizations (CIO), later to merge into the AFL–CIO. Some were successful in eliciting cooperation from management, but most experienced little or no success on that front. Some were visible and vocal; some were controversial in their views and activities in relation to Communism and Socialism, as well as in their relationships with church authorities. Yet, whatever their roles, affiliation, ecclesiastical rank, involvements, or effectiveness, all were popularly referred to as labor priests.

Popular opinion has it that there were only a dozen or so labor priests. Recently, however, several scholarly monographs on individual or groups of labor priests have made clear that there were many more.

In this study, as a result of a sixteen-year search (from a base at the University of Notre Dame) of academic, diocesan, and religious community archives throughout the nation, more than 100 well-documented labor priests have been identified, and there are traces of hundreds more.

Appendix II contains the names and locations of 107 labor priests for whom significant information was discovered in this research. Appendix III contains names and locations of an additional 326 labor priests discovered in correspondence or publications as involved in some manner in labor–management issues, but who could not be identified in any detail, despite more than 300 inquiries to diocesan, religious, and college/university archives.

Two questions arise: why the discrepancy in numbers, and why the paucity of information for the larger list? The responses, emerging from this research, include: failure of some labor priests to attach enough significance to their labor involvement to preserve correspondence, memos, notes, sermons, speeches, etc.; discarding of such material by unthinking or unsympathetic archival or local diocesan or religious officials; understandable inadequacies of archival facilities or staffing; and restrictive policies of some dioceses about access to archives out of concern for bad publicity related to some of the controversies in which labor priests were involved. Even so, the overall experience of this researcher has been a gracious welcome and assistance in almost all, save a very few, archives.

Several priests around the turn of the nineteenth century, provided assistance to workers and the growing labor movement, as will be indicated below. Labor priests, however, as a strong part of the social history of the Catholic Church in the United States, really began in earnest shortly after World War I—with the founding of the National Catholic War Council, later renamed the National Catholic Welfare Council (or Conference) (NCWC).

The purpose of this body was to draw all U.S. Catholic Bishops into voluntary consultation on matters of common interest and to provide an organizational framework for the participation of the laity in the national public life of the Church.

In 1966, the NCWC was renamed the U.S. Catholic Conference (USCC), and more recently the National Conference of Catholic Bishops (NCCB). Despite name changes, many of the early departments—for education, legislation, press, publicity, and social action—were carried over into the USCC and USCCB.

9

One important department initially supported the labor priests as a social movement, namely, the Social Action Department (SAD). But it was later reduced, for several reasons, to a one-man operation in the person of the late Msgr. George Higgins, who wore many hats until his retirement in the 1990s.

This research project began in 1996, when a fifty-two–item questionnaire was mailed to archives of all U.S. Catholic archdioceses and dioceses, colleges, and universities, as well as to religious community provinces, in search of any archival material about labor priests. The hope was that there would be ample returns of the questionnaires. Instead, there were only notices that here-and-there that some archival material existed and some opportunities to interview a few surviving labor priests or their acquaintances or protégés.

So, reliance had to be placed almost totally on archival material — biography, correspondence, talks, sermons, newspaper clippings, etc. Some archives were well organized with full-time directors and staffs. Others were staffed by part-time directors who were usually involved in other tasks. Some archives had much material, others had little. Some archival material included texts and media items, but sometimes these were not identified as to sources, dates, persons, locations etc. When several archival sources were available, each was cited as appropriate.

In addition to the archival material, information was gathered from published material in articles, books, dissertations, libraries, newspapers, etc. The gathering of all this data was made feasible thanks to a grant from Notre Dame University's then acting dean of Arts and Letters, Professor Christopher Fox, and thanks to the inspiration and guidance of Professor Daniel Myer, chair of Notre Dame's Department of Sociology.

Data was collected over a period of three years and was then organized into files on each labor priest. The files were all arranged initially in alphabetical order. From each file for each labor priest, "vignettes" were written from items about biography, correspondence, writings by, writings about, and testimonials on the labor
priests.

Where possible, each archival interview and published item has
been footnoted. Yet there is no assumption that all material in archives, interviews, or publications has been exhausted by the vignettes. Neither is there any claim that this work is an exhaustive
presentation of all U.S. labor priests. Indeed, inclusion or exclusion
of specific items from the archives may only reflect the researchers'
own biases and the purposes of the research—making known and
appreciated the activities and attitudes of labor priests.

The completion of this research project will be fully realized with
the appearance of five volumes, of which the first is this one, titled
Labor Priests and the Catholic Church. The second volume is tentatively titled *Labor Priests and Unions;* the third, *Labor Priests and Labor
Schools and Institutes of Industrial Relations;* the fourth, *Labor Priests
on Economic and Politics;* and the fifth, *Labor Priests' Vignettes.*

MSGR. JOHN A. RYAN

First Giant of the Social Action Department

T he first director, and architect, of the Social Action Department was Msgr. John A. Ryan. He was born on May 25, 1869, in Vermillion, Minnesota, and was ordained on June 4, 1898, for the Archdiocese of St. Paul–Minneapolis.[1]

Ryan spent a summer studying economics at the Catholic University of America, which at that time was under the influence of the progressive wing of the U.S. Catholic Church. The leaders of that wing were Cardinal William Gibbons of Baltimore, Bishop John Spalding of Peoria, and Ryan's own ordinary, Archbishop John Ireland.

Ryan was quite pleased when his first assignment as a priest was to study moral theology at Catholic University. There he was influenced by Fr. William Kerby and Fr. Thomas Bouquillon. Both insisted on the importance of the students becoming acquainted with data, especially that of economics and sociology, in order to evaluate correctly the moral aspects of social problems.

---

[1] Curran 1982, 26–30.

Significantly, Ryan's 1900 licentiate dissertation was titled *Some Ethical Aspects of Speculation*. His subsequent 1906 doctoral dissertation, titled *A Living Wage*, received wide acclaim in religious and secular circles. Richard Ely, a distinguished economist at the University of Wisconsin and a leader in the Protestant Social Gospel Movement, urged Ryan to have it published.

In 1919, Ryan, by then a member of the Catholic University faculty, wrote an important pamphlet entitled *Social Reconstruction: A General Review of the Problems and Survey of Remedies*. The pamphlet contained the reform program that he had been developing since the beginning of the century.[2] Ryan initially drafted the document as a speech to Knights of Columbus in Louisville, Kentucky, but then decided to put it aside as too lengthy. However, Msgr. John O'Grady, director of the National Conference of Catholic Charities, presented the text to the NCWC, where some changes were made and it was published on Lincoln's birthday, 1919, as the Conference's own statement.[3]

The proposals of this document evolved into the platform for SAD's call for "social reform." The platform included retention of wartime agencies like the State Employment Services and National War Labor Board, a living wage, organized labor, collective bargaining, federal loans to war veterans, curbs on monopolies in the commodities market, regulation of privately owned public utilities, heavier taxation of incomes and investments, wider opportunities for employee stock options, government elimination of child labor, and equal pay for work of men and women (despite Ryan's not favoring unnecessary female employment outside the home).

In September 1919, all the U.S. Catholic bishops met for the first time since 1884; in 1920 they issued a document titled *Pastoral Letter*. The document was somewhat different from, but not incompatible

---

[2] Cerny 1955, 7, fn. 9.
[3] Abell 1963, 199.

with, the Conference's 1919 statement, which became known as the *Bishops' Program*—popularly referred to as the 1919 *Program of Social Reconstruction*.[4] (In this volume we will shorten the title to the U.S. bishops' *Pastoral Letter of 1919*). Given the emphasis in the *Pastoral Letter of 1919* on the moral general principles relating to the social problem on which all Catholics should agree, it possessed a higher degree of moral authority than the *Bishops' Program*. Yet, it could claim to be the type of practical application of moral principles that were necessary for the conditions of U.S. society. In this sense, Father Ryan and the Social Action Department could call upon both documents in support of their work during the 1920s.

The two documents are often referred to as being identical.

A president of the National Association of Manufacturers decried the "radical" proposals in these documents as partisan, pro-labor union, and socialistic propaganda. A 1929 New York State Senate investigating committee labeled the pamphlet as the work of *a certain group in the Catholic Church with leanings toward Socialism*.[5]

Church opposition came from Cardinal O'Connell of Boston and some other members of the hierarchy. In fact, only four bishops were said to have signed the original statement.[6] Hence, when the very existence of the NCWC came under severe attack by O'Connell, the cardinal cited the *U.S. Bishops' Pastoral/Statement* as part of the problem.

One of the alleged reasons for O'Connell's attack was Ryan's position on social reform. Also, he deemed Ryan's support of a constitutional amendment prohibiting child labor as "Soviet legislation...[and] special privilege of J. A. Ryan, Jane Adams, and a few more socialistic teachers and writers."

---

[4] Cerny 1955, 103–104.
[5] Ellis 1987, 589.
[6] John M. Hayes, interviewed in Chicago in May 1999.

O'Connell had written to Baltimore's Archbishop Michael Curley, then chancellor of the Catholic University, to complain that the hierarchy should abandon "weakly our duty and turn it over into the hands of the Ryans ... [or demand] that these servants of the university and paid agents of the NCWC either cease their crooked and false activities or leave the University and the offices of the NCWC."

Curley, a member of the Catholic University Board and of the NCWC, disagreed. Ryan's NCWC Social Action Department work continued, but not without challenges from the likes of O'Connell and some others among the hierarchy, clergy, and laity.

When Peter Muldoon, bishop of Rockford Island, Illinois, and chair of the SAD, was organizing the department, Fr. Peter Dietz, a longtime associate of the AFL leadership, had hoped to lead the SAD's "sub-division for labor." But Muldoon refused to make the appointment, because the department's Executive Committee had vetoed it. In addition to being so closely identified with trade unionism, the *Bishops' Program/Statement* espoused both co-partnership and producers' cooperation, and Dietz regarded this as "delusionary."

By contrast, Ryan, soon to be SAD director, was prepared to vigorously defend the program. Operational by February 1920, SAD initially had three divisions: (1) Industrial Relations, under Ryan; (2) Education and Social Welfare, under a Dr. Lapp; and (3) Rural Life Bureau, under Fr. Edwin O'Hara. By the late 1920s those divisions had come together in Washington, D.C., under Ryan and remained so throughout the rest of SAD's history. So from early on the SAD was concerned with more than labor–management relations.[7]

Almost immediately, the SAD cautioned the AFL not to "aim wholly, or even mainly, at wage increases [but that it also argue that workers] should claim a significant share in management, profits,

---

[7] Cerny 1955, 107.

16

and ownership." The SAD also condemned the National Association of Manufacturers' and other management groups' *American Plan*, pushing for an "open shop" in industrial relations.[8] Also decried were judicial abuses stressing injunctions and opposition to protective labor laws, notably abolishing child labor and minimum wages—especially for women and minors. Adamantly, Ryan urged an amendment to the U.S. Constitution empowering Congress to enact social and labor legislation. Also, the SAD launched an increasingly comprehensive series of programs and services.[9]

Made available in print were Ryan's and others' ideas on the living wage, distributive justice, socialism, labor relations, social reconstruction, church and state relations, liberty and citizenship, economics and politics, doctrine and morality, and social charity.

Also published was a series of pamphlets on Catholic Social Teaching about specific social issues, all done in less detail than in the larger publications. In 1927 *The Catechism of the Social Question* (1921) was published for use in study clubs, one of over four hundred such pamphlets.

In the early 1920s, the SAD sponsored hundreds of lectures in Catholic colleges and universities—hoping to inspire students to prepare for careers in professional social service, which was described as "the most pressing need of the Catholic Church in the postwar years." In addition, popular versions of the papal encyclicals were provided in simplified and inexpensive formats, as well as U.S. bishops' statements, reprints of significant public addresses or magazine articles, and short discussions of aspects of the social problem.

A weekly *News Sheet* was distributed to Catholic newspapers and periodicals about current events, as interpreted in light of Catholic

---

[8] Abell 1963, 211–212.
[9] Ibid., 214–217.

social principles. And in 1933, the "Yardstick" appeared, a weekly column syndicated by the NCWC News Service until the 1980s.

Outreach to other Catholic organizations was begun. In 1921 the social study club movement was urged on many groups, like the National Council of Catholic Men and the National Council of Catholic Women, both national lay organizations affiliated with the NCWC Department of Lay Organizations.

In December 1922, the SAD organized the first Catholic Conference on Industrial Problems "to discuss and promote the study and understanding of industrial problems." Represented at the first gathering in late June 1923 was a cross-section of academic, industrial, and Catholic organizations, and of union leaders. Discussion sessions were organized on wages, collective bargaining, state and industry, workers and ownership, and women in industry. Catholic social action historian Aaron Abell has judged that these meetings, well attended by management and union leaders, were more instrumental than any other agency in acquainting the Catholic and non-Catholic public with the Church's social doctrine.

One Conference president, Frederick Kenkel, director of the German-American Association's Roman Catholic Central Verein, thought that these "travelling schools of social thought [had gone far] towards establishing a Catholic public opinion on questions pertaining to industry and labor."

Prior to the launch of such SAD publications and activities, Catholic public opinion about the few labor priests was at best indifferent and sometimes opposed as not "priestly" or as "dabbling in Socialism or Communism."

In 1927 annual national meetings of the Catholic Conference on Industrial Problems gave way to regional meetings, held at irregular intervals, in all parts of the nation. The entire organization was formally separate from the SAD, but Ryan's assistant, Fr. Raymond

McGowan, remained its secretary-treasurer and was deeply involved in planning the meetings with his staff.

However much the meetings provided a public platform for discussion of Catholic Social Teaching, the SAD was disappointed that the appeal to employers was significantly less effective than the appeal to employees, educators, and social workers. Such was evident from comments of an array of thirty business leaders, which revealed their coolness toward *Rerum Novarum* and the *U.S. Bishops' Pastoral/Statement*. Abell has cited a few of these comments: "It is the business of the Church to save souls and not be like the Protestant churches, butting into everyone's business.... What did Leo XIII know about digging subways with steam shovels and handling 'Wops' and 'Hunkeys'."[10]

Too often among some Catholic hierarchy, clergy, and publicists, the attitude was that Protestant ministers had to focus on "social work" because their teaching and preaching were too bereft of substantive theology. Ryan was friendly with, but somewhat aloof from, prominent Protestant theologians who were immersed in the "Social Gospel" of Walter Rauchsenbusch and others.

Critics of the SAD often alleged that many of its educators exhibited a "labor complex" and that "the greed and avarice of the employers" theme was overworked. There was also the opposition from some who suspected that Christian charity and scientific clarity were incompatible.

In addition, disparaging references to "Wops" and "Hunkeys" betrayed the bias among many business and clerical leaders with Irish family backgrounds. The Church at the time was dominated by Irish "powerhouses" in Boston, New York, and Philadelphia. This was a remnant of the turn-of-the-century battles between Irish and

---

[10] Ibid., 216.

19

other European bishops over "Americanization," Catholic University, papal representation, and other issues.

Nevertheless, due to the SAD's social surveys, over thirty dioceses established charitable bureaus. The SAD conducted or helped produce other financial surveys, especially in rural areas. Eventually, the SAD coordinated many of its interests and projects with the Rural Life Bureau, the National Council of Catholic Women, the National Council of Catholic Men, the National Conference of Catholic Charities, and other NCWC departments. In 1928, in collaboration with the Federated Colored Catholics of the United States, SAD sponsored an annual conference on "The Negro in Industry." In 1929 the SAD also formed a parish credit union committee.

Within a decade, under the leadership of the NCWC's first chair, Cardinal James Gibbons, many social service aspects of Ryan's pamphlet and of the *U.S. Bishops' Pastoral/Statement* were realized. Abell has said that insistence on the importance of industrial ethics regularly brought home to SAD that economic conditions were unsound and that while productivity was high the income of industrial, service, and agricultural workers remained low.

Further, in 1929 and in response to the Great Depression, the SAD was prepared to do its part in making the purchasing power theory into basic public policy.[11] Evidence of such readiness was apparent in the SAD's publications and programs, especially in Ryan's speeches and debates.

Ryan gave speeches to the members of numerous associations, including the National Child Labor Committee, the National Consumers League, the National Conference of Charities and Corrections, and the American Civil Liberties Union (in which he became the first priest-member since its founding after World War I.)

Especially notable were Ryan's public criticism of President Herbert Hoover, made in a speech at the National Democratic Committee, and his benediction at the second Inauguration of President Franklin D. Roosevelt in 1937 (the first time a Catholic priest gave the benediction).

Along with various Congressional testimonies and testimonials from the president, Supreme Court justices, senators, Congressional members and cabinet secretaries, there was also criticism from some sectors of the Catholic press. Although assured early in his career by an influential Roman cleric that his views were acceptable to Rome, and although later he was named a monsignor, Ryan was assailed in the earlier days by *America, The Brooklyn Tablet*, and *The Catholic World* as ascribing too much importance to government's role in public life.

After a 1914–1915 debate with Morris Hilquist, the leading socialist theorist of the time, Ryan's article, "Socialism: Promise or Menace" was published in *Everybody's Magazine*. Abell has called the article *by far and away the best short exposition of Socialism in the English language.*[12] Yet even unenlightened folks could discern that Ryan clashed sharply with Socialism's economic, philosophic, and theological assumptions. To uninformed and reactionary Catholics who thought his social program was tantamount to Socialism, Ryan responded that he was seeking "economic democracy" free from the abuses of Capitalism and Socialism.

Abell has said that Ryan excelled above all his predecessors and contemporaries in his "ability to combine economics and ethics into a virtually new science of social justice. [He] was not only a highly learned moral theologian but a professional economist of rare competence."[13] Abell further underlined that, in all his efforts, Ryan insisted that Catholics could not transform society alone, urged that

---

12 Ibid., 233.
13 Abell 1946, 130.

social work be correlated with social justice, and stressed that industrial reform was a necessary part in relieving poverty.

In the "Red Scare" after World War I, Ryan saw not only a grave injustice to innocent and ignorant foreign-born U.S. residents, but also a not-so-subtle attempt to discredit industrial reform. Referring to the industrial feudalism of the 1920s, Ryan stressed that it rejected economic liberty, was extolled by the Republican Party, and undermined interpretations of the Constitution's "due process" clause by judicial decisions.

In 1928, Ryan, more than many other economists and publicists, argued that the underlying causes of unemployment were over-production and under-consumption. The remedy, he added, demanded drastic measures to increase most people's buying power.

In Abell's mind, Ryan, in his *A Better Economic Order* (1935), adapted the English economist J.A. Hobson's under-consumption theory very skillfully to U.S. conditions. He believed that Ryan had great influence on the Roosevelt administration, as one of its philosophers, and "strongly supported the major proposals of the 'New Deal' while urging "higher incomes for labor and farmers, lower interest rates, and smaller shares of the national income for the owners of capital."

Abell also wrote about Ryan in an early 1947 article in the *Review of Politics* titled "Monsignor John A. Ryan, An Historical Appreciation."[14]

Ryan chided Catholics about their indifference to social reform, excepting Fr. Peter Dietz and a few others. Further, he urged that social work be correlated with social justice, even though the U.S. Catholic bishops, as well as prominent business and professional

---

[14] Ibid., 128.

leaders, opposed Ryan's support of a proposed Child Labor Amendment.

Abell has cited Ryan's autobiography to explain Ryan's desire to specialize in the parts of the Gospel that apply to social and economic issues, especially in view of the realization that the number of priests who were laboring in this portion of the Lord's vineyard was pitiably small.

In 1982, Catholic ethicist Charles Curran did extensive analysis of Ryan's Social Teaching. Referring to his *Economic Ethics (and) Methodology,* Curran quoted Ryan: "The...concept of social justice, adequately considered and comprehensively applied, would do more to bring about a reign of industrial peace and industrial justice than any other theory or formula that has ever obtained lodgment in the minds of men."[15]

Ryan emphasized the dangers of materialism and the role of the rich. As the editor of *Catholic Charities Review,* he focused not only on character problems but also on "scientific charity." Noting critics who cited Leo XIII's caution about limitations of government interventions, Curran wrote:

[From] Ryan's viewpoint as a meliorist the first steps were necessary and no further steps could build on these. One could almost hear the practical reformer saying that the better should never become the enemy of the good.[16]

Ryan insisted that the advocacy of definite methods of political organization, of agriculture, and finance lies outside the powers of the church. He distinguished three ways in which the authoritative teaching of the popes and bishops should function: (1) the Church lays down moral principles; (2) it declares some methods lawful or not; and (3) it might advocate certain methods without the binding

---

[15] Curran 1982, 38.
[16] Ibid., 63.

force of the previous two ways, because of the practical expediency involved.

Although Ryan stressed the need for lay involvement in social reform by pushing certain policies or participating in organizations like unions, he also stressed the leadership role of priests in social work and social action and the need for seminary courses in social thought, sociology, and economics. Quite aware of the estrangement of workers from the Catholic Church in Europe, Ryan thought it was in the Church's best interests in the United States to endorse social reform.

But Ryan distinguished the Catholic Church's social mission from what he considered exaggerated views of some proponents of the Protestant Social Gospel. Curran explained that Ryan stressed reason and natural law, while the Protestant Social Gospel leader Walter Rauschenbusch emphasized Christian faith and the Bible. Curran also recalled that in 1909 Ryan remarked that Protestant churches tended to identify religion with humanitarianism. For Ryan the mission of the Church was not to realize the kingdom of God on this earth, but by saving souls to make them fit for the kingdom.

Ryan was criticized for making too great a distinction between the natural and the supernatural, between this world and the next. Many Christians operated under such presuppositions and actually denied any social mission of the Church. Ryan may have given a weak justification in his writings, but he was a living witness in his actions. Nonetheless, he failed to have the holistic approach found in others like Fr. Virgil Michel, O.S.B., the Catholic Worker movement, and Catholic University's Fr. Paul Hanley Furfey, all of whom were deeply involved in social action and who included the liturgy, prayer, simple lifestyle, and personal change in their approach.

Further, Ryan advocated the use of theoretical deduction, unlike Fr. John Courtney Murray, S.J., who used a more historical and inductive methodology. Although Ryan admitted that order and harmony were not immune to a realistic tension in human affairs, there was more conflict than he admitted.

Ryan also failed to nuance self-interest and concern for others from proper self-love and proper self-interest, to admit possible conflicts between good economics and good ethics, and to articulate that human beings cannot be identified merely as "economic," "psychological," or "sociological." Yet, like every good social reformer, Ryan would ask himself if a particular measure was in accord with right reason and Catholic teaching and if it was wise and prudent to seek such a measure at a particular moment. Hence, he later opted for government intervention instead of the cooperatives he had hoped for earlier.

Yet, as an effective reformer, Ryan was tempted to overlook deeper issues of injustice, which he did not think allowed much hope of immediate change and reform, such as the role of minorities. Also, the authors of some doctoral dissertations written during the 1950s were not as enthusiastic about Ryan as were Aaron Abell and Charles Curran, although they did hold Ryan in some esteem. These assessments will be discussed below in some detail.

2

MCGOWAN, HAYES, HIGGINS, & CRONIN

Four More Giants

of the Social Action Department

P ioneering and essential as Ryan was in the Catholic social reform movement, he did acknowledge his debt to the work of
others, especially the SAD staff.

This staff was comprised of the four "giant" teachers of Catholic
social thought, pertaining to labor–management relations and kin-
dred economic-political issues: Fr. Raymond McGowan, Kansas
City Archdiocesan theologian-priest; Fr. John Hayes, Chicago Archdiocesan theologian-priest; Fr. George Higgins, Chicago Archdiocesan economist-priest; and Fr. John Cronin, Sulpician economist-
priest. All men were gifted writers and speakers and some had several books and published articles to their credit.

Yet, talented and experienced as Ryan, McGowan, Hayes, Higgins,
and Cronin were, their personal backgrounds made for differences
in their activities as labor priests, as well as in the policy nuances
that they espoused and expounded. Discussions below of various
talks, sermons, and activities of labor priests will reveal the giants'
influence in the advice, direction, and references given to mostly
untrained and inexperienced, but zealous and streetwise labor
priests.

Largely overlooked by some authors mentioned below was the fact that a very large portion of SAD's time was spent reaching out to labor priests through the Catholic Conference on Industrial Problems, Social Action Seminars for Priests, and exchanges of correspondence. Also overlooked is the keen awareness the SAD had of local politics and respect they had for the political practical wisdom of local labor priests. Noted, however, was the involvement of SAD staff in union, economic, legislative, political, peace, interfaith, and a wide variety of local and national Catholic gatherings. Whether, as former students or through regular meetings with Ryan, SAD itself conveyed his influence on their ideas and activities, although at times there were differences among themselves and Ryan.

Fr. Raymond McGowan

Ryan's first assistant director was Fr. Raymond McGowan, a self-effacing priest who readily acknowledged his deep debts of gratitude to his predecessor and later assistants. Yet, on several occasions McGowan received high praise. Indeed, it was Ryan himself in his 1941 *Social Doctrine in Action*, who said so authoritatively, namely, that SAD, the U.S. Catholic Church, and the social justice cause are "indebted to him [McGowan] in far greater measure than I could adequately describe."

McGowan was said to have done most of the planning and implementation for SAD's work, as well as originating most of its ideas and decisions. Ryan could not recall any important mistake that McGowan had made: "So pleasant and amicable have been our personal relations that my recollection does not cover any occasion on which a word of blame, complaint or annoyance passed between us."

Ryan was most grateful that, when he needed an assistant director of SAD, McGowan happened to be in Washington, D.C., and was unassigned.[1] Several years later, the first chaplain of the New York Catholic Association of Catholic Trade Unionists (ACTU), Fr. John Monaghan, noted that for thirty years McGowan had traveled in every industrial section of the United States and republics of South America. "Whatever general knowledge of Catholic teaching about the dignity of man and the rights of labor is common among us, under God, we owe it to the energy and faith of this man.... Father McGowan was the popular apostle of an unpopular cause."[2]

SAD moderator, Washington's Archbishop Patrick O'Boyle, said, "Few priests in the history of the United States have contributed as much as Father McGowan to the great cause of social justice.... [He] has proved himself to be a man of unusual intelligence and extraordinary vision."[3]

Father John Cronin, S.S., an assistant, called McGowan a man of "absolute integrity...tenacious and unbelievably stubborn to holding for what he considered to be the correct application of Catholic social principles. Arguments could not budge him, nor could pressure induce him to compromise."[4]

McGowan was born in Brookfield, Missouri, and was ordained for the St. Joseph (Missouri) Diocese in 1915, after theological studies at St. Bernard Seminary in Rochester, New York, the North American College in Rome, and Catholic University in Washington, D.C..[5] He was a parish assistant in Missouri and a military chaplain in World War I.

In 1919 he was assigned to the NCWC as assistant to Ryan, his professor at Catholic University, and was responsible for writing arti-

[1] Ryan 1941.
[2] NCWC News Service, August 1949.
[3] NCWC New Service, November 22, 1954.
[4] Kansas City, Mo., *Catholic Weekly*, November 17, 1962.
[5] Archives, Kansas City–St. Joseph Diocese.

cles and pamphlets on Catholic Social Teaching, especially on labor–management relations. He published *Europe and the United
States*, as well as *The Church and Social Reconstruction in Puerto Rico*.
He also initiated a regular column in many Catholic newspapers,
the very influential "Yardstick."

He was founder of the Catholic Conference on Industrial Problems,
Inter-American Committee, Catholic Association for International
Peace, Bishops' Committee for the Spanish-Speaking, Catholic
Council of the Spanish-Speaking, Bishops' Committee for Migrant
Workers, and Inter-American Catholic Social Action Confederation.
McGowan also served for many years as secretary of the National
Catholic Social Action Conference (NCSAC), an umbrella for organ-
izations of clergy, laity, and religious involved in a variety of social
issues.

Like Ryan, McGowan was friend and confidant, counselor, and advisor to the hierarchy, presidents, cabinet officers, legislators, management and union leaders, journalists, and people in various
walks of life. All the while, he guided SAD's assistants in their man-
ifold activities, especially on behalf of labor priests.

Becoming SAD director upon the death of Ryan in 1945, McGowan
assumed even more tasks. As active as he was in SAD's day-to-day
operations, McGowan also became involved in other tasks such as
accepting an invitation from the National Conference of Christians
and Jews to contribute officially to its Wednesday issue of a tri-
weekly column on social action subjects syndicated to the secular
press.

A second task was planning the fortieth anniversary of *Rerum Novarum*, which included a pilgrimage of hierarchy, clergy, and laity
to Rome. The task necessitated an extensive public relations outreach to Catholic seminaries, educational institutions, parishes, lay
organizations, Newman clubs, press, and radio. There were plans
for sermon outlines on the encyclical, prefaced with some major

points of the papal encyclicals, which would reject individualism's excessive competition, but insist not only on the "rights" but the "responsibilities" of private property in light of the common good.[6]

A third task was the effort to pass the highly controversial child labor law amendment. After a federal law was declared unconstitutional, there was a later discussion of SAD's options, given Catholics' suspicions about any state or federal power over children in anyway. In addition to the legal and political concerns, he had to address the negative publicity about some Church opponents to the legislation.

A fourth task, which consumed much of his time, was planning and administering Summer Schools of Social Action for Priests in several dioceses throughout the nation.

A fifth task arose in response to efforts by Baltimore's Archbishop Michael Curley to have McGowan and Ryan dismissed from NCWC and the archdiocese, allegedly because of their advocacy of Franklin Roosevelt's New Deal policies and programs. Ultimately, the threats subsided after mediation efforts that would involve the NCWC Administrative Board and the Apostolic Delegation.

A sixth task, destined to have great ramifications later, was conducting a survey of priests and priests groups about Communism in their areas.

A seventh task occurred with efforts to enlighten the Detroit "radio priest" Fr. Charles Coughlin, by accepting his invitation to have McGowan write a weekly column in Coughlin's widely distributed newspaper, *Social Justice*.

An eighth situation arose with occasional budgetary disputes, publishing, and jurisdictional issues with NCWC officials and some of

---

[6] McGowan, Raymond, letter to Bishop Edwin O'Hara, Episcopal vice-chair of SAD, March 28, 1936. Archives of the Kansas City–St. Joseph Diocese.

the hierarchy over authority to attend or represent the SAD at ecumenical and civic organizations' gatherings, as well as extensive assurances and assistance for some of the labor priests.

In 1954 McGowan retired as director, continuing work on Inter-American affairs in San Antonio, Texas. He died in November 1962.

Msgr. John Hayes

The least heralded of SAD staff was Fr. John Hayes, at least until 2010 when Kimball Baker wrote *America's Labor Apostles* for Marquette University Press.[7] Born in Chicago in 1906, Hayes studied at Chicago Archdiocesan Quigley and Mundelein seminaries. After ordination in 1920, he pursued doctoral studies in Rome, taught at Quigley Seminary, and briefly served in St. Angela's Parish, where he became interested in problems of the steel and stockyard workers then being organized by the CIO. Also, he was invited by McGowan to speak at gatherings of the National Association of Social Action Conference (NASAC) in Milwaukee and Chicago.

In 1940, at the invitation of McGowan, Hayes joined the SAD staff. Ryan was said to be courteous in welcoming him, but left Hayes to work with McGowan. Since specific plans were not available, Hayes drafted his own program. Not interested in organizational tasks or speaking engagements, Hayes devoted his efforts largely to correspondence with labor priests, editing *Social Action Notes for Priests*, SAD's bulletin (initiated by McGowan), and attending and assisting meetings, especially of the National Catholic Rural Life Conference and the Catholic Peace Conference.

Approximately one hundred pieces of correspondence between Hayes and a wide variety of people on a variety of issues have been located. An amazing number, given Hayes's term at SAD of only four years. The people were mostly labor priests throughout the

---

[7] Chicago Archdiocesan Archives.

United States. Yet, there was contact also with labor leaders, politicians, ecclesiastics, journalists, educators, parish priests, government officials, etc.

The issues addressed in their correspondence ranged from the war in Europe, assisting others' research on labor, worker education, priests' social action studies and activities, advice to union leaders, cooperation with interfaith groups, concerns of Labor Schools, partisan politics, government agencies, right-to-work laws, SAD pamphlets and other information sources, newspaper campaigns against labor unions, sermons and teaching on labor unions, immigration problems, government surveillance, priests in the midst of labor controversies, internal union struggles, disagreement with the Association of Catholic Trade Unionists, Communism and the church, racial discrimination, editorial battles with the Catholic and secular press, Catholic Charities, War Relief Fund, the papal plan and industry council plan, internal Church controversies, etc.

Hayes resigned from SAD because of tuberculosis, perhaps due to a lack of sleep from writing pamphlets late into the night. After some surgery, he moved to the warmer climate of the Southwest, serving as chaplain and teaching for the Sisters of the Incarnate Word in San Antonio, Texas. While there, he became reacquainted with San Antonio's archbishop, Robert Lucey, and wrote sometimes controversial articles in the archdiocesan newspaper, with Lucey's silent approval. Hayes also came to the aid of organizing efforts of the International Ladies' Garment Workers Union (ILGWU) and the Amalgamated Clothing Workers Union (ACWU), as well brewery and meatpacking workers. In addition, he wrote articles for Catholic publications like *Commonweal, Orate Fratres,* and *Today.* He also took part in discussions in New York's Corpus Christi Parish with Frs. Ford (a cultured and liberal pastor based near Columbia University), Hillenbrand, and Monaghan (chaplain of the New York ACTU).

33

From 1953 to 1958, Hayes was chaplain at Chicago's Mercy High School. From 1958 to 1968, he served St. Carthage's Parish, formerly an Irish but eventually a Black parish. From 1968 until his death in 2002, he served in Epiphany, a totally Hispanic parish.

In May 1999, this researcher interviewed Hayes at Epiphany Parish. Between telephone calls and requests, mostly in Spanish, he reminisced about earlier days in the Catholic Church and during his short retirement in San Antonio, while McGowan was also there. Higgins was described as possessing good personal and organizing skills, a genius for writing and lecturing, and a sharp mind. "So he took my place, and a man of great talent and intelligence, so it worked out all right."[8]

Hayes referred to labor priests as only "journeymen" and said that their greatest work was involvement in labor, due to their personal inclination and the Gospel mandate to help the needy. He insisted that SAD was the focal point of the labor priests, since "save for a few dioceses there was no other source."

Msgr. George Higgins

George Higgins was born in Chicago on January 21, 1916. As a youth he would rush home from school to read to his nearly blind father from *America, Commonweal,* and the writings of Christopher Dawson and Jacques Maritain.[9] In 1930 Higgins entered Quigley, the Chicago Archdiocesan Preparatory Seminary, and in 1934 Mundelein, the major seminary, where he and many progressive Chicago priests were influenced by the rector, Msgr. Reynold Hillenbrand.

After ordination in 1940, Higgins studied economics, with a first minor in political science and second minor in sociology, at Catholic

---

[8] Hayes, John M., Interviewed in Chicago, May 1999.
[9] Costello 1984, passim.

University. His doctoral dissertation, *Voluntarism in Organized Labor in the United States: 1930–1940*, was directed by Msgr. Francis Haas, renowned in Catholic social services and national labor–management relations. In April 1944, McGowan invited Higgins to assist part-time, while Hayes spent the summer in San Antonio trying to recuperate from tuberculosis. In September 1944 Hayes's health had deteriorated and he had to resign from SAD. So Higgins was appointed McGowan's full-time assistant and began editing *Social Action Notes for Priests* and SAD's pamphlet series.

After Ryan's death in September 1945, McGowan's workload increased so much that he also had to step down and Higgins took over as SAD's director. Many of McGowan's duties had been already been assumed earlier, such as administrative tasks within NCWC, public presentations of policies and practices, as well as almost endless correspondence. Such tasks never curtailed his wide range of intellectual acumen, apostolic zeal, and pastoral care. Many bishops, priests, religious, and laity benefited. So did members of various academic, economic, interfaith, political, union, and other sectors of society—at home and abroad.

Perhaps none benefited more from his acumen, zeal, and care as the labor priests—the many bishops, priests, and religious involved in responding to the labor–management challenges from the 1940s to 1970s—a period that witnessed the U.S. Catholic Church's most intense commitment when the "social problem" was the "labor problem."

As with Hayes, Higgins's correspondence with labor priests revealed much about assistance to so many people. Although Higgins's longer tenure in SAD would account for the larger volume of correspondence, the nature of the correspondence was similar to that during Hayes's much shorter tenure. Examples abound of several hundred writings with labor priests and more than a hundred with others about labor–management and related issues. The voluminous collection of articles, columns, interviews, sermons, and talks made recounting almost impossible.

Here, attention will be paid mostly to available material with implications for the Catholic Church and labor–management issues by one of its most distinguished labor priests. They reveal not only an informed theological and ecclesial perspective, but also an intriguing grasp of the economic, political, and labor–management facets of American workers and of the wider world. Some highlighted his interfaith, peace-making, church, political, and other involvements.

Higgins's many awards were also noted—appointment to the preparatory commission for Vatican II, delegate to the 1971 World Synod of Bishops' discussions on the priesthood, adviser to a 1977–1978 Belgrade Conference on International Human Rights, the "Presidential Medal of Freedom," Notre Dame University's honorary doctorate and the Laetare Medal, and other church civic, union, and local honors.

Given the volume of Higgins's correspondence, other volumes in the Catholic Labor Priests series will focus on more significant events and issues—agricultural workers, civil rights movement, Communism, controversies over political leaders, defense of union leaders, differences involving labor issues, misunderstandings with ACTU, forced retirement from NCWC, and subsequent commendations.

On May 2, 2002, the day after Higgins died, many tributes were paid to him. His friend and theologian, Fr. Charles Curran, writing in *Commonweal*, noted Higgins's criticism of the new breed of the 1960s for not respecting the competency of the laity and for indulging in too much moralizing: "While he realized the need for the Church to take stands on controversial issues, he also recognized that such stands did not necessarily end disagreement or the need for further research."

Gerald Renner's article in the *National Catholic Reporter* quoted from one of Higgins's "Yardstick" column. Calling failure by the Catholic community to respect employees' rights and dignity a contradiction in terms, recognized by the workers themselves, Higgins added, "That is not to say workers must belong to a union to have a sense of their own dignity. It is to say, however, that their right to organize must be recognized."

A few days later in Chicago's Holy Name Cathedral, the eulogy was given by Boston Archdiocese's Fr. Bryan Hehir, who served with Higgins in the Catholic Bishops Conference a few years earlier. Compliments were given about his place in the social ministry of the Church. The most striking was this: "The very center of his commitment to the Social Teaching was what Leo XIII called the rights of workers.... The labor movement was a community second only to his church.... George Higgins dedicated his life to forging strong, public, effective bonds between labor and the church."

Fr. John Cronin, S.S.

As laudatory and distinguished as was Higgins's life and accomplishments in his later years, he was never one to slight the contributions of others in SAD, especially the last addition to the SAD staff, Fr. John Cronin, S.S. Cronin was born on October 4, 1908, in Glen Falls, New York.[10] In 1923, he wrote an essay entitled "Coal Situation," a description of different types of coal and the unfair and dangerous working conditions of mining. Published in the Glen Falls *Post Star*, the essay showed the great influence of his father, a strong union man.

---

[10] Donovan .

After two years at the College of Holy Cross, Worcester, Massachusetts, Cronin won a scholarship to Basselin College in Catholic University. Upon completing a Masters of Art degree in philosophy in 1928, he entered the Sulpician Seminary in Baltimore, Maryland. In 1932 he was ordained a priest and entered the Sulpician Novitiate in Catonsville, Maryland. From 1933 to 1935, he studied for a doctorate in economics at Catholic University, under Msgr. John A. Ryan and Msgr. Francis Haas.

After McGowan retired, Cronin became assistant director. By July 1946, Cronin admitted that he had had some differences with Haas, McGowan, and Ryan, most importantly about the correct analysis and application of the "vocational groups" mentioned in Pius XI's *Quadragesimo Anno*. In making changes on some of the minor points, Cronin was able to win over bishops and priests who might have been turned off by the social program precisely because they were convinced of certain facts that were denied or minimized.

Higgins and Cronin might have disagree on factual matters and their relevance or on particular emphases when presenting the truth, but with *these principles, we can catalogue differences* over the degree and method of emphasizing Communism, the best approaches to reactionary Catholics, and faults in the labor movement and Roosevelt administration.

During graduate studies and afterwards, Cronin was quite busy teaching and writing. At the Sulpician St. Mary's Seminary, he was said to have taught the first full-length course in economics ever taught in any seminary. Articles in the *Pittsburgh Catholic* and *Sign* were followed in 1939 by publication of *Economics and Society*. In 1944 he wrote several articles in the Baltimore Archdiocesan newspaper, *Catholic Review*.

For the U.S. bishops, he completed *The Problem of American Communism in 1945: Facts and Recommendations*. The U.S. Chamber of

Commerce supported his 1946 eight-page booklet, entitled *Communist Infiltration in the United States: Its Nature and How to Combat It* (1946). A second booklet for the Chamber appeared in 1947, *Communists within the Government: The Facts and a Program*. A third Chamber booklet, which Cronin authored with the AFL's John Frey, was entitled *Communists within the Labor Movement: A Handbook on the Facts and Countermeasures*. Several of Cronin's publications singled out for praise by Toledo bishop and NCWC chair Karl Alter, including *Communism: World Menace*, the magazine *Plain Talk*, *Economic Analysis and Problems* (1945), and *Catholic Social Action* (1948). In 1962 *Communism: Threat to Freedom* was published.

Cronin's writings were imbued with the teachings of Leo XIII and Pius XI and clearly contrasted with those put out by the Populists and Fr. Charles Coughlin, Detroit radio orator. Instead of insisting on currency reform, Cronin urged democratizing industry, as *Quadragesimo Anno* recommended, meaning industries should be compelled to base decisions in part on the rights of labor and the public interest, because cutting off economic power at its source would diminish banking influence.

He rejected the notion of the U.S. economy "as an automatic machine, self-regulated by inherent checks and balances," but endorsed the need for government intervention. Like SAD and the labor priests, he did not look for relief from the Great Depression in Communism, as some Americans did. Also, unlike some priests, he did not favor blanket condemnation of the labor movement, although there were communists in the CIO and a small segment of the labor movement had been affected by racketeering in the AFL. In a July 1941 issue of *Sign*, he said, "One wonders why not long ago union leaders have not asked us why we are so free in advice to them and so sparing in admonitions to corrupt politicians of our own faith and nationality."

Aside from concerns about communist presence and power in the United States, amidst some partisan political involvements and complications, Cronin's attention to labor unions was never as focused as George Higgins's. In 1938 and 1939, however, Cronin established Labor Schools for the education of clergy of Baltimore (Maryland), Richmond (Virginia), and Washington, D.C. Later, parishes hosted Labor School programs, attended by twenty-five to forty parishioners. The threefold agenda was to (1) explain Catholic Social Teaching; (2) train lay leaders; and (3) combat Communism and other subversive influences in the labor movement.

The many-pronged curriculum in the Labor Schools included teaching about the right and necessity of unions, collective bargaining, wages, hours, working conditions, mutual rights and duties of capital and labor, the right and the duty of the Catholic Church to teach with authority on such issues, and the place of religion in society.

By 1941, Cronin took charge of the Institute of Catholic Social Studies at the Catholic University. He also wrote many articles and gave radio and other public addresses on labor issues.

3

CRITICISM & RESPONSE

Accomplishments of the

Social Action Department Priests

Several recent studies have examined the Social Action Department (SAD) and its "giants," the labor priests, and the Catholic Church's relationship to the U.S. labor movement.

In 1981 a Rutgers University doctoral dissertation of Douglas P. Seaton (revised and published by Bucknell University Press) offered a negative and dismissive evaluation. Higgins submitted a critical review of Seaton's ideas to *America* on July 27, 1981.[1] The entire dissertation is beyond the scope of this research period (1920s–1980s), yet, some points of Higgins's review are included because Higgins regarded the dissertation as "tendentious" because it discounted the positive accomplishments of labor priests, Labor Schools, and Association of Catholic Trade Unionists (ACTU) and in an unscholarly manner.

---

[1] Higgins 1981.

According to Higgins, Seaton argued, "almost *ad nauseam,* that partisans of the Church" and specifically the now defunct ACTU, were a, if not the, crucial factor in determining the "conservative" direction taken by the CIO unions during the period 1937–1950. In fact, Seaton fell into the trap of "proving too much and proving nothing," revealing a tinge of "an unprofessional personal pique and personal hostility that Catholic Social Teaching...is, by his standards, hopelessly 'conservative'." Calling Seaton's standards "avowedly subjective," Higgins said they "are not and never have been the standards adhered to by the mainstream of the American labor movement." Seaton's definitions of "radical" and "conservative" seemed "to beg the question which the rest of the book purports to answer."

According to Seaton, "radicals" were committed to the class struggle and Socialism as a political, social, and economic system, while "conservatives" rejected the class struggle, spurned Socialism strictly so-called, and aimed primarily to defeat the radicals. Msgr. Ryan was called a half-hearted and illogical progressive. Seaton's writing abounded in misconceptions of ACTU. ACTU's original "militantly pro-worker attitude" was said to have given way to nonviolence, mediation, and class harmony. Loyalty to Catholic Social Teaching led ACTU to obsessive anticommunism, eventually making it "virtually the sole issue which occupied the organization."

Seaton's positions, said Higgins, were based too much on the New York ACTU archives and failed to report differing views of other ACTU chapters about fighting Communism. Seaton viewed ACTU as monolithic and exaggerated its "national" character, justifying his preconceived conclusions and placing several Labor Schools under ACTU's umbrella. Higgins pointed out some of Seaton's glaring mistakes: CIO president Philip Murray was made to be a Republican; UAW (United Auto Workers) opponents were considered to be followers of Fr. Coughlin; the World Federation of Trade Unions

(WFTU) was deemed to be "socialist;" leaders of communist-dominated CIO unions were valued as authentic militants, while anticommunist CIO leaders were labeled as inferior union leaders; ACTU's anticommunism was "adopted" by the CIO, and without ACTU the CIO would never have expelled the communists. Granting that Seaton's dissertation was worth reading, Higgins said that the well-grounded research of most scholars who wrote about the ACTU–CIO connection disagreed with Seaton. So much for "the allegedly 'conservative' orientation of the U.S. labor movement."

In an interview in the early 1990s George Higgins told this researcher that some evaluations of Ryan and SAD, which minimized the principles or discredited "corporatism" and "industry councils," seemed unfair for several reasons.

Catholic Social Teaching, unlike Fascism and Communism or even Capitalism, did not pretend to be an ideology, save for the brief excursion of Pius XI, Pius XII, and some in SAD into corporatism and industry councils. Higgins would say reject the method, but not the principles, especially because later U.S. Catholic Social Teaching had very decisively limited itself to teaching principles and making only policy recommendations, as evident in the 1980s U.S. Catholic bishops' pastoral on peace and pastoral on economic justice.

To say the SAD failed because it did not "provide adequate political theory" and to "ignore [the] political implications" of its teaching is to ignore the elephant in the midst of society, evident in the continued opposition of the world of business and finance to labor unions and government guidance, let alone regulation. Such opposition became such an insurmountable obstacle that not even embracing laissez-faire individualism would have been remedial and/or preventive for society's problems prior to 1945 and ever since, let alone for acceptance of the teaching and activities of labor priests.

Even without implicit or explicit, conscious or unconscious bias, the critics of SAD offered nothing other than some tinkering with Capitalism and/or Socialism. Labor priests' efforts at implementing Catholic Social Teaching—save corporatism or industry councils—were often frustrated by the ever-prevalent political chicanery of established capitalists and ideological socialists. Witness the continuing blind and/or rapacious opposition to "institutionalist economics" in some professional journals and academic appointments.

Any understanding of the political scientist's task—"to suggest means of organizing society so that in practice the tension between social authority and individual liberty can be resolved"—betrays the ideology of some social scientists, some of whom are determined and/or confident that they will eventually come to know and control, with scientific certitude, all the variables of persons' choices, whether acting alone or in groups. Labor priests never fell into that trap and only once did SAD, with its design for reforming society by corporatism and industry council.

Ryan, Higgins, and Cronin were professionally trained economists, but McGowan and Hayes were professionally trained theologians. All five were politically attuned priests, fundamentally interested in spreading and implementing Catholic social justice—a social ethical system, not a political theory or ideology. Hence, they should not be held to the canons of such "social science," whether in economics, politics, sociology, or what have you. Rather, they were searchers and users of the best data social science and social philosophy could provide.

Catholic social justice actionists from a variety of social "institutions or movements" periodically voiced important differences over policies and legislation—some more overarching than others. On the one hand were Ryan and SAD. On the other side were the Association of Catholic Trade Unionists (ACTU), Dorothy Day and Peter

Maurin's "Catholic Worker," Catholic University's Msgr. Paul Hanley Furfey's Catholic Radicalism, Benedictine Fr. Virgil Michel's Liturgical Movement, and William Englen's Roman Catholic Central Verein. Some reduced social reform to personal and spiritual reform and/or specific legislative reform.

SAD's staff chose to inform and motivate—not to command or compel—Catholic hierarchy and clergy, religious, and laity about social justice principles and possible policies and programs to reform society along social justice lines. The SAD staff's only comprehensive and overarching effort—eventually abandoned, as will be explained below—was to provide a blueprint for reorganizing society according to Pius XI's and Pius' XII's "corporatism."

In addition to Abell's above-mentioned comments and the harsh criticism of Seaton, David O'Brien judged that aside from Ryan's pioneering work on minimum wage he contributed little that was original to the social reform movements of those times.[2] Ryan's major function (according to O'Brien) was as a mediator, helping to erase the image of the Church as "reactionary and tied to the political machine" and to relieve the fears of some Catholics by educating them about their social responsibilities, especially with regard to the role of the state and the reform efforts of the Protestant majority.

O'Brien's main criticism was that Ryan failed to offer a politically wise plan to implement his ideas. This was something for which Ryan had little time, however, given his influence and ongoing association with Democratic political leaders. Indeed, O'Brien offered faint praise by quoting Ryan's colleague and friend, George Shuster: "[Ryan] happened to be a good, square-shooting priest who helped turn the face of American Catholicism toward the future."[3]

---

[2] O'Brien 1965, 129–130.
[2] Ibid.

45

Finally, O'Brien's comment on Ryan's very important work on the living wage appears rather stingy, inasmuch as that concept is still at the core of Catholic Social Teaching and Ryan's creation and direction of SAD was an important contribution to the labor movement in one of its most perilous days.

In his Yale doctoral dissertation Karl Cerny wrote, "Monsignor John A. Ryan and the members of the Social Action Department represented the most important segment of American opinion during the period under review [1920 to 1945]."[4] In a concluding chapter titled "Evaluation," Cerny discussed the elaboration of goals or objectives and the means of achieving these objectives, which Ryan and SAD considered to be their most notable contribution and which they contrasted and compared with other schools of thought.

According to Cerny, SAD offered a solution that refused to sacrifice liberty to authority (collectivism) or authority to liberty (individualism). The former led to denial of liberty and equality; the latter led to inequality and full liberty only for the privileged few. Thus, SAD's conviction that unfettered Socialism and Capitalism resulted in practice to the denial of U.S. political tradition. SAD's interest in Catholic tradition focused on the social problem, which at that time meant labor.

Yet, there was still the failure to address the practical implications and applications of SAD's principles and proposals. For Cerny, missing was any serious consideration of the political effect of SAD's "theory" of the "corporatist system" and/or "occupational groups."[5] The central problem of further analysis, Cerny thought, would be to discover if SAD ever considered the political effect of as "theory" and recognized the necessity of revising the conception of "occupational groups," sometimes referred to as a "corporatist system." As Higgins indicated, the real issue is confusion about

---

[4] Cerny 1955, iv.
[5] Ibid., 243–33.

what was the purpose and difference of SAD's ethical system, as contrasted with a political theory.

Neil B. Betten's doctoral dissertation at the University of Minnesota, in its chapter 5, "John Ryan and the Social-Action Department," offered a more benign account and traced the development of the social thought of Ryan and SAD. This dissertation is important here because it presented a synoptic overview of the social thought, which in time became the larger content of the labor priests' lectures, speeches, and writings. Betten began by stating that there was a swing to the left by "Catholic social actionists during the 1930's, which was reflected both in the new Catholic institutions [or movements that]...arose in response to the Depression and the old ones, which often modified their outlook."[6] Some of the new and old "institutions or movements" were mentioned above in references to Cerny's dissertation.

Also, infrequently and privately, there were differences between SAD and "institutions" represented by NCWC committees and their chairs, as well as local bishops who were zealous to protect their autonomy and Vatican officials zealous in protecting their authority. Later volumes in *Catholic Labor Priests* will make it clear which were old and which were new. Yet, of the development of the social thought of Ryan and SAD, Betten said, "John Ryan...remained the paramount figure in the organization, as its changing role in great part reflected Ryan's own intellectual development.[7]

Earlier, Ryan did not neglect society—he deemed "the good life of the individual" as its end—but he focused on society as it affected the individual, especially the worker.

As early as 1906, he argued the worker had a right to a living wage, as a personal prerogative and not his share of the social good. It

---

[6] Betten 1969, 72.

[7] Ibid., 75.

47

belonged to the worker as a person and not as a member of society. A living wage was natural and absolute! The state was obligated to provide for the common good by minimum wage legislation, public-supported employment agencies, social security against unemployment, sickness and old-age benefits, housing projects, and laws guaranteeing the right of labor to organize. Favoring industrial unions over craft unions, Ryan expected workers to take the initiative in organizing unions, with government assistance. Thus, he also favored unionism, strikes, boycotts, closed shops, and even featherbedding.[8]

By 1916, Ryan had shifted his focus from simply the individual worker's welfare to the whole of society. He accepted private property, both personal and real, as limited in a way that it did not violate the rights of either the community or non-owners. Assuming fair competition, he maintained that capital had a right to a fair share of profits after labor received its due. Yet, he argued for strong antitrust measures to keep corporate units competitive and small, although capital as a practical necessity could accept interest in the capital economic system. A worker was entitled to a family wage through minimum wage legislation, but income beyond the minimum necessary for living should be determined by productivity, ability, and the common good.

Besides accepting responsible labor scales aided by strong unions, Ryan viewed organized labor as a major means to economic fulfillment, checking the narrow materialism of the AFL craft unions. For unions sometimes could be so member-oriented that they violated the rights of capital and the public. Government functions were to pursue minimum wage and antitrust legislation. While he supported unions, he also favored private associations, cooperatives,

---

[8] Ibid., 76–77.

profit-sharing programs, and co-partnership between labor and management.[9]

Many of Ryan's principles and thinking, ante-dating the establishment of SAD, echoed the U.S. bishops' *Pastoral Letter of 1919*. In 1944, he summarized its main points. Betten argues, however, that the bishops' program "was virtually ignored" in SAD's earliest years. SAD, he said, developed "a far more conservative stance than the potential of the Bishops' Program suggested." Ryan was much more cautious about support of unions, urging them to go beyond material goals, acquire a social vision, support for the Child Labor Amendment, and government supervision, and/or ownership of some natural resources. He labeled AFL leadership as "neither adequate nor effective" and criticized restrictive work rules that earlier he would have approved of. He stressed more cooperative decision-making on the plant level, profit sharing, eventual sharing of ownership, higher wages, and stock-sharing plans.[10]

Several reasons were alleged for SAD not advancing Ryan's and the bishops' earlier progressivism in the 1920. First, bishops, clergy, religious, and laity "were [not] convinced that our industrial system should be reorganized" in a radical manner. Second, SAD had to dissipate its energies in other priority campaigns, such as parochial schools targeted by Nativists, and immigration restrictions and threats that affected immigrant workers. SAD was also busy providing the numerous services mentioned earlier—publications, lectures, surveys, study clubs, and press conferences—for the benefit of child welfare, credit unions, social work, "Americanization" of immigrants, ethnic groups' loyalty, and industrial relations. Third, as a very young and somewhat unusual organization in the Church, SAD needed some functional reorganization, which did not appear until 1928 when education and other services were spun

---

[9] Ibid., 77–78.
[10] Ibid., 78–81.

off. Fourth, some lay organizations, such as the National Conference of Catholic Women and the National Conference of Men, were quite parochial in outlook. There were efforts to create private boarding for working women and settlement houses, as well as social clubs. These activities could be described only as social service and not social reform. Fifth, the concerted hostility of governments, courts, and management's "Open Shop" campaign distracted SAD from more progressive aspects of industrial relations. SAD was involved in several interfaith investigations of strikes in mining, railroads, and textiles. The fault usually lay with capital, but SAD did more than deplore such opposition to unions.

As early as 1922, SAD took steps to pursue one of the primary objectives of Catholic Social Thought—unity of interests between labor and management and within labor. A prime example was the "Catholic Conference on Industrial Problems," which organized annual meetings on a regional basis to bring capital, labor, and outside experts to discuss the problems of labor and capital in the light of Catholic Social Teaching. Discussed were wages, collective bargaining, the role of women in industry, and the prevalent types of labor–management cooperation. Mild as SAD's progressivism was in the 1920s, it surpassed that of other Catholic organizations at that time.[11]

With the Great Depression and its social-economic fallout, SAD took a more radical turn. Thanks to *Quadragesimo Anno* in 1931, Ryan's prestige improved among many in the hierarchy, who were usually reluctant to offend the Vatican. He taught that the Depression was caused by under-consumption and over-production, namely, "bad distribution of purchasing power." In a 1937 address to the National Catholic Social Action Conference (NCSAC), he outlined his plan for recovery.

---

[11] Ibid., 81–85.

Some of the more salient aspects of his plan were these: significantly increased public works programs, paid for by highly graduated higher income and inheritance taxes; a thirty-hour work week; minimum work hour law; a minimum wage law; a new government farm policy; the prevention of monopolies; price controls; interest rate deductions; and a greater distribution of ownership. He also wanted the reinstatement of the National Recovery Administration (NRA) with more power to labor and its extension to agriculture and professions with more government oversight. He called for little NRAs at the state levels to fill the vacuum for intrastate industry, as well as the establishment of a federation of all separate industries for improved relations among themselves and for the entire nation. In addition to structural changes in any restored NRA, Ryan had regulatory programmatic changes in mind: production quantity, prices, employment, wages, hours, training, social insurance, work methods, interests, capitalization, profits, and credit. Both Ryan and McGowan conceded that the NRA did not go far enough in planning.[12]

Thus, by the end of the 1930s, Ryan was an enthusiastic New Deal supporter and a thorough Keynesian, advocating deficit financing to support greater government spending. Praise for competition and smallness were replaced by the necessity for regulation and planning.

He also assumed that Capitalism as it existed was doomed unless it underwent radical modifications such as those recommended in *Quadragesimo Anno*, which he understood in more millennial terms than many socialists. He associated with several socialists, was an active member of the Public Ownership League, and offered to serve as editor of its journal. Yet, he was also uncomfortable in their company, was refused permission to speak before several of their

---

[12] Ibid., 86–87.

groups, and felt constrained from serving on some of their commit-tees.[13]

Most significant for this present research were Ryan's attitudes about the U.S. labor movement. By the 1930s there was no longer any ambivalence: unions were needed to achieve something like quality in bargaining power; yellow-dog contracts were unreasonable; closed shops were necessary; and sit-down strikes were equivalent to picketing inside—neither confiscation nor larceny.

Very friendly with John Brophy and Phil Murray, and defender of David Dubinsky and Sidney Hillman against red-baiters, Ryan supported industrial unionism, but was officially neutral in the AFL and CIO conflict. Insisting there was room for both, he said, "Undoubtedly, the ideal form would be industrial, in as much as it exemplifies the cooperation of the strong with the weak."

He still championed the Child Labor Amendment, as well as the Social Security Act, the Wagner Act, and limits on labor injunctions. He also served on several work-oriented and pro-labor organizations. Examples included the National Unemployment League, the American Association for Labor Legislation, the Association for Social Security, the "Citizens Committee to Aid in the Struggle of the Employees of the *Wisconsin News* against Hearst," and numerous federal government advisory positions in relation to labor.

Betten added that Ryan's economic outlook evolved from the individual to the social and his labor outlook from ambivalence and criticism to total support, especially of the CIO. Betten ended: "The Social Action Department continued to follow Ryan's direction for more than a generation after the New Deal," which concentrated more on policy matters, his assistants ran the programs and services. His statements, whether official SAD policy or not, were taken as such, "thus giving his declarations the aura of hierarchical

---

[13] Ibid., 87–89.

approval." After *Quadragesimo Anno,* his pro-labor statements took on greater importance for Catholic clergy, who quoted him at labor rallies and in Labor Schools. SAD's Catholic Conference on Industrial Relations evidenced greater attendance and different emphases—moral and practical effects of the Depression, higher wages, lower unemployment, measures for relief, government responsibility, union rights, economic planning, reform of Capitalism, lower profits, federal regulation of hours and wages, and greater social actionists' involvement.

Other SAD policies and services gained in momentum, scope and emphasis, including women in industry, increased wages, fewer work hours, collective bargaining, unemployment insurance, major public works programs, and bona fide unions. There were several interfaith campaigns on behalf of specific strikes, NRA, Wagner Act, higher income taxes for wealthy, unification of AFL and CIO, social insurance, and cooperative planning. Such efforts to change social conditions had effects that will be evident in a later volume in *Catholic Labor Priests* on Labor Schools and Institutes of Industrial Relations.

4

CATHOLIC SOCIAL TEACHING

Sources for the Five Giants and

Other Labor Priests

T hroughout the preceding discussion of SAD's history, staff, and policies, there have been recurring references to Pope Leo XIII's *Rerum Novarum*, Pope Pius XI's *Quadragesimo Anno*, and the U.S. bishops' *Pastoral Letter of 1919*. While much could be said about the influences of these seminal documents in Europe,[1] the focus here is on their impact on U.S. labor priests.

Understanding SAD's policies, as part of what the labor priests taught, is impossible without understanding the papal and episcopal documents that made up the state of Catholic Social Teaching at that time. Only then can there be intelligent analysis of leading labor priests' talks, sermons, publications, correspondence, and other material on labor–management and related issues.

Here, attention will focus only on the Catholic Social Teaching itself, not on the specifics of applications to economic, political, or union situations. Such will be explored in later volumes. It is noted that many insights of these seminal documents enjoyed Scriptural (New and Old Testament) and Patristic support, but it was not until Vatican II that such older sources had such a prominent influence.

---

[1] O'Brien 1965.

While primary and authoritative voices were heard in popes, conciliar, episcopal, and related documents, in many instances labor priests learned Catholic Social Teaching from secondary and lesser authoritative sources. Such would include occasional statements of bishops and religious superiors; correspondence from SAD staffers; meetings of Catholic Conference of Industrial Relations; newspapers of some local ACTU groups; and periodicals like SAD's *Social Action Notes for Priests, America, Commonweal, Social Order*. Other secondary sources were articles and books—some by Catholics and some not—that amounted to commentaries on Catholic Social Teaching or its possible applications to specific issues. Talks and sermons, especially of labor priests with academic experience, were spiced with references to such books and authors.

Citations noted from the twentieth-century labor priests who will be noted in the volumes in this study were from Leo XIII (seventy), Benedict XV (five), Pius XI (ninety-eight), Pius XII (twenty), John XXIII (twelve), Paul VI (four), and John Paul II (four). Such large numbers of citations from Leo XIII and Pius XI are understandable, since both chartered new territory with the initiation and expansion of the industrial revolution's problems for workers. Also, both were the most well known in the time period of most labor priests' activities.

The smaller number of citations from Pius XII is also understandable, given his preoccupation with World War II and its aftermath. Nevertheless, although Pius XII did not write an encyclical on labor issues, he produced many addresses and letters on the subject.

The fewer citations from John XXIII, Paul VI, and John Paul II are similarly understandable, given the labor priests long practice of citing the writings of Leo XIII and Pius XI, as well as the distractions of the cold war. Nonetheless, despite the significant role of John XXIII and Paul VI in Vatican II's and/or the Synod of Bishops' expressions of concern for labor issues, both men issued some crucial encyclicals and/or apostolic letters that contained teaching on labor issues.

The same can be said of the writings of John Paul II, even thought he had played a much more subdued role as a bishop at Vatican II and at the Synod of Bishops. Never to be forgotten is John Paul II's encyclical *Laborem Exercens* (On Human Labor), especially that most powerful statement that "Labor unions are absolutely indispensable in industrial society."

It also must be kept in mind that by the time of the pontificates of John XXIII, Paul VI, and John Paul II, most of the labor priests had disappeared from the scene. Also, with few exceptions, labor priests were not on the scene during the pontificate of Benedict XV, a pope so preoccupied with achieving peace before and during World War I. Thus, the content of the labor priests' sermons and talks, books and articles came almost completely from Leo XIII, Pius XI, and Pius XII.

The overwhelming numbers of citations were from *Rerum Novarum*. The labor priests' citations from this encyclical referred to motivation and strong support for labor movement involvement, defense of the rights of workers to organize and to join unions, support for collective bargaining and union strikes, concern about jobs/wages and prices/profits, calls for a family or living wage, openness to both craft and industrial unions, models for Labor Schools and Labor–Management Conferences, ideas for the Association of Catholic Trade Unionists, topics for Labor Day sermons, harmonization with the U.S. bishops' *Pastoral Letter of 1919* and the spirit of the United States, compatibility with the National Labor Relations Act and the International Labor Organization, preparation for *Quadragesimo Anno*, more condemnation of Communist Socialism than criticism of laissez-faire capitalism, neglected in Catholic colleges and seminaries, reminder of the importance but limitations of the role of government in labor–management relations, support of the right to and social responsibility of private property, the ideal of labor–management harmony, and warnings about management greed and union corruption.

Few references were made to Benedict XV: the impact of economic conditions on the faithful; the importance of priests' involvement in social and economic issues; support for labor, the challenges of mediation and arbitration of labor–management relations; and approval of the Association of Christian Workers. There was reference to Pius XI's *Singulari Quadam*, which allowed Christians to join "neutral unions," though separate Catholic unions were preferred. That encyclical also included some principles enunciated in the U.S. bishops' *Pastoral Letter of 1919*.

References to Pius XI's encyclical *Divini Redemptoris* (Atheistic Communism) included the duty of priests to assist people to obtain temporal goods with justice and charity; Communism as a satanic scourge bent on destroying Christian civilization; the impossibility of Catholics' collaborating with Communism; the need for courses that provided a foundation for social education essential for a democratic system; and a primary concern for the remedies of the economic evils responsible for spreading Marxism and Communism spawned by the excesses of Capitalism.

As the numbers mentioned earlier show, references to Pius XI's *Quadragesimo Anno* were abundant. The encyclical addressed issues such as support for the rights of workers to form and join unions, to bargain collectively, and to strike; the need for "ample sufficiency" and "adequate family income" for workers; the role of government in ownership; the necessity of social responsibility joined to the right of private property; the importance of Labor–Management Conferences; the absence of a "natural right" to share in management—even in the terms and conditions of employment; a call for balanced prices for stabilizing prosperity and social justice; the applicability to the economic and political aspect of democracy; the importance of the principle of subsidiarity; support for the goals and programs of the International Labor Organization (ILO); the need for industry councils or occupational groups; the feasibility of labor–management harmony; the need for continuing labor–management collaboration within and across industries and approval of the 1940 AFL and Railway Workers Unions policies.

A social justice theology emerged from *Quadragesimo Anno* as a source for the possible greater reconstruction of the social order, with the support of the encyclical by the U.S. bishops and labor leaders and inspiration of labor priests. Yet it was not without attendant challenges: the persistent communication and acceptance without winning the popular mind for social reform; pastoral need for outlines of the encyclical; inadequate teaching in Catholic colleges and seminaries; misinterpretations by the radio orator Fr. Charles Coughlin; awareness of the Catholic Church not possessing the mission nor equipment to offer technical reforms; confusion in using papal statements on Fascism as applying to U.S. governmental power over labor–management agreements strikes; hostility toward the labor movement among Catholics; the indictment of anti-unionism as "criminal injustice;" implicit disapproval of "right-to-work" laws; and obstacles of a "messianic redemption" for the poor.

Quadragesimo Anno provided comparisons of Communism or Socialism and Capitalism, seen alternately as collectivism and individualism, as the "twin rocks of shipwreck." It described the role of Capitalism's failings in generating dire economic conditions; the Great Depression as the maladjustment among production, distribution, and consumption of wealth; consequences of the "individualistic spirit;" "economic dictatorships" of dominating trustees and international imperialism; widespread lobbying and confusion of civil governments; Communism as a degeneration of Socialism; irreconcilability of Catholicism with the U.S. Socialist Party and the U.S. Socialist movement; goals and programs of social reform and

59

Socialism compatible with Christian principles; Socialism modifying some tenets of class struggle and private property; need for collaboration with Socialists on human nature, ownership, and the function of government; importance of cooperation with people of goodwill; Henry Wallace's more radical policies on jobs, prices, and unions than in *Quadragesimo Anno.*

Several of Pius XII's statements were cited. In the 1930s he issued an allocution to Spanish refugees during the Spanish Civil War, decrying race prejudice and discrimination as the heresy of pride and race. A 1938 letter called for justice in the social order. His 1944 Christmas Message addressed many socioeconomic issues. His post–World War II prohibition against voting for communists in Italian elections was considered an exception to the traditional Catholic call for nonintervention in partisan elections. His 1950s encyclical *Menti Nostrae* decried excesses of Capitalism. A 1953 Easter Address sought fortitude, patience, and perseverance in seeking justice and peace. At various times, Pius XII's strong support for labor unions and the ILO was voiced: allowing a degree of codetermination or joint labor–management, but not supporting a claim of a natural right of workers to share in management, even terms and conditions of employment; cooperating with good-willed people; critiquing Liberalism, laissez-faire economics, individualism, Social Darwinism, and Physiocratic economics; tracing the history of Catholic Social Teaching; modeling Catholic labor institutes; and instituting the Feast of St. Joseph the Worker.

Statements from John XXIII' came especially from *Mater et Magistra* and *Pacem in Terris,* which proposed more radical views on private property than Leo XIII; calling for the Church to be more relevant to the modern world and in interfaith issues; the State's obligation to enhance workers' rights; mentioning Communism only once in *Mater et Magistra;* accepting movements to realize human aspirations; stressing labor–management peace, supporting and challenging labor, approving collective bargaining and strikes, and urging adequate family income; advocating stewardship, technological advances, and human economic progress; endorsing the labor priests' anticipation of ecumenism in the 1930s.

Cited also were Paul VI's statements concerning the creation of SODEPAX; the teachings on three economic systems of Capitalism, Communism, and Socialism; and the widespread dissent in the wake of his encyclical *Humanae Vitae*.

Citations from John Paul II included the human dignity and moral aspects of work in *Laborem Exercens*; focus of service in work; support for labor–management peace; praise for Catholic Social Teaching on labor–management relations; and the indispensable role of labor unions in modern industrial life.

Besides papal teaching, labor priests cited Vatican II's *Church in the Modern World* that rejected radical causes; emphasized economic and social life; encouraged sharing in management and profits of business and private property by workers; called for the Church to take an active role in social and economic reform; and blessed the earlier efforts of labor priests in labor–management relations and ecumenism. The 1971 Synod's *Justice in the World* was also cited.

Labor priests cited U.S. Catholic bishops' statements, as well as those by individual bishops and religious superiors on labor–management issues. Most frequently mentioned was the U.S. Catholic bishops' *Pastoral Letter of 1919*, noting its incorporation of the principles of *Rerum Novarum*; its relevance to the National Religion and Labor Foundation; its inspiration for earlier labor priests; its usefulness as a source for teaching on wage justice and unions' rights to exist; as an antidote to the "hysterical crises of Socialism," "reform" or "readjustment," but not a real "reconstruction," "backbone of the New Deal," or "implicit pattern" for the New Deal.

Also cited was the U.S. Catholic bishops' 1940 Statement, *Church and Social Order*, which was called "one of the most important" statements of the U.S. Catholic bishops on social and economic issues, was seen as providing an extension of *Rerum Novarum's* advocacy for wage justice, and was linked to protests over racial prejudice and discrimination. In addition, there were citations of the 1951 *U.S. Catholic Bishops' Statement* for its "thinly veiled" condemnation of McCarthyism. Also mentioned was a draft of New York's Cardinal Patrick Hayes's planned 1938 Letter, *The Church and Social Justice,* which his successor Cardinal Spellman never adopted, perhaps due to planning for the 1940 statement. Finally, cited several times were the Jesuit superior general Joseph Jansens's *De Apostolatu Sociali* and the Jesuit southern provincial's statement on race.

Utilization of such authoritative sources by almost forty labor priests illustrates their knowledge of Catholic Social Teaching about labor–management issues.

Let us now turn to some specific examples from the most influential labor priests, who all relied upon such papal and hierarchical documents for their arguments.

In 1940, Hartford Fr. Joseph F. Donnelly addressed a Catholic Conference on Industrial Problems on Pius XI's "Corporatism." Shortly before the end of World War II, Donnelly referred to Leo XIII's description of Socialists in *Rerum Novarum* as people who "[worked] on the poor man's envy of the rich, endeavor[ed] to destroy private property and maintain[ed] that individual possessions should become the common property of all, to be administered by the State or by municipal bodies." Later, Pius XI in *Quadragesimo Anno* declared that Communism, once in power, became "degenerated Socialism" and he mentioned its destruction and hostility with regard to the Church. "Even more severely, must be condemned the foolhardiness of those who neglect to remove or modify such conditions as exasperate the minds of people and so prepare the way for the overthrow and the ruin of the social order."

Pius XI's encyclical *Atheistic Communism* declared that Communism was a satanic scourge bent on destroying Christian civilization, a false messianic idea, and a deceptive mysticism, despite its outlawing of all religions. Pius XI cited examples of Communists' efforts to worm their way into religious and humanitarian organizations without changing their ultimate principles or goals. He said, "See to it, Venerable Brethren, the faithful do not allow themselves to be deceived! Communism is intrinsically wrong, and no one who would save Christian civilization may collaborate with it in any undertaking whatsoever."[2]

During his eulogy for Donnelly, Msgr. George Higgins said that Donnelly was par excellence precisely the type of apostle Pius XI had in mind when in *Quadragesimo Anno* he instructed bishops of the world "to assign specially qualified priests to the social apostolate." Further, he heeded the instruction of Pius XI's *Atheistic Communism*, "A priest...who has the duty of administering temporal goods must bear in mind that he is obligated not only to observe the laws of justice and charity, but also that he must make a particular effort to show himself a real father to the poor."

In a 1947 dispute with Los Angeles Bishop Manning, Fr. George Dunne, S.J., sought permission to assist a dissident but honest Hollywood union, the Conference of Studio Unions (CSU). Deplored by Pius XI was a false prudence by which "priests had been afraid to preach the doctrines of *Quadragesimo Anno*...because certain wealthy Catholics in their parishes would take offense." Daniel Marshall, with a Los Angeles law firm, defended Dunne in a letter to the Jesuit assistant general, because an executive of one of the largest airplane manufacturers had accused Dunne of being disloyal to the Church and spreading Communism by supporting the Fair Employment Practices Committee. Words of Benedict XV were

---

[2] Catholic University Archives, Washington, D.C., and Hartford Archdiocese Archives, Hartford, Conn.

cited, "Let no member of the clergy imagine that such activity lies outside his priestly ministry because that is the economic sphere. It is precisely in this sphere that the salvation is in peril."

The book *King's Pawn: The Memoirs of George H. Dunne, S.J.* (1919) dismissed Pius XI's oft-quoted words in *Quadragesimo Anno* that "no Catholic can be a true socialist." Dunne stated that Pius XI did not distinguish between socialist philosophy and programs, but implicitly accepted the Marxist thesis, saying, "Programs often strikingly approach the just demands of Christian social reformers." John XXIII's *Pacem in Terris* was cited: "Who can deny that those movements, in so far as they conform to the dictates of right reason and are interpreters of the lawful aspiration of the human person, contain elements that are positive and deserving approval."[3]

In a 1935 *America* article, Milwaukee Fr. Francis Haas said Leo XIII believed that most workers thought the capitalist technique for wage determination was essentially unjust. Yet Leo's writing about the natural right of workers to form unions had to be interpreted primarily as a vindication of the right to bargain collectively and of governments' obligation to protect such an inherent right, as evident in Leo's lamenting the destruction of the Workmen's Guilds in the eighteenth century with his regret that "no other organization took their place." In 1938 Haas drafted a pastoral letter, *The Church and Social Justice,* for the ailing Cardinal Hayes, with the draft closely adhering to *Quadragesimo Anno* and serving to offset communist propaganda, which deceived many Catholic workers.

In October 1941, SAD's Hayes noted that in *Quadragesimo Anno* and *Atheistic Communism* Pius XI "talked a lot about social education for all classes as an essential of any successful democratic system." Hayes sent James Martin, of Yale Divinity School's branch of the National Religion and Labor Foundation, copies of the 1940 U.S. bishops' statement, *The Church and the Social Order.* Hayes told Doris

---

[3] California Jesuit Archives, Los Gatos, Calif., and Dunne 1990.

64

Hassell of Collier's New York Readers Research Bureau about the U.S. bishops' *Pastoral Letter of 1919* and *Church and the Social Order* (1940) He referred to Fr. Smith's article about Henry Wallace's criticism of "income producing property" and "unearned income." Hayes thought Wallace had gone much further than Pius XI's *Quadragesimo Anno*, but Hayes regarded the topic to be "a poorly-mapped-field."

Months later, Hayes recommended to A.H. Clemens the pamphlet *Jobs, Prices, and Unions*, which attempted to assess public awareness and acceptance of principles stressed in Leo XIII's and Pius XI's encyclicals. An inquiry by Fr. Michael Quinn of Brooklyn's Confraternity of Christian Doctrine about studying "Catholic sociology" drew Hayes's response about the special importance of the heavy obligations of people "under Catholic democratic principles of Leo XIII and Pius XI, to create right institutions in economic and political life—organizations of employers and employees, legislatures, and government agencies."

Hayes criticized the negativism of George Donahue, editor of the New York ACTU's *The Labor Leader* toward a federal official who came in for harsh criticism, and especially toward top leaders of the AFL, CIO, and Railway Unions. Hayes said that despite much rank-and-file indifference and strife among the leaders, their policy decisions "showed striking similarities to Pius XI's teachings."

A year later, Hayes congratulated Fr. John Cronin, S.S., for holding a discussion with ten priests and for comparing England's Beveridges Plan to Leo XIII's and Pius XI's encyclicals on labor. Promising to incorporate the event in the next issue of *Social Action Notes for Priests*, Hayes alluded to the English Catholic *Blackfriars* and other journals. "[With] all our tradition of authority it took almost a personal disaster, calamity really felt, to get English Catholics interested in *Rerum Novarum*." He added that McGowan noted how few followed "the conviction of SAD to begin with and judge their publications by the encyclicals."

Hayes responded to San Francisco attorney John Doran's request for a clarification about whether or not the Church had a comprehensive and coherent plan. The answer was lengthy, but at its core was this statement: "The Pope [Pius XI] laid down only some general principles...clear and distinctive enough to indicate broadly a new system of...collaboration between labor and management [and] industry-wide and inter-industry collaboration." Also, Hayes cautioned another priest about being too hard on Communism, since some papal documents admitted communists did have some acceptable goals and he did not know of any Catholics who incurred any Church censure for joining the Communist Party. Though Pius XII had said a Catholic may not be a socialist and a fortiori communist, this was never stated explicitly.

In 1945, SAD's Higgins said the greatest contribution of ACTU's *Wage Earners* was its emphasis on Pius XI's industries and professions system. He told a *Commonweal* editor that in discussions about Socialism and Catholic Social Teaching one had to distinguish between the "doctrine" of Socialism and Socialism's economic program. "For, the very heart of the problem was not specific planks which might be quite ethical and consonant with encyclical teaching, but what was central to *Quadragesimo Anno*, if implemented effectively in time."

He insisted Catholics and socialists "must work together harmoniously and sympathetically for greater economic justice.... [Also] conservative Catholics and socialists alike have something to learn from a closer study of *Quadragesimo Anno*—not merely about the ownership of property, but also about the nature of man and the function of government." Higgins said Pius XI's encyclical *Atheistic Communism* was "primarily concerned with positive remedies for the economic evils which are at least partly responsible for the spread of Marxism."

At Jesuit Fr. Benjamin Masse's funeral on September 30, 1978, SAD's Higgins said that Masse had followed Popes Leo XIII, Pius XI, John XXIII, and Paul VI in remaining adamant that struggles between labor and management could never be resolved unless and until labor's right to organize and bargain collectively was recognized in principle and guaranteed in practice. In early 1966, he spoke on "Economic and Social Life" during an international conference of experts and observers at Vatican II.[4] He focused on "Church and the Modern World."

SAD's McGowan hailed Leo XIII's *Rerum Novarum* as something to be proud of and meriting "the honor and gratitude of every Catholic and above all of the Catholics who are close to the industrial life today." In a 1937 article in Fr. Coughlin's *Social Justice*, McGowan cited *Rerum Novarum* in support of compromise in a controversy between industries in the North and the South, as well as between the AFL and CIO over wages and hours. He also noted Pius XI's encyclical's reference to the government's obligation to help the guild system. Quite firm about failing businesses closing, he cited Leo XIII: "In the last extreme, counsel must be taken whether the business can continue, or whether some other provision should be made for the workers." Pius XI, he added, called employee–employer, management–union collaboration "a near guild," demanding balanced prices for steady prosperity's sake in a program of social justice.

A 1961 document entitled *Notes on Social Justice* was basically McGowan's commentary on *Quadragesimo Anno* and represented his theology of social justice. At a McGowan 1962 Memorial Mass, Higgins said his mentor and predecessor had advanced a plan eventually called the Industry Council Plan, almost ten years before

---

[4] Miller 1966, 489–497.

Quadragesimo Anno. He said, "Gompers was sympathetic with the idea, but unfortunately died before he was able to do anything about it in a practical way."[5]

In *Seven Troubled Years,* SAD's Ryan noted Pius XI's comment, "Paradoxically, Capitalism can be saved only by becoming transformed into a system that apparently could not properly be called Capitalism," but also included such a system in his scheme of occupational groups. For Ryan, there were two Socialisms: one more extreme (Communism), which Leo XIII condemned, and another more moderate, which showed varying degrees of moderation. Of the more moderate, if the mitigation continued, Pius XI said, it would "no longer differ from the desires of those who are striving to remold society on the basis of Christian principles." In that context, Pius XI said some kinds of property should be under government control, because in private hands they would not serve the general welfare, so powerful their impact on society.

Yet, Ryan thought the U.S. Socialist Party and Socialist movement still retained enough false philosophy about society and hostility to religion to render them contrary to Pius XI's *Quadragesimo Anno.* Ryan was neither an advocate for the status quo nor a radical. Yet he thought the U.S. Catholic bishops' *Pastoral Letter of 1919* on "Social Reconstruction" was misnamed, because, it called for a considerable amount of reform, readjustment, and improvement, but there were no changes envisioned to warrant the notion of "reconstruction." Some thought Ryan did not pay enough attention to Leo XIII's warnings about the limitations for government interventions. Yet Ryan was quite aware of the need for an initial role for government. His position on private property differed somewhat from that

---

[5] Kansas City–St. Joseph Archdiocesan Archives, Kansas City, Mo.; Catholic University Archives, Washington, D.C.; and Detroit Archdiocese Archives, Detroit, Mich.

of Leo XIII, but Ryan anticipated Vatican II's insistence on the common destiny of the goods of creation to serve the needs of all.[6]

Bishop Cleveland Schrembs insisted on Leo XIII's statement on the right of labor to organize, a right reasserted and reemphasized by Pius XI. As episcopal moderator of the National Council of Catholic Women, Schrembs insisted they become acquainted with *Rerum Novarum*. At a 1937 Youngstown Steel Workers Organizing Committee (SWOC) event, he referred to the popes and the Wagner Act, saying that "there should be no fundamental differences between employer and employee that cannot be smoothed out by friendly conversation...[but] no individual claim conflicting with [community]...rights shall be valid."[7]

To those who insisted that encyclicals were too vague, New Orleans–based Fr. Louis Twomey, S.J., explained that although the encyclicals presented some problems for moral and theological interpretation "they are thought out very carefully in the light not only of Catholic theological reasoning, but also in the light of developing phenomena in the existential world." In May 1947, he noted that Pius XII's declaration that no Catholic could support the Communist Party was an exception to the official Church policy of not taking an official stand in elections. The pope did not dictate "a mandatory choice among the other contending parties."

In 1948 Schrembs gave six steps to follow in conducting discussion groups. One of them called for bringing the force of "Christian principles to bear on the critical maladjustments in our social, economic, and political life [which] call...for a serious study of what these encyclicals contain [*Rerum Novarum* and *Quadragesimo Anno*]." In 1950, he wrote about the Fair Employment Practices Committee (FEPC) with a reference to the U.S. bishops' *Pastoral Letter of 1919*,

---

[6] Abell 1946; Broderick 1963; Curran 1982; Gearty1953.
[7] Archives of the Cleveland Diocese, Cleveland, Ohio; Grand Rapids Diocese, Grand Rapids, Mich.; and Toledo, Diocese, Ohio; and Poluse 1991.

"which became the backbone of the social legislation since the New Deal era began in 1933." In 1951 he referred to the U.S. bishops' *Pastoral Letter of 1919*, which "proposed a social program which later proved to be the pattern, at least implicitly followed, in New Deal legislation."

In 1953 he referred to Pius XI's phrase about "an individualistic Spirit" creating a vacuum in the souls and stomachs of hundreds of millions across the world. Also cited was *Quadragesimo Anno* on individualism and collectivism as the "twin rocks of shipwreck." He spoke of the "third way" of encyclicals. In 1953, he hoped the New Orleans Institute could move "significantly toward the reconstruction of the social order to which Pius XI speaks in *Quadragesimo Anno*."

In the 1960s, John XXIII's *Mater et Magistra* mentioned Communism only once and in passing. Twomey explained: "John XXIII is telling us to quit pushing the panic button and be quick about removal of social evils in which Communism got started." In a 1965 Labor Day sermon in Toledo, Ohio, Twomey cited *Rerum Novarum* and *Mater et Magistra*, about strikes and real collective bargaining, stewardship of creation, human economic progress, and technological advances.

5

INSTITUTIONAL RESOURCES

Media, Church Institutions,

Catholic Labor Schools, & ACTU

I n addition to recourse to authoritative Catholic Social Teaching, labor priests could draw from abundant storehouses of resources not readily available to workers. These included media outlets, abundant opportunities to utilize Church facilities, and access to institutional resources such as the Catholic Conference on Industrial Problems, Labor Schools and Institutes of Industrial Relations, Association of Catholic Trade Unionists, and other lay organizations.

Labor priests themselves were often the generators or focus of media. At other times they cited or explained the media sources. One source for Catholic workers to become acquainted with labor priests' activities and Catholic teachings on labor–management relations were archdiocesan and diocesan weekly newspapers, Although their coverage of labor priests was rather cursory. Arranged by geographic regions, there were eight in the East, ten in the Midwest, five in the Far Northwest, and four in the Southwest.

A second source was Catholic periodicals or journals (75), most of which were monthlies rather than weeklies. These periodicals appealed mostly to better-educated readers and thus their readership was somewhat circumscribed. Yet, their audience was more focused on labor–management issues, especially labor leaders—not all of whom were Catholic.

A third source was secular newspapers, usually in cities where the labor movement was most active. A fourth source was secular periodicals or journals (81). A fifth source was labor-oriented periodicals or journals (115), some of which were Catholic in nature (79). A sixth source was books and pamphlets (220). Some of these were autobiographies or biographies of labor priests (15); others dealt specifically with labor–management relations/issues (115). Few dealt with aspects of Communism (20).

Church facilities were available to spread the news of labor priests. These included parish and campus churches during Sunday Masses through sermons, announcements, and bulletins. A few archdioceses and dioceses had placed strictures on sermons and media reporting about principles of Catholic Social Teaching concerning labor–management issues. Motivations for such strictures were varied and complex. Sometimes there was an expressed fear of alienating parishioners opposed to Catholic support of the labor movement. Sometimes the fear was implied in actions taken against labor priests' sermons or speeches, writings or actions in which they expressed such support. Widespread exceptions were in dioceses that permitted the reading of the "Labor Day Statement" from SAD or from the local ordinary and scheduled sermons at Masses on Labor Day or on the Sunday of the Labor Day weekend. Local labor leaders, many non-Catholics, often attended these services. Frequently, the celebrants were the local ordinaries, with sermons preached by notable labor priests.

Parish schools and halls were often scenes of union meetings for organizing drives, strike votes, boycott, demonstration planning, or public forums on labor–management issues. These sites were typically equipped with telephones and copying machines for "getting out the word." Dinners honoring labor or business leaders in the community were held on college and university campuses and commercial hotels. These were also the site for large conferences of Labor Schools and Institutes of Industrial Relations. Chapters of the Association of Catholic Trade Unionists regularly aided the teachings and activities of the labor priests). Other lay Catholic organizations, such as the Catholic Worker Houses, Holy Name Society, Knights of Columbus, National Council of Men and National Council of Women, also supported the labor priests in this manner..

Launched in 1922 as an annual event, the Catholic Conference on Industrial Problems numbered seventy regionally by 1939. The sessions, which were organized at the invitation of local bishops, focused on the character, origin, basic purposes, and detailed standards of economic life, means of establishing order and justice. Programs of education in Christian Social Teaching were also held. A typical program would feature presentations on "American Economic Life," "Youth in Industry," "Age in Industry," "The Right to a Livelihood," "Employer–Labor Cooperation," "Legislation," and "Ways and Means to Promote Christian Social Teaching." Speakers and attendees came from academia, business, government, labor, and religion.

Though these events allowed ample opportunity for questions and answers, the Conference's constitution forbade passing resolutions or voting on industrial policy issues. Publications containing the speeches and discussions of the Conferences were occasionally made available. Labor priests would sometimes be presenters at the Catholic Conference on Industrial Problems (CCIP) meetings, usually on the topic of the Church's Social Teaching, but on other occasions about economic, political, or union issues. The conferences gave labor priests, management, and labor leaders a chance to become better acquainted with Church teaching and related important issues. On one occasion, when the executive secretary, Detroit's Fr. Raymond Clancy, was asked about the achievements of the Conference, he responded that there was no yardstick, save the surfacing in communities of special knowledge and talents on labor–management relations.

The most common and enduring institutional arrangement to reach workers, especially union leaders and rank-and-file members, were the Labor Schools and Institutes of Industrial Relations. Their numbers are disputed—ranging from the 100s to the 200s—because differences among the sources and authors. Many of schools and institutes arose and faded quickly due to local and national developments. Focus here is limited to the origins, goals, programs, obstacles, demise, and achievements of the Labor Schools and Institutes of Industrial Relations.

In the early twentieth century three priests—an East Coast Jesuit by the name of Terrence Shealy, a Midwest diocesan by the name of Peter Dietz, and a West Coast diocesan by the name of Peter Yorke—pioneered efforts to establish schools for workers in order to teach Catholics about labor–management relations. Between the 1902 and 1936 such schools were few in number, but by 1936 one of the most important, effective, and long-lived institutions was founded, the Xavier Institute of Industrial Relations (XIIR), based in New York's Manhattan Jesuit Xavier Military School. According to Notre Dame's Fr. Mark Fitzgerald, C.S.C., director of one of the last Labor–Management Conferences, by 1949 there were over one hundred such schools and institutes.[1]

Some of the schools and institutes were strictly parish entities, usually with some diocesan supervision. Others operated diocesan-

---

[1] Fitzgerald 1954.

wide under the guidance of a director appointed by the local ordinary; others were established by and operating on the campuses of Catholic colleges and universities. Another variant were general programs of adult education that offered a few courses on labor–management relations. Finally, a type that Fitzgerald omitted: his own Labor–Management Conferences, which met less frequently than the schools and institutes.

Initially, members of both management and unions joined the schools or institutes. Later, management's interest subsided, as the Church's support of unions became apparent; students then were mostly workers, unionized or not. Participants represented a wide range of levels of age, education, interests, occupation, religion, and union or no nonunion membership.

Evident in many of Fitzgerald's comments were references to Labor Schools and Institutes of Industrial Relations run by the De La Salle Brothers, Holy Cross Fathers, Oblates of Mary Immaculate, Redemptorists, and Holy Ghost Fathers. There were also approximately twenty Jesuit sites, which were celebrated in a March 2000 article by the recently deceased Fr. Edward F. Boyle, S.J., director of the Boston Labor Guild, the sole surviving site.[2] Preferring the title "institutes" to "schools," Jesuit efforts represented a response to Leo XIII's *Rerum Novarum*. They took a leap into the competition — but with a strong spiritual base — between those of a socialist or communist bent and were testimony to the social and economic malaise created by the Great Depression and the response of New Deal legislation. Jesuit directors, like some of the other directors, were also mediators and arbitrators, lecturers to Church and civic organizations, worker retreat directors, and writers.

Variously phrased, the goals of Labor Schools and Institutes of Industrial Relations were many. First, impart the principles and facil-

---

[2] Boyle 2000, 1–7.

itate the application of Catholic Social Teaching to workers and employers. Second, train workers and management in basic skills necessary to successful labor–management relationships. Third, make sure that harmonious relations in industry and business were taken for granted as technology developed. Fourth, assist labor unions, especially the CIO, which had not yet developed its own worker educational programs. Fifth, prevent the repetition of the mistakes of the Catholic Church in Europe, which had diminished the attachment of so many workers to the Church during the Industrial Revolution. Sixth, build a sound social order by creating understanding and cooperation between labor and management. Finally, offset communist and extreme socialist inroads into the labor movement.

Depending upon the goals, differences arose in titles, procedures, and courses. A change in titles from Labor Schools to Institutes of Industrial Relations, initiated by Jesuit directors, was dictated by the desire to make very clear that the doors were open to employers as well as employees, management as well as union personnel. For the same reason, most classes were open to both employers and employees. Degrees, credits, and examinations were not featured in most programs. Certificates and awards were presented at year-end dinners, however, as evidence of attendance for employers, unions, and families. Faculty came largely from academia, business, law firms, and unions—usually on a voluntary and non-compensatory basis. Monies were ordinarily not accepted from corporations; expenses were usually covered by funds from dioceses or religious communities who sponsored the programs, as well as for small fees paid by the workers, companies, and unions.

The most frequent courses taught were—public speaking, parliamentary procedure, debate techniques, industrial ethics, labor history, and basic economics. Classes were held one or two evenings a week for a period of ten or more weeks. It was hoped that most students would stay enrolled for two years. Larger programs included courses in arbitration/mediation, collective bargaining, contracts, grievance procedures, stewardships, and other types of nuts-and-bolts material.

Obstacles to the conducting of these programs were numerous, some accidental and some deliberate. Greater detail will be provided on these matters in future volumes, but here seven general explanations are provided. First, some Catholic workers and organizations became apathetic, especially in times of "full" employment. Second, some business opposed the very existence of the labor movement. Third, communist groups attributed sinister goals to the Catholic programs. Fourth, business complained about excessive emphasis on workers' "rights" and the great neglect of workers' "responsibilities." Fifth, some AFL officials became suspicious about the programs' bias toward CIO unions and about an ultimate goal of creating "confessional unions" (Catholic/Protestant), as in Canadian and European settings. Sixth, workers were distracted by the advent of television and by competition from other clubs. Finally, funds became scarcer as enrollment declined due to the loss of jobs and dioceses and other institutions were not able to provide personnel to serve as directors and faculty.

Considering these obstacles helps make it clear why the Labor Schools and Institutes of Industrial Relations eventually faded away. The most noteworthy reasons include these six: One, the communist attraction and threat subsidized. Two, educational programs in most CIO and AFL unions expanded in number. Three, degree and non-degree programs arose in the extension programs of many state universities and in such distinguished institutions as UC Berkeley, Cornell, Harvard, Illinois, and M.I.T. Four, negative popular perceptions of the labor movement intensified. Five, difficulties increased for labor organizing and bargaining from business, governmental, executive policies, and the judiciary. Finally, insecure union leaders feared a better educated rank-and-file membership.

In a later volume, details of the successes of some Labor School and Institutes of Industrial Relations will be discussed. Here, eight general observations are presented, although an overall assessment is extremely difficult. First, Catholic Social Teachings about labor–management relations were advanced, especially among union rank-and-file membership and leadership. Second, common misconceptions that all unions were communist and corrupt were dispelled. Third, confidence was gained in the information provided about labor–management issues. Fourth, respect increased for the Catholic Church's concern for the workers. Fifth, many individuals were inspired to choose union careers. Sixth, some of the institutional ties between the Church and the labor movement, locally and nationally, were retained. Finally, understanding increased about the linkages between the economy and the larger social fabric: addiction, crime, family, health, violence, etc.

Drawing on other sources, SAD's Higgins agreed with most of Fitzgerald's conclusions, but added two clarifications. Labor Schools were not supposed to build up pressure groups within unions and, save for two directors, there was explicit discouragement of the slightest move "in the direction of intra-union sectarianism." It was impossible to assess accurately the accomplishments of the Labor Schools, but there was general agreement that they contributed to arousing among workers a greater loyalty to the trade unionism.

Discussion of institutional arrangements for labor priests would be incomplete without reference to the Association of Catholic Trade Unionists, which played an important role in the Church's involvement in the labor movement. Meetings in Church basements and parish halls provided opportunities for ACTU chapters to reach workers and union leaders, but less frequently for labor priests' activities and teaching. This limitation was not dictated by hostility or opposition to labor priests, but because ACTU was a lay organization. Priests, appointed by a local ordinary, would serve as chaplains, spiritual guides, and occasional lecturers on Catholic Social

Teaching about labor–management relations. The exact number of ACTU chapters is not clear. Chapters waxed and waned in different areas and at different times. This research indicates that thirty might be a reasonable number.[3] Here, interest is in ACTU's origins, organizational structure, goals, and labor priests tie-ins.

On February 27, 1937, five lay social reformers—John Cort, George Donahue, Edward Scully, Edward Squitire, and Martin Wersing— held an initial organizational meeting of ACTU around a kitchen table in Dorothy Day's Catholic Worker headquarters in New York.[4] They did so, because they thought the Catholic Worker Movement was too utopian or millenarian and not sufficiently anticommunist. Soon, autonomous chapters with similar purposes were formed in Boston, Chicago, Detroit, and San Francisco, seeking little more than a blessing of the local ordinary. By 1940 eight chapters sent delegates to a convention in Cleveland in an effort to establish a loose national organization with a salaried national director and plans to meet twice a year. Each chapter was autonomous and expressed its own emphases and approaches to ACTU's goals.

At a convention in Cleveland, "Articles of Federation" were formulated that set standards required of all chapters for affiliation with the national organization, without prejudice to each chapter's local control.[5] The role of the national council, which was made up of two members from each local chapter, was "to establish and maintain liaison among the chapters, gathering information as to policies and problems of each chapter, and to distribute the same to other chapters by means of regular memoranda." ACTU's basic doctrine was

---

[3] Favorable and balanced writings are: Ward 1958; Betten 1969; Harrington 1960, 231–263; Taft 1949, 210–218. Favorable but partial writings are in Kelly 1948, 298–302; McKenna 1949, 453–45. An example of unfavorable and strident writing is Seaton 1975.

[4] Betten 1969, 124–145, *in passim.*

[5] Taft 1949, 210–218, *in passim.*

Rerum Novarum's mandate to create, side by side with unions, "associations zealously engaged in imbuing and informing their members in the teaching of religion and morality, so that they in turn may be able to permeate the unions with that good spirit which should direct all their activities." In fulfilling Leo XIII's mandate, ACTU chapters made several pledges: abide by the teachings and practices of the Catholic Church, especially as in papal documents; oppose fascists, Nazis, communists, and racketeers; attend union meetings regularly; maintain good standing in the organization. Individual members (ACTUists) had to be practicing Catholics and members of a bona fide union, as well as indicating the church they attend and the name of the pastor.

Chapters were divided into smaller groups, called industry councils, whenever five or more members worked in a particular industry. To claims that ACTU constituted a faction or political caucus within a given union, Taft admitted the theoretical possibility, but pointed to ACTU's record as a convincing denial. ACTU attacked Catholic labor leaders, supported socialist and Protestant candidates against Catholic candidates for union office when convinced the former would better serve the union than the latter, espoused decent and progressive unionism, and opposed union racketeering and abuses.

Acting in accord with papal mandates, ACTU insisted on the rights and duties of workers. Rights included jobs; adequate family living wages; collective bargaining; shares in profits after wages and a reasonable return to capital; nonviolent striking; peaceful picketing; and dignified working hours and conditions. Obligations were joining a union; striking only for "just cause" after other methods of settlement had been exhausted; refraining from violence; respecting private property; maintaining strict honesty within the union; fighting for a fair deal for all regardless of color, creed, or race; and sponsoring a Catholic Labor Defense League.

In aiding workers to achieve such rights and to fulfill such obligations, ACTU became involved in myriad activities, including conducting mass meetings in parishes and communities to publicize papal teaching on labor; establishing speakers' bureaus for clubs and parishes; operating Labor Schools; and publishing reputable and influential newspapers in local ACTU chapters. Over the years, such activities, in fulfillment of papal mandates, led ACTU to endorse various policies or campaigns such as profit sharing in industries; increasing social security benefits; initiating family allowances; supporting the Missouri Valley Authority modeled after the Tennessee Valley Authority; investigating the desirability of placing certain industries under government ownership; criticizing the Taft-Hartley Act; guaranteeing an annual wage for workers; becoming involved in organized labor battles; and fighting for civil rights.

Perhaps the most controversial aspects of ACTU were opposing communist inroads into unions and fostering papal "corporatism." The Pittsburgh chapter, for instance, became embroiled in fights with communist leaders in the United Electric union; the Detroit chapter, with communist leadership in the United Automobile Workers of America. Similar battles took place in Connecticut, Maryland, New York, and elsewhere. For many years communists and liberals accused ACTU members of being "clerical fascists," maintaining a grip on the CIO hierarchy on behalf of the Catholic Church. Another volume in this series will say more about this controversy.

A forthcoming volume in this series will address the issue of ACTU and corporatism in the context of labor priests and "corporativism." Sufficient here is a condensation of Taft's remarks on ACTU and corporativism. Due to attempts to identify the papal plan with the "corporate state" of Mussolini, Franco, and Salazar, Taft defined "corporativism" essentially as an economic and not a political arrangement, constituting an organic arrangement of economic corporations embracing whole industries and comprising workers and

81

investors. Unlike in corporate states, single industries would not be departments of government, but members of a corporate body, obligated to serve the public interest in a particular field of economic activity. Each industry would be governed by a board of directors, setting conditions of work and prices. All corporations would be federated into a National Economic Council. Both workers and owners would be represented on the board and the Council would set up rules for the economy in conformity with the laws of Congress. For ACTU, these would be known as Industry Councils. Similar arrangements, endorsed by Philip Murray and the CIO and to be known as Guilds, would have labor and management representatives, be chaired by a government representative, and empowered to direct production in their respective industries. One hears echoes of the ill-fated National Industrial Recovery Act of early New Deal days.

Most pertinent here were ACTU's tie-ins with labor priests, however divergent their approaches to Communism or interpretations of corporatism. An obvious connection between ACTU and labor priests, as indicated above, would be service as chaplains or lecturers. Labor priests were often allies with ACTU in various union struggles and economic campaigns, and they were often writers of ACTU articles, especially in the New York chapter's *Labor Leader* and Detroit chapter's *Wage Earner*. Consequently, one would expect some mutual influences between these laypeople and priests — sometimes positive, sometimes negative. Search of archival materials revealed that some labor priests were associated with ACTU in ways that will be analyzed in forthcoming volumes about union, economic, and political contexts.

From the late 1920s to the early 1960s, Catholic organizations, in one way or another, involved labor priests. Some of these organizations claimed labor priests as regular members; some assisted labor priests in their varied activities; some entertained labor priests as speakers or awardees; some received praise or criticism from labor priests; some required much time; some meant simply carrying the names of labor priests on their membership rolls. They were quite diverse, though non-Catholics and other civic groups were not included. Labor priests had limited involvement in or acquaintance with Catholic organizations such as Dorothy Day's Catholic Worker, Holy Name Society, Knights of Columbus, National Catholic Social Action Committee, Confraternity of Christian Doctrine, National Council of Catholic Men, and National Council of Catholic Women.

6

RELATIONSHIPS WITH RELIGIOUS LEADERS

The Vatican, Diocesan Officials,

Religious Superiors, & Others

A nother essential ingredient of the history of the labor priests is their relationship to religious authorities and influential figures. As participants in a religious, as well as a social, movement, labor priests had to relate to religious leaders. Here, the term "religious leaders" embraces Catholic Vatican officials, diocesan officials, and religious community officials, as well as, occasionally, leaders from the Protestant, Jewish, and other religious groups. We treat religious leaders under two headings, Catholic and non-Catholic. The two subdivisions under the Catholic heading—diocesan and religious communities—are both important because they reflect involvement in teaching and acting. Relationships were positive, negative, and mixed over time. Overall, religious leaders were more supportive than opposed or indifferent. Examples follow.

The Vatican

In 1889 San Francisco's Fr. Peter Yorke had a private and warm audience with Pope Leo XIII. When asked how Protestants in the United States were disposed to the Church, Yorke replied, "Holy Father, all love the Pope of the great encyclicals." The U.S. bishops' *Pastoral Letter of 1919* on social reconstruction was produced by SAD in 1919. Bishop Peter Muldoon of Rockford, Illinois, its chair and holder of various NCWC leadership positions, shepherded the document through the U.S. bishops' meeting that established the NCWC. On June 23, 1920, Muldoon had a private audience with Pope Benedict XV, who spoke highly of the NCWC and predicted favorable things for the organization.

Yet, by February 1922, detractors of the NCWC among the U.S. hierarchy prevailed upon the Vatican to close down the organization. On April 25, 1922, the NCWC Administrative Committee, of which Muldoon was the vice chair, protested the decision to Pius XI, defending the NCWC's work in communications, education, lay organizations, and social action. Yet, since the original decree had not been promulgated officially in *Acta Apostolicae Sedis* and the wording was sufficiently vague, Muldoon and associates continued to organize the various NCWC departments. Cleveland Bishop Schrembs was dispatched to Rome to argue the majority's case and Muldoon submitted to the U.S. hierarchy a petition for their signatures requesting the Holy See to reverse its stand. Thanks to the visit and the petition, the decision was reversed in June 1922 and Pius XI in July 1922 gave full approbation to the NCWC. Had the plea gone unheeded, it is hard to imagine how labor priests and Labor Schools and Institutes of Industrial Relations would have survived, since opponents in the hierarchy were objecting to "intrusion" into the power of local bishops and were little interested in labor priests or social action. On June 8, 1922, in recognition of work on behalf of the NCWC during World War I, Muldoon was appointed assistant to the papal throne.[1]

Schrembs, in Rome after the death of Pope Benedict XV, convinced Pius XI not to dissolve the NCWC, very aware that Cardinal DeLai was influenced by the opinion of the NCWC's opponents—Boston's Cardinal William O'Connell, Milwaukee Archbishop Sebastian Messmer, and Brooklyn Bishop Charles McDonnell. Their argument earlier to Benedict XV and DeLai was that the NCWC might cause the U.S. Church to become too independent of the Vatican. Quite aware that 90 percent of the U.S. hierarchy supported the NCWC, Schrembs chastised DeLai for his limited view of the U.S. hierarchy, contending that "Rome's mentality was that it was easier to deal with bishops individually than with an entire hierarchy." On June 23, 1922, Schrembs wired the NCWC Administrative Committee, "Fight is won. Keep program Bishops' meeting September. Official notice will be cable next week. Hard struggle. Complete victory. At farewell audience Pope blesses Bishops and Welfare Council."[2]

Subsequently, the NCWC's name was changed from "Council" to "Conference" to avoid confusion or competition with universal Church Councils.

By almost unanimous acclamation, Msgr. John A. Ryan is recognized as the foremost leader in social justice in the United States. Although said to be a "papalist" because of his devotion to papal encyclicals, Ryan encountered some tension within the U.S. Catholic Church. Assured in his earliest career by an influential Roman cleric that his views were acceptable to Rome, Ryan was named a domestic prelate in 1939. Yet Boston's Cardinal William O'Connell was so upset with Ryan's position on a child labor amendment before the U.S. Congress that he tried to have Ryan dismissed from

---

[1] Ellis 1952, 302–305, 415–420.
[2] Poluse 1991, 248.

the faculty of Catholic University. Though unhappy with Ryan's support of Roosevelt and the New Deal, the chancellor of the university and Baltimore Archbishop Michael Curley defended Ryan, perhaps due to Ryan's shrewd praise of the academic freedom he had experienced at the university. Not so placated, however, were some Catholics who represented publications such as *America, Catholic World* (especially its editor, Fr. James M. Gillis, C.S.P.) and Brooklyn's *The Tablet* (especially its editor, Patrick Scanlan). All of them thought Ryan ceded too much importance to the role of government in public life.[3]

In 1939, Fr. Jerome Drolet of New Orleans reported to Dorothy Day about having written and sent a report to Archbishop Rummel on the sessions in Mundelein. The gist was that New Orleans ought to have "something like the ACTU or Catholic Labor Schools." Yet, any intended letter of complaint to the apostolic delegate was delayed, since Rummel was busy denying accusations of being involved in some scandals. The FBI had been investigating Rummel for protecting some planters, generous benefactors of the Church, who were charged with hiring child labor or underpaying workers. Eventually, he sided with a Fr. Coulombe, who dug up evidence on the planters and was scheduled "to be railroaded out of the diocese, but the AAA and Secretary Wallace got in touch with the delegate, and as a result he was only moved, and is now stationed about 15 miles from here and carrying on."

Fr. James Vizzard, S.J., lobbyist for NCRLC and Chavez's United Farm Workers Association (UFWA), in 1968, was sent the Benemerenti Medal and citation from Archbishop Bennelli, on behalf of Pope Paul VI.[4] Pius XII instituted that award for persons who

---

[3] Curran 1982, 29–30.

[4] Vizzard File, Stanford University Libraries, Department of Special Collections, University Archives, Bennelli to Vizzard, March 22, 1968.

through great deeds merited a papal testimony for their accomplishments.

Diocesan Officials

Labor priests' relationships with diocesan officials contrasted with their relationships with Vatican officials, who appeared to be much more supportive of labor priests but had far fewer contacts with them. As the years rolled on, however, some earlier opposition or indifference to labor priests by diocesan officials gave way to more support.

For example, in the 1890s Fr. Peter Yorke of the San Francisco Archdiocese was appointed chancellor and editor of its paper, *The Monitor*, showing the confidence Archbishop Patrick Riordan placed in him.[5] During the tenures of Riordan and his successor, Edward Hanna, confidence in Yorke grew and waned, as he became involved in multiple and diverse causes such as defusing the American Protestant Association (APA); freedom for Ireland; corruption in city government; labor–management controversies; and conflicts with the Ancient Order of Hibernians. During the APA battle, Yorke "basked in the favor of his archbishop...the path to a prelacy seemed wide open...Riordan years later spoke with evident feeling about these stormy yet happy days."

Two years later, however, Yorke, no longer chancellor and editor, fell out of favor with Riordan.[6] As early as 1895—as the "American heresy" was falsely hatched—a very harsh *terna* (affidavit about fitness to be a bishop) was prepared at Riordan's request charging that Yorke tended to "modernize" and "Americanize" theology. The author of the *terna*, a Jesuit, was accused of doing a "hatchet job" on Yorke, taking quotations out of context, ignoring the spirit in which they were written, and failing to note their polemical character. He

---

[5] Brusher 1971, *in passim*.
[6] Ibid., 35.

"composed sometimes overnight in the white heat of religious controversy, not intended to be scholarly, definitive tracts."[7] While Riordan praised Yorke, he felt he needed better maturing and judgment through more years of experience before he would be "a suitable candidate for the dignity and responsibility of the Episcopacy." Also, he was said to have been too entangled in politics, been dismissed as chancellor, and had attacked Catholic University. On July 11, 1898, Yorke wrote a fiery letter protesting Riordan's "shameful charges." Yorke concluded that he had no other choice but to resign as chancellor and editor. Riordan tried to get Yorke to reconsider, but he adamantly and publicly refused to do so.[8]

On four other occasions, he was turned down for the episcopacy because he had a habit of saying "what he felt ought to be said was more dear to Yorke than Episcopal purple."[9] Yet, when Yorke opposed the election of James Phelan, a millionaire, as mayor of San Francisco, Riordan conceded that as a private citizen, a priest could express his political preferences. On another occasion, Riordan "seemed to be convinced that Yorke was wasting energy and arousing unnecessary ill-feeling to flog a dead horse."[10]

As mentioned above, Yorke had a private and warm audience with Leo XIII in 1899. Yorke was reportedly stirred by the audience, and Leo seemed to be impressed by Yorke.[11] Yet, on returning to San Francisco and being feted by laity, nuns, and priests, he felt a chilling indifference from Riordan, who failed to give him an assignment, even as an assistant pastor. Some thought Yorke was a has-been at thirty-four and too proud of this earlier successes.

---

[7] Ibid., 39.
[8] Ibid., 42–42.
[9] Ibid., 40–41.
[10] Ibid., 50.
[11] Ibid., 52.

Brusher felt otherwise: "[If] ever a priest practiced humility and accepted humiliation without calling press conferences to denounce unfeeling bishops, it was Yorke at this time."[12]

After the death of a local pastor four years later, Riordan appointed Yorke an "irremovable pastor," an assurance of gratitude and loyalty. In July 1911 Riordan was present at Yorke's jubilee of ordination and appointed him as irremovable pastor to St. Peter's Parish, where he had started his priestly ministry as an assistant pastor. Both occasions were marked by very complimentary and warm exchanges of letters between Riordan and Yorke. Brusher said of Yorke's relations with Riordan's successor, Archbishop Hanna, "as far as we can ascertain neither was as ambivalent or as interesting. As far as can be known, Yorke got along well with the outgoing, loving Hanna."[13]

Other authors had different views on Yorke's relationship with the religious authorities. Mary Lyons, focusing on Yorke's representation to the Irish community, felt that the more he alienated himself from the Church hierarchy and City Hall, the more he endeared himself to the masses and was their "Pope" and "president."[14] Fr. Richard Gribble, C.S.C., singled out Yorke and Hanna as the two individuals most prominent in Catholic efforts to help labor in San Francisco. Yorke was described as a "brash and uninhibited man who spoke and wrote in a highly polemical style...not the type of person to work gracefully and tactfully within the system." Yorke's "swash-buckling approach" contrasted with Hanna's "discrete approach." Placing their efforts in the larger Catholic context, Gribble likened the two to Fr. McGlynn of New York, Msgr. John A. Ryan, the U.S. bishops' *Pastoral Letter of 1919*, and Fr. Husslein, S.J.[15]

---

[12] Ibid., 57–58.
[13] Ibid., 151–155.
[14] Lyons 1987.
[15] Gribble 1993, 152–157.

In an article in *The Way* G.M. Bergman asked whether a priest interpreting *Rerum Novarum*, should play the role simply of a "father" social conciliator of all or champion of the cause of labor. With reference to Yorke's speeches and actions in the 1901 San Francisco strike, Bergman said that Yorke used *Rerum Novarum* to assail employers as greedy and determined to deny workers' their rights. "When an employer...asked Riordan to silence Yorke in the strike, that Archbishop answered that the priest was explaining the encyclical."[16] In a second article Bergman called Yorke a strong figure in social activism and in the radical traditions of the Church, a precursor of Vatican II's statement that the Church should actively "grapple with the great questions troubling the minds of men." Bergman noted that Yorke in San Francisco in 1902 and Padre Roncalli, later John XXIII, used *Rerum Novarum* and "represented a progressivism in the Church, then submerged, even suppressed."[17]

A little known, but influential, labor priest in the United States and the wider world labor movement, Cincinnati Fr. Peter Dietz, in 1914 formed a committee with Catholic University's Fr. William Kerby and an AFL official to visit Baltimore's Cardinal Gibbons, seeking an official "Catholic Policy" on the labor movement to be formulated in the U.S. bishops' *Pastoral Letter of 1919*.[18] Gibbons promised to refer such a proposal to the archbishops and asked Dietz to draw up a comprehensive list of topics. Dietz obliged with a list of unions rights and responsibilities, as well as the suggestion that there be a conference called, similar to what would later become the Catholic Conference on Industrial Problems. The prospects for the pastoral looked bleak, because St. Louis's archbishop, John Glennon, was sure that the bishops would not approve of the AFL "as such." He suggested instead a statement of principles.

---

[16] Bergman 1970, 35–40.
[17] Bergman 1978, 37–52.
[18] Fox 1953, 70 ff.

Kerby, however, pushed for a national document more practical than merely speculative. Despite their efforts and Dietz's plans for a national conference of lawyers, canonists, sociologists, union leaders, and judges presided over by a delegate to the hierarchy, the work of the committee came to naught. Useless were Dietz's warnings about the "anarchy of secularism," more insidious than Socialism, unknowingly winning over workers who viewed religion and labor as separate pigeon holes in a desk. Furthermore, Gompers's AFL did not want to become embroiled in Catholics conflicts with socialists in the labor movement.

Dietz established an American Academy of Christian Democracy (AACD) after World War I. The AACD aimed to provide social studies and social services, in conjunction with similar local agencies, in several locations and with several donors and problems. The academy, which was located in Ault Park, Cincinnati, Ohio, and afforded Dietz opportunities to mediate so many labor disputes and union organizing drives that his emphasis shifted more to labor unions than on social services. The plan was to establish itself along parish lines and irrespective of types of crafts, in order to insure solidarity among Catholic trade unionists. When the U.S. Chamber of Commerce inaugurated its "American Plan" to stifle the formation of union shops, Dietz announced a National Labor College at Ault Park. The National Labor College never materialized, because after a visit by Chamber of Commerce officials to Henry Moeller, Archbishop of Cincinnati, Dietz was ordered to close the academy and leave the archdiocese. Other reasons alleged for the archbishop's action were Moeller's advanced age and ill health, as well as Dietz's support of Warren Harding's presidential campaign and public opposition to the League of Nations, despite its approval by the pope and Baltimore's Cardinal Gibbons. Intercessions by Gibbons, Msgr. John A. Ryan, top AFL officials, and employers not opposed to unions and collective bargaining were all futile. Indeed, all Dietz's plans had been submitted to Moeller and the guidance committee and were judged by reliable people as strictly in accord with principles of theology.[19]

A striking dissent to Harrita Fox's interpretation of the Moeller–Dietz falling-out is contained in an August 7, 1953, letter she received from SAD's Fr. Raymond McGowan.[20] After praising Fox's book for resurrecting the important contributions Dietz had made in spreading Catholic Social Teaching and supporting the labor movement, McGowan listed differences he had with her account. Many of these focused on Fox's failure to mention other serious preoccupations of the hierarchy and several policy differences Dietz had had with NCWC and SAD. Dietz had also misinterpreted some bishops' actions, especially Muldoon's reasons for choosing Ryan over Dietz as SAD director. Also important was Fox's ignoring Moeller's crucial role, along with that of Schrembs and Muldoon, in preventing a Vatican dissolution of the NCWC.

McGowan said Fox's book would have been a better book "if you had analyzed the Moeller case better, the environment in which Father Dietz worked, and Father Dietz's final concentration on the unions and the AFL unions at that, to the neglect of other parts of Catholic Social Teaching." McGowan gave five examples. First, the time was not ripe for Dietz's plans. Second, instead of governmental action, Dietz thought joint boards of employers and unions could handle just about all conflicts. Third, Fox failed to stress sufficiently Dietz's articles on the League of Nations and Harding's campaign. Fourth, by the summer of 1920 SAD had attacked the antiunion drive of the U.S. Chamber of Commerce. Dietz did so in November. Fifth, McGowan thought Moeller had made a big mistake in dismissing Dietz, but "not on the grounds you indicate."

Br. Bernard Kelly, F.S.C., (Elzear Alfred), president of La Salle College, Philadelphia, Pennsylvania, from 1928 to 1934 was said to

---

[19] Ibid., 100 ff.
[20] McGowan to Fox, August 7, 1953, Catholic University of America Archives.

have become a persona non grata to Dennis Dougherty, the Cardinal Archbishop. During this researcher's interviews with Christian Brothers at the College, it was rumored that Kelly had refused to hand over the property of the original La Salle College, a piece of valuable estate along Philadelphia's Broad Street, after the college was relocated to suburban Olney. Archival search revealed no direct support for that rumor, but correspondence with a real estate agent for the Cardinal revealed a desire to sell, rather than to donate, the valuable property to the cardinal, because of the college's heavy indebtedness in the Depression.[21] Another rumor was that the cardinal was displeased with Kelly as director of La Salle's labor–management educational program, because in attendance were communists, especially in the struggling CIO unions in the area. Lending support at the time to such an allegation was the all-too-prevalent practice among some Catholic leaders of smearing anyone assisting CIO workers. Yet, several pieces of correspondence support such a rumor.[22]

After his presidency of La Salle College, Kelly served as director of its Labor–Management Education Program and established a Civic and Social Congress, responsible for much labor and management peace throughout southeastern Pennsylvania. A March 18, 1944, letter from the assistant superior general and overseer of the Brothers in the United States to Kelly's provincial set the scene for Kelly's removal from the Philadelphia area. The report was based on the report of Kelly's successor. Alluding to Dougherty's displeasure with Kelly's labor union involvement, the provincial said, "The Cardinal feels that La Salle is a hot-bed of Communism—Russian variety—and that devotion to the cause of labor has blinded the

---

[21] Elzear Alfred File, La Salle University and Baltimore Province of Brothers of Christian Schools Archives, Dougherty to Provincial, August 2, 1930.

[22] Elzear Alfred File, La Salle University and Baltimore Province of Brothers of Christian Schools Archives, Provincial to Hickey, February 10, 1952.

Brothers to the truth and he, the Cardinal, blames the Brother president of the College for allowing it to continue and furthermore that this must stop."

A June 2, 1944, letter of the provincial to Kelly reported the gist of a telephone conversation with the assistant general in New York City in which the Brothers were ordered to discontinue the Civic and Social Congress and similar activities in Philadelphia and elsewhere. On November 18, 1945, Kelly had hoped to interview the assistant general during the presentation of an award in Washington, D.C., by Auxiliary Bishop McNamara to a distinguished American. So, Kelly told the assistant general he had the responsibility of removing "the stigma of an untrue and unjust charge being attached to the most important school of the Institute in the Baltimore District." Thus, he should allow the presentation of the National De LaSalle Gold Award by McNamara. On November 23, 1945, the assistant general sent Kelly's letter to the provincial with caveats about the wording, purpose, and permissions of the ordinary/provincial/college for the presentation and Kelly's lack of authority with regard to the award, as well as the need to limit Kelly's activities to the Novitiate at Ammendale, Maryland.[23]

Seven years later, in 1952, the provincial wrote to Thomas Hickey, executive director of the Philadelphia-based La Salle Endowment Foundation. Hickey was then busy organizing a fundraising campaign among labor union leaders to honor Kelly. Expressing his esteem for Kelly and his work, the provincial added, "he fell afoul of ecclesiastical authority and as a result he had to be transferred from Philadelphia. His return in any prominent position or celebration would be embarrassing, I fear. Of course, I count on you to keep these background facts in confidence."

---

[23] Elzear Alfred File, La Salle University and Baltimore Province of Brothers of Christian Schools Archives, Assistant General to Provincial, November 25, 1945.

96

Excerpts from an unpublished manuscript in the La Salle Archives shows that some unnamed opponents of Kelly's activities had complained to Dougherty, "Brother's work was Communistic, Socialist, unfavorable to Capitalism, etc."[24] In the absence of official Philadelphia Archdiocesan documents, however, "nothing more can be said and His Eminence thought it best to have Brother Alfred removed from the Philadelphia scene." Yet, the authors of the excerpts related that Kelly was permitted to send Dougherty an affidavit on August 8, 1945, in which Kelly solemnly swore, "La Salle College Congress [Civic and Social] and its classes, both week-day and Sunday, have never been Socialistic or Communistic, either in theory, in practice or in implication of any kind." Along with the affidavit, Kelly sent testimonials from business, civic, FBI, law enforcement, political, and other leaders.

Throughout early 1937, SAD McGowan was busy reporting to Bishop Gerald O'Hara, SAD Chair, about travels to various dioceses planning Catholic Industrial Conferences and/or Labor Schools for priests. Apparently a letter O'Hara sent to all the U.S. bishops angered Baltimore's Archbishop Michael Curley. Thus, from April 12 to December 24, 1937, there was a dispute between Curley, O'Hara, and McGowan. The occasion was O'Hara's letter, but the focus was Curley's disagreement with Ryan and especially McGowan. However, Ryan was protected but McGowan was not. Ryan was incardinated [making him a full-fledged member] in the St. Paul–Minneapolis archdiocese, but McGowan was subject to Curley as archbishop of the Baltimore Archdiocese. Curley thought McGowan was "a first class 'omadan'" and although "an Incardinated Priest of this Archdiocese," Curley had decided to take McGowan out of the NCWC in June 1937.

---

[24] Elzear Alfred File, La Salle University and Baltimore Province of Brothers of the Christian Schools Archives; Ignatius and Joseph. Date unknown.

O'Hara had referred the information about McGowan's relation to NCWC to Msgr. Michael Ready, its general secretary. Yet, McGowan was determined to tell the whole story and informed O'Hara of a visit with Bishop LeBlond of St. Joseph, Missouri, who was quite willing to do anything that included incardinating McGowan in the St. Joseph Diocese, whether or not Curley took the threatened action. LeBlond had chatted with Curley and understood that Curley would take no action, which McGowan surmised. Yet, McGowan thought there was a possibility Curley might take action and even take a first step without warning, "by publishing the announcement of a transfer, which would be a scandal. I don't know what to do."

Several options were available to McGowan. He might wait until June or August to ask Curley for excardination [making him no longer a full-fledged member of the Baltimore Archdiocese]. Yet, LeBlond thought it better to have O'Hara or Detroit's archbishop and NCWC Administrative Board chair, Mooney, to do so at the appropriate time. LeBlond might inform Curley that incardination in the St. Joseph Diocese was open to McGowan and said, "He'd do anything he could."

Shortly afterwards, the chancellor of the Baltimore Archdiocese told McGowan that Curley would grant the Letters of Excardination under two conditions: he would be assured that McGowan would be incardinated only in the St. Joseph Diocese and that once McGowan became incardinated in the St. Joseph Diocese, McGowan would have no clerical faculties in, or perform any functions in, or reside in the Baltimore Archdiocese. McGowan expressed his willingness to be so incardinated and, as a matter of courtesy, said he would not reside in any diocese where he was not wanted. At the same time, Ready updated O'Hara on developments in the case. Enclosing the correspondence exchanged, Ready said McGowan spent three days in Baltimore trying to see Curley, "but the Archbishop would not see him." Noting that a canonist advised McGowan not to prejudice his canonical status by accepting any parish as a benefice, Ready said, "There is reason to believe that the Archbishop gave permission for Father McGowan to come to this jurisdiction, in order to work at the National Catholic Welfare Conference. So far as can be ascertained, there was no explicit incardination." Ready suggested that he and O'Hara discuss the problem."

McGowan sent a memo to O'Hara, Alter, and Ready, reciting efforts to find a religious priest to run a parish until the time of new assignments and enclosing a copy of his gracious note to Curley. McGowan sent another memo. He enclosed Curley's sarcastic reply about McGowan's inability to run a parish, yet he offered presumptuous advice about running a diocese. McGowan suggested a draft letter to Curley, repeating his offer to find a religious priest to run a parish, while he continued work at NCWC. If nothing suitable could be arranged, he would proceed with a canonical case, despite his hope the matter could be settled more amicably and be of service to Baltimore.

There were letters and conversations exchanged between McGowan, Alter, O'Hara, Ready, and Ryan about the latest developments on the issue. After conferring with Ryan, McGowan decided to visit the chancellor and put before him all the developments. The last discoverable move in the controversy was a McGowan December 24th memo to Mooney and O'Hara. Later, LeBlond and Ready relayed the recommendation of McGowan's canonist. According to McGowan, on December 21st, Fr. Howard Smith of Cleveland wrote "a very long and very good letter" to Curley, requesting that the matter be placed before the apostolic delegate. If Curley refused, Smith would do it himself. Whatever the other correspondence or appeals, McGowan remained at SAD and in a January 29, 1938, letter McGowan told O'Hara it was noted that any discussion of plans for a *Social Action Quarterly* be delayed "until I [McGowan] got the mattered straightened [out] at Baltimore."

Around the same time, there was a memorandum from McGowan to O'Hara, on a proposed constitutional amendment to prohibit child labor, addressing the negative reputation the Church acquired when it took on startling issues. Examples were given of hierarchy in Massachusetts—Boston's Cardinal O'Connell and Fall River's Bishop Cassidy—who had been labeled as reactionaries because of their objection to the Child Labor Amendment, despite their generally good records on social justice.[25]

In late 1954, NCWC News Service announced McGowan's retirement from full-time service at SAD. Among many testimonials to his greatness was that of Washington, D.C., archbishop and chair of SAD Patrick O'Boyle, who understood that ill health prevented McGowan from remaining at NCWC, but praised the thirty-five years of efficient and effective service. "Few priests in the history of the United States have contributed as much…to the great cause of social justice.… From the very beginning he has proved himself to be a man of unusual intelligence and extraordinary vision.[26]

Ryan's fate in this unfortunate controversy was not so troublesome. For later in 1939 Ryan was made a domestic prelate and an influential Roman cleric reassured him that his social justice views were acceptable in Rome.[27] As indicated above, most of his life, he was known as a "papalist," like most of the progressive Catholic writers of that time. Yet, progressive stands caused him some tensions with some of the hierarchy. Boston's Cardinal William O'Connell was so upset with Ryan's position on child labor that O'Connell tried to have Ryan dismissed from the Catholic University faculty. Yet, Michael Curley, Baltimore archbishop and Catholic University chancellor, defended Ryan. Although Curley was unhappy with Ryan's support of Roosevelt and the New Deal, Curley eventually became

---

[25] McGowan File, Catholic University Archives, McGowan to O'Hara, March 26, 1936.
[26] McGowan File, Catholic University Archives, NCWC News Service release.
[27] Curran 1982, 29–30.

reconciled with Ryan. Perhaps, another reason for Curley's support was Ryan's shrewd praise of academic freedom at Catholic University.

In mid-1941 Detroit's Archbishop Mooney responded to Baltimore Archbishop Curley's complaints about NCWC News Service's publication of Ryan's negative comments about the *Brooklyn Tablet* and Fr. Charles Coughlin.[28] Mooney was perplexed by the fact that those who most resented Ryan's letter were the ones who publicized it. Mooney believed that a quiet letter to O'Hara, SAD chair, would have elicited an apology from Ryan. "[Then] the entire matter would have been settled without having a lot of good ordinary people all worked up about it. If one had a suspicious mind he would be inclined to look for ulterior motives behind the publicizing of an offensive private letter." During an interview on June 16, 1999, Msgr. John Hayes, formerly with SAD, added further evidence of Ryan's brushes with the hierarchy. After explaining Ryan's role in conceiving of the Catholic Conferences on Industrial Problems, Hayes said, "Cardinal O'Connell did not approve of him because Monsignor Ryan had supported the child labor law, but everywhere else [outside Boston], Ryan talked.[29]

At Ryan's funeral in September 1946, Detroit's Cardinal Edward Mooney called Ryan a brave pioneer, who in fighting the battle of justice and freedom, "trod a lonely path with unflinching courage." Ryan supported the living wage, human rights, responsibility and rights of private property, and economic democracy, as well as the economic and political means to implement them. He was said to be no stranger to dissent and controversy and was respected for his integrity and sincerity of purpose by business, civic, and industry leaders. Noting the critical hour in which the nation faced serious and soul-searing tasks, Mooney closed, "We may well pray that the

---

[28] Mooney File, Archdiocese of Detroit Archives, Mooney to Curley, May 29, 1941.
[29] Hayes interview, June 16, 1999, Archives of the Archdiocese of Chicago.

spirit which burned so brightly in him continue to inspire us to justice for all, tempered by the gentle charity of Christ."[30]

In 1930, Bishop Hugh Boyle of Pittsburgh interviewed the future Fr. Charles Rice to determine if he would be a suitable candidate for the priesthood in the Pittsburgh Diocese.[31] Boyle was very impressed by Rice's Irish background, voracious reading habits, and broad acquaintance with classical and contemporary literature. So, later, "Boyle would give Rice his special protection when others wanted the young priest restrained or disciplined. Such lasted until 1948, when ill health caused Boyle to be eased out of office." In 1935 Rice taught undergraduate courses in psychology at Mount Mercy College, but, when Rice was told his services were no longer needed and another priest was immediately hired to take his place, Rice was convinced that the "cause" of the firing was his involvement in the Catholic Radical Alliance, labor–management, and interracial issues in the area.

In 1937 Cleveland Bishop Schrembs invited Rice to address CIO steelworkers in Youngstown, Ohio, despite accusations of a suburban pastor that the CIO was communist. Rice defended his speech as in keeping with papal teaching on labor–management. Despite criticisms of Rice, Schrembs and Bishop Boyle of Pittsburgh continued their vocal support of him. Schrembs invited Rice back two years later to address the National Catholic Social Action Congress in Cleveland. Although Schrembs admitted that the CIO and other labor organizations had both virtues and vices, he also said that they were generally beneficial to the workers.[32]

In the same year, Msgr. J. F. Minihan, secretary to the Boston Archdiocese's Cardinal William O'Connell, wrote to Valery Burati of the

---

[30] Mooney File, Detroit Archdiocese Archives, "Tribute to Monsignor Ryan," September 16, 1945.
[31] McKeever 1994, 24.
[32] Poluse 1991, 200–202.

CIO–Textile Workers Organizing Committee (TWOC), indicating the cardinal's refusal to allow Rice to address a mass meeting on the Commons in Lawrence, Massachusetts. Five months later, Rice told Fr. George Sullivan of Beechview, Pennsylvania, that Rice and Fr. Karl Hensler had tacit permission of several bishops to speak in their dioceses — Boyle in Pittsburgh, Lucey in Amarillo, McNicholas in Cincinnati, Ritter in Indianapolis, and Schrembs in Cleveland.[33]

Also in early 1938, Rice contacted Bishop P.A. Bray, C.J.M., of St. John, New Brunswick, Canada, who had requested Rice's advice. Rice admitted that, with permission from his own bishop, he had been active in labor circles. Rice found no disagreement with Bray on the principles involved, but laid out six necessary clarifications — mostly about combating Communism in the labor movement.[34] One month later, the vicar general of the Albany Diocese, Fr. Edward McGinn, said that Albany's Bishop Edmund Gibbons approved Rice's and Hensler's proposed address to workers at the General Electric plant in Schenectady, New York. In mid-year, Milwaukee's Archbishop Samuel Stritch thanked Rice for "your very great contribution to the success of the National Catholic Social Action Conference."[35]

At the same time, Fr. George Mulcahy, chancellor of the Harrisburg, Pennsylvania, Diocese, told Rice that in the absence of Bishop George Leach, "I feel that it would be most inadvisable for the Church to identify with either side in the controversy [union workers or employers in a Hershey, Pennsylvania, plant]."[36] Rice awaited the bishop's return and then told him that he disagreed with Mulcahy's suggestion that in addressing the meeting he would be identifying the Church with the CIO. Rice, after all, would be speaking

---

[33] Rice File, University of Pittsburgh Hillman Library Archives, Minnihan to Rice, September 7, 1937, and Rice Interview with Sullivan, February 3, 1938.

[34] Ibid., Rice to Bray, February 25, 1938.

[35] Ibid., Stritch to Rice, May 12, 1938.

[36] Ibid., Mulcahy to Rice, July 18, 1938.

only as an individual Catholic priest from outside the diocese, as he had done on numerous other occasions, and would not immerse the diocese in any particular squabble. The purpose of the meeting was simply to prove that the CIO was not antireligious or communist.[37]

In autumn, Fr. David Cunningham, secretary to Bishop Foery of Syracuse, New York, sought information on the Industrial Union Council, which had invited Rice to speak in Syracuse. "The Bishop will expect to have a manuscript of your proposed talk before he sends you permission for that engagement."[38] A month later, Rice was informed of the diocesan policy that requiring speakers to provide information about the sponsoring group and only to "present the principles of social justice as formulated in the Papal Encyclicals without recommendations of particular unions or individuals, or associates of the unions."[39] Noting that some union members had the impression that Rice was not being allowed to speak in Syracuse, Cunningham said, "[You] understand that this is not correct and at no time were you refused permission to address this group in Syracuse. He told Rice to avoid needless and possibly embarrassing entanglements."[40]

Things had changed for Rice in Pittsburgh by 1950, however. For Bishop "Iron John" Dearden had succeeded Boyle as Pittsburgh's ordinary. Rice was moved from the House of Hospitality to a parish in Natrona, Pennsylvania, a forty-five-minute automobile drive from Pittsburgh; was relieved of a teaching position in Duquesne's Management-Labor Institute; and was informed that his column in the *Pittsburgh Catholic* had been cancelled. Before 1958, Rice felt he had been out-of-the-loop, but McKeever calls this Rice's "exile theory," one developed among Rice and close friends and a part of

---

[37] Ibid., Rice to Mulcahy, July 25, 1938.
[38] Ibid., Cunningham to Rice, October 13, 1938.
[39] Ibid., Cunningham to Rice, November 14, 1938.
[40] Ibid., Cunningham to Rice, December 3, 1938.

Rice's subjective interpretation of facts and "tendency to romanticize the past."[41] Yet, the diocesan radio station called on Rice to debate the birth control issue and he was later appointed to a larger and more affluent parish, though a location even farther removed from Pittsburgh.

When Dearden became Detroit's archbishop in 1959, his replacement—the more congenial Bishop John Wright—reappointed Rice to the Diocesan Board of Consultors. Finally, on Rice's ninetieth birthday, a Mass and dinner were organized to celebrate the occasion. (The events were held in conjunction with a memorial of Pennsylvania's 1892 Homestead Battle.) Rice received plenty of compliments from academics, ecumenical and labor leaders, as well Pittsburgh Bishop Donald Wuerl.[42]

In the Midwest, in the late 1930's Fr. Francis Eschweiller, professor of Catholic Social Teaching in Milwaukee Archdiocese's St. Francis Seminary, assisted in St. Rita's Parish.[43] At one point during the Mass he made a "harmless" reference to the long-running labor–management dispute in nearby Racine between the UAW and Allis-Chalmers, "Let us pray that this dispute will be settled peacefully and justly," he said. The next day he was summoned to the Chancery Office, removed from the seminary faculty, and assigned to an undeveloped rural parish. So his brother, Fr. Edward, explained during an August 2000 interview with this researcher.

Author Paul Wilkes's earlier interviews, however, revealed that Eschweiller thought the action was due to his attendance at UAW meetings without official permission.[44] He noted that in the 1930s and early 1940s he had received several notes saying, for example,

[41] McKeever 1994, 134.

[42] No author, *Pittsburgh Gazette*, 1998.

[43] Interview with Fr. Edward Eschweiller, August 2000, St. Francis Seminary, Milwaukee, Wisconsin.

[44] Wilkes 1973 and Wilkes date unknown.

"Frank, you were quoted as saying thus and thus. Lay off." Nevertheless, the Allis-Chalmers strike really got him in hot water after members of the UAW Bargaining Committee came to him for advice and this became known to Church authorities. It was then obvious to Eschweiller that Chancery officials did not want priests to mingle with labor union folks; they were clearly on the side of management, "from where the big money came."

Eschweiller was removed from seminary teaching and sent out of town" to Kewaskum, an isolated place that was seen to be culturally and intellectually barren. There was no way to fight back as a marked man [pp. 13–14]. In spite of such experiences and aware of Church's flaws and pathologies—due to some hide-bound and insensitive people—Eschweiller viewed the Church, like other institutions, to be a necessary and viable structure within which people are called to grow and work. For him, the priesthood was the opportunity for persuasive influence on people. He would not "jump over the wall or drop out," only strive to make the Church better. "I admit to my own lack of faith...always wanting things to germinate overnight.... But if you are true to yourself, you really cannot lose. You look like a loser for ten or more year, but ultimately the day of vindication comes" [pp. 24–25].

After years in "liberal causes"—liturgical reform, the peace movement, open housing campaigns, and opposition to Church teaching on contraception—vindication came. In 1991, his third archbishop, Rembert Weakland, O.S.B., presented him an award for a lifetime of dedication to social issues, despite letters calling him a communist, worthy of an FBI investigation.

Way down south in New Orleans, from January 1939 to April 1941, Fr. Jerome Drolet corresponded with Dorothy Day about Archbishop Joseph Rummel discouraging some of Drolet's social justice activities. For example, Herb Welch, director of Day's New Orleans House of Hospitality, was discouraged by Drolet from approaching

New Orleans Archbishop Rummel about refusing an order to close soup kitchens, clothing stores, and rooms for the poor. Drolet told Day that he felt the archbishop had no canonical right to order the closing of the house. Drolet hesitated to complain to the apostolic delegate. "I don't care a [tinker's\ damn about consequences, to me at any rate, but for your protection I want to know what you think first." Drolet also typed out part of Rummel's letter, which had request Drolet "not to encourage the establishment of similar institutions anywhere in the archdiocese in the future."

Another complaint had to do with Rummel's refusal to permit Drolet to give an invocation at the National Maritime Union convention in New Orleans. Drolet had suggested that *some* priests be allowed to attend, but the answer was always the same, "no." Pointing out how hard it was to fulfill Leo XIII's cry, "Go to the worker," Drolet spoke of his gradual indifference and pessimism. "I'm having a hard enough time convincing myself that the Church means what she says in the Encyclicals." Once again he thought about writing to the apostolic delegate and "let the chips fall where they may." Although admitting that he might be wrong, Drolet thought Rummel suffered due to crass ignorance and a thick bourgeois background.

Despite being allowed to attend, along with some other New Orleans priests, the Priests' School of Social Action at Mundelein Seminary in Chicago, Drolet said, "I'm strangely unimpressed with the utility of it all for anybody with a guy like that over us." After the internal problems of the National Maritime Union (NMU) were resolved, Rummel attended its convention. He understood its implications: "[So] he pointed me out to the boys, said some very complimentary things about me, and they all gave me a good hand, which tickled me to no end, or made me feel like having a good cry, I don't know which."

Later, a company union supporter complained that Drolet had distributed about five hundred copies of Haas's booklet, *Labor Unions*, but Rummel reprimanded the complainer. Thus, Rummel was not as severe as he had been in earlier times. "I think maybe all the 'hot-oil' and other local scandals have drawn him slightly closer to the common people. Drolet referred vaguely to plans for a future diocesan 'social justice' program, 'when the right time comes.' Here's hoping!"

Yet, another Rummel reprimand passed down through the chancellor was called "the crazy thing." This action had to do with the pleasure Rummel took in closing the Catholic Worker House and forbidding Drolet to reopen it "or any similar establishment." Drolet was ordered to refrain from engaging in any social work, whether in person or in correspondence, and to devote himself to parochial work "under the direction of your reverend pastor.... This is to be the last notice; next will be acknowledgment of penalties if there are any violations." Drolet visited the chancellor, only to find the monsignor hemming and hawing about no new violations and being in impossible circumstances. Under the circumstances, Drolet would have been surprised if Rummel had allowed anything like a Labor School or ACTU chapter in New Orleans.

Thus, Drolet wearied of being so alone! He also told of his pastor's efforts to undermine Drolet with the parishioners, even though he tried his best to abide by the archbishop's strictures. While Drolet could do some things secretly and moderately from the pulpit, he could not understand how some people could trifle with something as sacred as suspension. He was torn between laughing or crying, staying or leaving, especially when an elderly priest was shipped out for helping "sharecroppers" at the instigation of wealthy cane growers who had the ear of the archbishop. Yet, Drolet was reminded that he and others were co-victims as Christ's "co-priests."

Later, when allowed to attend strike meetings, Drolet found Rummel to be better disposed, evidenced by his authorizing a Labor Institute to train workers and reading of his statement to the Young Men's Business Club by a judge before sentencing an executive for overworking girls. Rummel wanted to send Drolet to the Summer School of Social Studies at Catholic University, but Drolet had trouble getting his pastor's permission to attend. The pastor said he needed to know that "the archbishop really wanted [Drolet] to go." Despite feeling he would learn what he had not already experienced, Drolet believed that if he behaved himself a little longer, Rummel would allow him to work in social action—openly helping unions—provided he did well at the Summer School.

In early 1943, Drolet told Hayes about how Rummel learned much about "the lack of assistance from Church circles" in removing a communist regional CIO director and planned to correct the situation. However, Drolet also noted that he had been given permission to produce a series of articles on Catholic Social Teaching derived from forty to fifty topics and four volumes of papers presented at the Summer School for Priests at Mundelein. Many of the articles had already been published in the local CIO newspaper with the archbishop's approval. Contacts had been reestablished with an archdiocesan official close to Rummel, Msgr. Wynhoven. Yet, when he wanted Drolet to retain the former title of the column, "Warning to Americans," indicative of Wynhoven's identification with Brooklyn's Fr. Curran and Christian Front people—a very conservative Catholic lay group, Drolet refused.

He expressed disappointment over the lack of encouragement for Labor Schools, especially by Fr. Reintjes, chair of the Social Action Committee. "I'm afraid the complete lack of stimulation from above has about taken the heart out of Fr. Reintjes for a while; I'm willing, but have no authority whatever to do anything. Until I get some recognition on our so-called Social Action Committee my hands are tied. I hope I am wrong."

He also noted that he was mentioned in an issue of *Business Week* as having been involved in the Robertson–Bridges controversy over the International Longshore and Warehouse Union (ILWU). Yet, he was afraid, "The Abp. is likely to imagine that I told the reporter about my being 'head of the New Orleans ACTU', which of course is nonexistent here. I wish the guy had consulted me before printing the thing so I could have stricken out a few things." Yet, at the same time, a letter from Hayes to Donnelly noted that during a visit to San Antonio, Texas, Drolet claimed Rummel approved a permanent organization of Catholics and non-Catholics, but not limited to labor representatives. Hayes added, "I do believe Rummel has shown him more favor of late."

Thomas Becnel noted that in 1944 that the New Orleans Association of Commerce leaders sent Rummel a copy of a flyer Drolet had distributed to textile workers he was trying to organize.[45] Rummel's response was, "[Surely] there can be no objection to the presentation of the right and duty of employees in industry to safeguard their common interests though legitimate organization." Later, sugar growers from Bayou LaFourch asked Rummel to remove Drolet as pastor of St. Charles Parish.[46] The immediate excuse was Drolet's statement on the rights of labor, testimony before Senator Estes Kefauver's crime investigation committee, and the campaign against an infamous Thibodaux "Jeanette's" brothel. When the planters conferred with Rummel, he made them make their charges in the presence of Drolet. When there were loud criticisms of Drolet, Rummel interrupted to ask if the charges about prostitution were not true. Even the complaints of influential parishioners about Drolet did not result in his removal. Drolet also told SAD's Higgins that during a sugarcane workers strike, Rummel had privately deposited a couple of thousand dollars in the strike relief funds to help

---

[45] Becnel 1980.
[46] Ibid.

defray some of the workers' food, housing, and legal costs.[47] Drolet himself raised over $10,000 from several area unions.

In 1944, Detroit Social Action Director Fr. Raymond Clancy told Higgins that he had given no sermons on the social question, due partially to former Bishop Duffy of Buffalo, New York.[48] At an earlier Catholic Conference on International Peace, Duffy stated that Sunday Mass was not the occasion "to sell Catholic principles to the public. [So] many whose minds were not too open, would immediately close them, with a feeling of resentment that the priest was attempting to take advantage of the fact that they have to be present to fulfill their Sunday Mass precept." Duffy maintained study clubs, lecture courses, and talks before service clubs (Lions, Rotarians, etc.) as "perhaps one of the most fruitful approaches to non-Catholic or mixed groups." Clancy referred Higgins to the series of sermons SAD's Hayes had written for use in the Brooklyn Diocese many years earlier. Neither was enthused about Duffy's stand.

As bishop of Amarillo, Texas, in the 1940s, Robert Lucey championed the cause of labor unions and the New Deal administration, with support from New York's Cardinal Hayes and Cincinnati Archbishop McNicholas. Boston's Cardinal O'Connell and Cleveland's Bishop Schrembs withheld their support, warning against militant unionism, despite management's refusal to recognize unions and to bargain in good faith. While Lucey agreed with Chicago Cardinal Mundelein, Bishop Sheil, and Detroit's Archbishop Mooney, he differed with Newark Archbishop Walsh and Toledo Bishop Alter.[49]

---

[47] Drolet File, Catholic University Archives, Drolet to Higgins, November 18, 1953.
[48] Clancy Folder, SAD File, Catholic University Archives, December 16, 1944, Clancy to Higgins.
[49] Bronder 1982, 41–64.

In early 1959 Higgins expressed regrets that he would be unable to attend the silver jubilee of Lucey as archbishop of San Antonio.[50] Referring to the inspiration Lucey had given to countless clergy and laity in social action work and his tremendous contributions to the cause of social reconstruction, Higgins concluded, "I would single out...your untiring efforts to improve the lot of the migratory workers. If and when the migratory problem is ever brought to a reasonably satisfactory solution, history will undoubtedly give the lion's share of credit to Your Excellency." Higgins recalled that he first met Lucey in the summer of 1940 at the Priests Summer School of Social Action in San Antonio. "From that time to this you have done so many favors for me and have been such an inspiration to me in my work at the NCWC that I don't know how to thank you adequately."

SAD's Hayes told Hartford's Fr. Donnelly of the New York cemetery strike and how Cardinal Spellman had accused the ACTU lawyer representing the strikers of being a communist and sent his seminarians to dig the graves in late 1949.[51] Hayes said, "I had better not enter the realm of Card Spellman without police protection." He did not think the "bad business" had been given much publicity in Washington, D.C., but the New York media spread pictures of coffins piling up in Catholic cemeteries and busloads of Dunwoodie seminarians entering the cemetery. It was an example of the extreme unwillingness of Church officials to lose control of the work scene, even when dedicated Catholics like the ACTU lawyer merely trying to implement the right of all workers in all work sites to exercise their natural and God-given right to unionize.

---

[50] Lucey File, San Antonio Archdiocese Archives, Higgins to Lucey, April 15, 1959.
[51] Hayes File, Catholic University Archives, Hayes to Donnelly, December 2, 1944.

San Francisco Archdiocese's Fr. Donald McDonnell and Fr. Thomas McCullough, in 1958, directed the "Hispanic Mission Band," established by Archbishop John J. Mitty.[52] The priests supported the beginnings of the Agricultural Workers Association (AWA), which in 1959 became the Agricultural Workers Organizing Committee, established by the AFL–CIO. They made great strides in aiding organizing, but were soon opposed by farmers, growers, and pastors. Although Mitty stood behind them, some pastors and growers soon began calling the priests loose cannons. The critics then decided to pressure other California bishops with the canard that the Catholic Church was anti-farmer. So, before traveling to El Centro, California, in the San Diego Diocese, McDonnell and McCullough informed Bishop Charles Buddy of their plans.

However, when a local newspaper told of them stirring up trouble among the braceros and claiming to represent the bishop, Buddy vigorously denied such a role, reasserting his belief that priests should limit their activities strictly to the spiritual care of the workers. As justification, Buddy cited the complaints of the farmers and growers who insisted that priests be kept out of the camps, "They are agitators and troublemakers." Buddy sent a stern letter to McDonnell and McCullough, seeking an explanation for their actions, including giving invocations and leading some hymns in Spanish and "Glory Alleluia, the Union Makes Us Strong." They replied and offered a clarification, but a cloud still hung over the two priests.

Three factors contributed to the eventual closing of the Hispanic Mission Band. First, San Francisco was split into three dioceses. Second, the Hispanic Apostolate shifted to a newly created Archdiocesan Catholic Council for the Spanish Speaking, modeled after the 1945 U.S. Bishops' Committee for the Spanish Speaking. Third, after

---

[52] Dolan and Hinojosa 1994, 219–220.

113

Mitty's illness and death, his successor, Bishop Leo Maher, was not enthusiastic about the Hispanic Mission Band so he let it expire.

Some differences of opinions arose over the reason for Haas's move from Washington, D.C., to become bishop of Grand Rapids, Michigan.[53] In November 1982 Msgr. William Murphy of the Grand Rapids Diocese mentioned that Haas, on different occasions, had referred to the "unholy crowd" in Washington who clamored for his removal. Haas's closest friends "admit that his administration was un-imaginative...safe rather than experimental." Murphy added that Haas's predecessor, Bishop Joseph Pinten, had caused great hatreds and deep divisions among the clergy. "The diocese needed a healer at that time more than a brilliant administrator. And a good priest that he was, Haas...his administration had its high moments too."

Shortly thereafter, Higgins agreed that Haas was a "healer" and should be honored for being such.[54] Murphy may have been correct about people clamoring for his removal from Washington, but Higgins stressed that "it will probably take historians to clarify this point—given the reluctance of the Holy See to open its archives to research scholars." He thought the Vatican had made a great mistake, but Haas reluctantly took the assignment in a sense of loyalty and obedience. He would have preferred to stay at Catholic University. Furthermore, Higgins did not agree with the rumor that Haas had been removed because of his position as the chair of the Federal Fair Employment Practice Committee. Instead, Higgins maintained that "Cardinal Mooney of Detroit, who greatly admired him and, in general, shared his social outlook, wanted him close at hand in Michigan as a trusted adviser on labor–management relations and

---

[53] Blantz 1982.
[54] Ibid.

other socioeconomic problems." In closing, Higgins said it was fortunate that a very conservative Haas died "before the theological and pastoral floodgates burst open following Vatican II."

In New York's 1949 cemetery strike ACTU supported the strikers. Its chaplain and cofounder (with eleven laymen), Fr. John Monaghan, was another who incurred the wrath of Cardinal Spellman. Convinced by Patrick Scanlan, editor of the *Brooklyn Tablet*, that ACTU was supporting communist strike leaders, Spellman questioned the ecclesiastical loyalty of ACTU and Monaghan, who felt it very deeply.[55]

In the 1950s Marshall Tito of Yugoslavia jailed Archbishop Alois Stepinac and Spellman expressed outrage. Monaghan told Spellman that the spiritual life of the Church was never better than when bishops were jailed.[56] Earlier, with the assistance from Msgr. Ryan, Monaghan persuaded New York's Cardinal Patrick Hayes, a signer of the U.S. bishops' *Pastoral Letter of 1919* on social reconstruction, to endorse ACTU.

Spellman's chancellor, later cardinal archbishop of Los Angeles, Francis McIntyre, was never comfortable with trade unionism, but accepted it as a legitimate Catholic interest, thanks to Monaghan. He told labor priests in New York to respect McIntyre, but stand up to him. "His bark is worse than his bite.... He'll never agree with you but he may surprise you by doing what you want or even by changing his mind." Several priests were in trouble with the Chancery Office because a group of lay activists had aided strikers during a labor action by Wall Street clerks against the New York Stock Exchange and the 1947 Catholic Charities drive.[57] Yet, in 1948, McIntyre asked Monaghan to represent the archdiocese at a meeting of two thousand telephone workers. When McIntyre was told

---

[55] Lynch 1997.
[56] Kelly 1989.
[57] Ibid.

that he might not like what Monaghan would say to the workers, McIntyre retorted, "I don't care what you say. They tell me some Jesuit from Brooklyn [Fr. William Smith] is going to appear there, and if anyone is going to get credit for being on the side of the workers, it isn't going to be a Jesuit from Brooklyn."[58]

In the late 1950s, Fr. Sherrill Smith was a troubleshooter for San Antonio's Archbishop Robert Lucey, a very dedicated apostle of workers and the poor, though a rather sarcastic one at times. For example, when Smith failed to send a detailed report on some labor corruption and other related matters, Lucey voiced disappointment at a priest who had privilege of "doing graduate work."[59] In January 1959 Smith apologized for his carelessness and mentioned that although he had sent a report to Bishop Leven, who said he would forward the report to Lucey, a censure was deserved because Smith should have been sent a copy directly to Lucey. A few days later, Lucey thanked Smith for his report of January 26 and suggested that the matter be dropped.

For a few years, beginning in 1959, Lucey complimented Smith for his dedication to workers and the union movement. In May 1966, he also congratulated Fr. William Killian, editor of San Antonio's *Alamo Messenger*, for his April 29 editorial about some "shouting and turmoil" over Smith's encounter with the San Antonio City Council. Lucey deemed the controversy profitable for San Antonio in its war on the power structure, which was "taking a lovely beating" in fighting decent wages, "but they don't seem to know it." Many leaders had begun giving wages serious consideration as never in the past. "I realized that if priests in Latin America had put

---

[58] Ibid.
[59] S. Smith File, San Antonio Archdiocesan Archives, Lucey to Smith, September 19, 1959.

on the gloves with the employers down there 150 years ago it probably would have saved the Church from being abandoned by 200 million people."[60]

In late 1966 relationships between Lucey and Smith began to cool. In October 1966, Lucey admonished Smith in a two-page memo on a number of counts, including active involvement in union contract negotiations, damaging the image of the Church by discouraging and even disgusting "honest men and friends of ours," and making unwise remarks before the San Antonio City Council about taxing churches, engaging in controversies with John Birchites, and offending personally the archbishop of San Antonio. Lucey first complimented Smith, and his coworker and editor of the archdiocesan newspaper, Fr. William Killian, as the only two priests in Texas with an intelligent appreciation of organized labor. However, Lucey ended his admonishment of Smith about making enemies of the Church unnecessarily and shattering his influence for good. "It is one thing to preach social justice and make reactionaries mad. It is quite another thing to take over a layman's job and act as a representative of a labor union. That is not Papal teaching."

In early November 1966, Smith replied to Lucey with a very pained and frank, but respectful, fourteen-page letter. The letter opened with some delight in the opportunity to put in writing ideas and feelings that Lucey was said to dismiss with a wave of his hand or by appearing not to be listening. Smith was dismayed by the misinformation, contradictions, and insensitivity found in Lucey's letter. His reply represented a classic record of tensions and controversies in the aftermath of Vatican II, especially in terms of the mutual relations between freedom and authority in the Church.

---

[60] S. Smith File, San Antonio Archdiocesan Archives, Lucey to Killian, May 3, 1966.

In San Antonio the record culminated in a request that Rome seek Lucey's retirement. Rather than taking the position of a neutral negotiator, Smith had been asked to participate by the federal mediator and the workers demanded his involvement. Rather than being harmed, the Church's "influence was good in San Antonio and the Southwest had never been stronger." Rather than disappointing or disgusting "good men or friends," the question should be who they were and what they stood for; rather than hurting the San Antonio archbishop. Smith recalled Lucey's maxim about controversy: "its presence, and especially its virulence, are a sure sign of no small degree of effectiveness." Rather than being imprudent for calling for taxing churches and public disclosure of wages in church institutions, Smith explained that "obedience, like love, should be two-dimensional; if it isn't...it dead-ends in selfishness." Lucey was reminded that neither bishops nor priests exist for themselves, but for the Church.

In June and July 1966, Fr. James Vizzard, S.J., lobbyist for César Chávez's National Farm Workers Association (NFWA) and the AFL–CIO's Agricultural Workers Organizing Committee (AWOC), was in a controversy with Monterey–Fresno, California, Bishop Aloysius J. Willinger. The controversy started during the middle of a battle between NFWA–AWOC and the California Growers and between NFWA–AWOC and the Western Conference of the Teamsters.[61] Vizzard called Willinger's statement "untimely, unsound, and damaging." The bishop's statement came after visits with Einar Mohn, director of the Western Conference of Teamsters, and a letter from DiGiorgio and other growers asking Willinger's intervention in the Delano dispute. The letter was released around the time the Council of California Growers had requested Willinger's intervention.

---

[61] Vizzard File, Sanford University Libraries, Department of Special Collections and University Archives, Vizzard–Willinger exchanges.

Willinger's statement contained terminology that the growers themselves had used earlier: "[In] publicly charging certain Church spokesmen [including Chicago's Archbishop Cody and the Archdiocese of San Francisco] of attempting to destroy the democratic processes by 'favoring one union over another'." Vizzard charged that Willinger's statement "Could be interpreted only as echoing and reenforcing the growers' line...and was seized by DiGiorgio and others to justify their subsequent unilateral and fraudulent 'election'." Vizzard cited several supporters of the growers who echoed a similar theme about Willinger's statement being "a realistic solution to the apparent stalemate, "recommendation for a speedy election held in a neutral place by an impartial agency," and was "mystified [at] how so-called champions of social justice can applaud unilateral agreements that find the farm workers without any opportunity of choice on their part."

Vizzard also presented "internal" evidence that Willinger "had finally openly revealed himself as their [the growers'] ally. In characterizing the Delano situation as a "farm worker dispute" rather than as a "labor–management dispute," Vizzard said Willinger "abets confusion deliberately created by growers." Vizzard explained the source of the confusion in terms of labor–management relations. Willinger's protestations to the contrary, workers and owners clearly perceived his statement as "an open endorsement of the growers' views and propaganda." Vizzard characterized the statement as "pretty miserable" because it identified with the farm workers' opponents and "entirely gratuitous" because of its "snide remarks" about so-called champions of social justice.

In his response to Willinger's statement on July 19, 1966, Vizzard commented on a two-week visit to California and two newspaper stories, providing further support for his charge that Willinger, willingly or not, had fallen into the growers' trap. DiGiorgio's choice of Fr. Roger Mahoney as an "impartial observer," he said, would be a joke if the issues were not so serious. It was an insult to the truth, Vizzard claimed, to suggest that Mahoney was impartial. The same was true of other priests and ministers who had been openly condemned by NFWA–AWOC. Vizzard criticized one newspaper's total or selective silence on some crucial aspects of the controversy: growers' delinquencies, charges of fraud in the "election," recommendations of fair procedures for a new election, a report of an Interfaith Committee, and failure to mention a priest observer's refusal to sign a certification of the fairness of the "election." He concluded that there was a "consistent pattern of Bishop Willinger's lending authority and [the] prestige of his office and the pages of the diocesan paper to the growers' side of the Delano controversy."

Finally, later in the Delano strike, *Ave Maria* published an editorial entitled "Delano — Another Selma?" After listing Vizzard's achievements and the challenges he faced, the editorial focused on the opposition of Willinger to clergy involvement in the controversy. Vizzard's statement of beliefs at the time echoed those of the bishop of Mobile–Montgomery, Alabama, during the Selma Civil Rights march. Vizzard's immediate problem was that Church authorities were frozen into their cautious noninvolvement because of their fears that if they took a stand the growers would hit them in the pocketbook.

Vizzard's statement, as imbedded in the larger Church institutional setting, warrants being cited. "No ecclesiastical superior has any right to forbid me to be concerned with gross injustice and destruction of human dignity just because the specific problem exists within the territory under his jurisdiction. Nor can he rightfully forbid me to express concern in writings, speeches, or personal presence." Noting the Church's need for financial support for its institutions, Vizzard added that these did not exist for themselves or just for affluent, comfortable, or powerful donors. On some occasions members of the institutional Church might be forced to choose the implications and consequences of belief, whatever personal or institutional setbacks this may cause. "I think it would be more to the honor of the Church and, to the service of God that [buildings] remain unbuilt or unfinished or even closed rather than that the Church should knuckle under to the threats of those who demand that the Church 'keep out its nose out of their business'."

When SAD's Higgins officially retired in 1980, Phoenix's Bishop Rausch, formerly of USCC–NCCB, commented on how Higgins presided over evening sessions involving the USCC–NCCB staff: "I was getting an education that George never knew he was giving on Jewish–Catholic relations, on the whole labor question, on the church in politics, and on economics. Some of the best classes I even attended took place sitting in the recreation room of the staff house."[62] Yet, in October 1978, Rausch's successor as general secretary, Bishop Thomas Kelly, O.P., announced that for budgetary reasons Higgins's office was going to be closed in December 1979 and Higgins would be retiring a year earlier than had been planned.

The announcement was so stunning that it gave rise to protests by telephone calls, letters, visits to ecclesiastical leaders, and in media announcements by representatives of the academic, civil rights, ecumenical, political, religious, and union communities. The effect was too much to allow the decision to stand. The USCC–NCCB Plans and Programs Committee changed that the decision and announced publicly the decision had been due to a "misconception."

A variety of other explanations surfaced. Covering the spectrum was an article by the *National Catholic Reporter* editor one month after the decision to "retire' or "oust" Higgins.[63] First, his official position, secretary of research, was to be phased out, but he would be free to continue his labor, interfaith, and social legislation activities. Second, administrators of some Catholic institutions were angry

---

[62] Costello 1980, 42–46.
[63] Jones 1978, 1 ff.

about his criticism of their opposition to unionization and collective bargaining. Third, NCCB–USCC administrators exhibited incredible incompetence. Fourth, there was culpable insensitivity and/or gross ignorance that his national and international stature and influence, competence and contributions far exceeded his personal budget of $50,000. Finally, some in the hierarchy grumbled about Higgins's relative lack of accountability and freedom of operation, especially on the farm workers issue in California and elsewhere.

Other writers and speakers have suggested that criticism from the left was also involved, since Higgins had been timid when criticizing the hierarchy on other issues or denied the move represented a retreat from social activism by the NCCB–USCC? Higgins appeared to be quite calm, but cautioned about using the incident as a church–labor rallying cry for organization or protest campaigns. In stressing that no one was out to get him, Higgins may have offered an implicit reason for the move against him and revealed an aspect of his character: he never worried about success because he felt this would be self-defeating. He also realized that he had been part of the Bishops' Conference for so long that "people couldn't push me around and I was able to do things like helping the farm workers."

Yet, there were honors galore, such as the Presidential Medal of Honor and the Laetare Medal, Notre Dame University's highest award.[64] Higgins's ordinary, Cardinal George of the Chicago Archdiocese, said "Higgins integrated in practice over many years the principles of respect for the worker and the dignity of work. Because the freedom of workers is integral to a free society, the bestowal…is well deserved." Along with Notre Dame University's Fr. Theodore Hesburgh, C.S.C., Higgins was one of ten Americans Pope John XXIII selected to serve as members of the preparatory commission of Vatican II.

---

[64] No author, *Catholic New World*, 2000.

Early in 1982 Higgins's close friend Fr. Vincent O'Connell, O.M.I., commented that during the CIO "Sun Belt" Campaign to organized sugarcane workers, not once did a provincial or diocesan official even hint that O'Connell should not help the workers, except when he touched the "untouchables" — the Louisiana Sugar field workers. In 1939 when O'Connell became interested in organizing Polish refugees who had been brought to Louisiana to work in the sugarcane fields, New Orleans Archbishop Joseph Rummel remarked to O'Connell, "You know the growers are not going to like it. The field workers are Negroes and Baptists. But see what you can do."[65]

By the mid-1970s a different refrain was heard. O'Connell was notified by his provincial, Fr. Charles Barrett, S.M., that in a May 31, 1971, letter Baton Rouge's Bishop Robert Tracy said he wanted O'Connell out the diocese by June 21.[66] Tracy gave no reason to Barrett, but told O'Connell a grower had made a complaint about his attendance at a workers' meeting called to protest the workers' housing conditions on a plantation in St. James Parish [County]. Others misrepresented the housing conditions. In forbidding O'Connell to exercise any kind of ministry — clerical or otherwise, Tracy was quite adamant, stating that his reasons were personal and he was not obliged to debate them with anyone. He simply felt that O'Connell's work and his place of residence were not in the diocese's best interest. Tracy persisted, "[Everybody] minds being hurt by a fellow human being, but it hurts even more when it comes from a friend." Much earlier, O'Connell had assisted Tracy in St. Leo's Parish in New Orleans in a Confraternity of Christian Doctrine program out of Loyola University–New Orleans.

Barrett arranged for a June 16–17 meeting between O'Connell and Tracy, but denied knowing about any pressure on Tracy. On June 13, 14, and 18, the Diocesan Communications Office denied that

---

[65] O'Connell File, University of Notre Dame Archives, January 12, 1982.
[66] O'Connell File, Marist Provincial Archives, Washington, D.C.

Tracy had removed O'Connell because of his involvement with sugarcane workers. Cited were examples of Tracy's support for social justice causes,[67] including his approval of and assistance to the Southern Mutual Help Association (SMHA) and the Farah Slacks boycott, his approval of the manner in which a parish committee had handled the cause of sugarcane workers, and the devoting of one-tenth of the diocesan budget to social justice causes during the previous five years. Allegedly, the central reason was "jurisdiction." O'Connell ministered to the Plantation Adult Basic Education Program in Thibideau in the New Orleans Archdiocese, but resided in Plaulina in the Baton Rouge Diocese.

Despite regular, but confidential, exchanges between the Marist provincial, the Baton Rouge bishop, and several Marists serving in that diocese, O'Connell was said to have worked in the diocese without an assignment, a request from his provincial, or any discussion with diocesan authorities. O'Connell's views were echoed in several newspapers, including the New Orleans *Times Picayune* and *States Item*; *Daily Comment*, and *Morning Advocate*. A June 19, 1973, copy of the *States Item* quoted O'Connell as saying, "The Bishop has now backed off. I'm told he no longer has any objection to my remaining here."[68] Noting he moved in with a sugarcane worker and that thirty-one Marists in a provincial council meeting had praised and backed his work, O'Connell maintained that pressure from growers on diocesan officials would not get him to move. "They're going to have to shoot me.... It should be clear now to the executives of the sugar industry that they can no longer use church authority to force me out of my work."

On June 25, 1973, a diocesan spokesperson denied that Tracy had backed down, but the executive director of the SHMA and the Sisters' Councils of the Lafayette and Baton Rouge dioceses and the

---

[67] Ibid.
[68] Ibid.

124

New Orleans Archdiocese endorsed and praised O'Connell's assistance to the sugarcane workers.[69] The *National Catholic Reporter* ran several articles during the controversy. Especially revealing was an extensive September 14, 1973, article by Jerry DeMuth, entitled "Dispute spotlights plight of cane workers."[70] Cited first was James Bolner, associate professor of political science at Baton Rouge's Louisiana State University, who charged that rich landowners very often used the official Church. Instead, "[The] Catholic hierarchy should be actively supporting [O'Connell]. Opposition to him is based precisely on the proposition that he is effective. He is not the Sunday Catholic, paying dues, keeping to himself, and deploring from afar the plight of his fellows." Also cited was Sr. Lorna Boug, founder of SMHA, who claimed that more assistance came from Protestant and Jewish groups than from the Catholic Church. "The Catholic Church is responsible for problems. Most growers are Catholic. But the church hierarchy has done nothing to change the situation."

DeMuth said that when O'Connell mentioned his expulsion from the diocese during Agriculture Department hearings in Houma, Louisiana, growers in attendance applauded. More evidence of growers' tactics and of Church support for priests helping sugarcane workers appeared in *Labor, Church, and the Sugar Establishment*.[71] For example, O'Connell was cited as discerning a "kind of cop-out" by not challenging the political, social, and economic power structure to solve social problems, but merely going through the motions without effecting real change [p. 56]. Yet, New Orleans Archbishop Rummel created the Social Action Committee, with O'Connell as chair and Fr. Jerome Drolet and Charles Chapman, S.J., as members. "All three of these young priests were to play important roles in labor relations for many years" [p. 61]. O'Connell's

---

[69] Ibid.
[70] Ibid.
[71] Becnel 1980, 56–63.

activities drew criticism from commercial interests, but Rummel seldom interfered. The Knights of St. Gregory (usually big donors) confronted O'Connell and received no support from Rummel.

Back up north in July 1984, Fr. Philip Carey, S.J., told SAD's Higgins about the background of the film *On the Waterfront*, and John Corridan's support for New York–area longshoremen.[72] Director of the film, Bud Schulberg, for artistic reasons, wanted to introduce the notion that Corridan was persecuted by the Church. Carey disagreed because Cardinal Spellman may have been "cautious," but never opposed to Corridan's involvement.

Referring to a later controversy, Carey noted, "Had we Spellman here, we'd never be having the horrible mess the Hospitals and Nursing Homes have with 1199 [local of Service Employees International Union (SEIU)]. I had tried to set things up for Cardinal Cooke but he wanted committees, and working papers, and all that jargon. He blew it."

During the May 1989 eulogy at Carey's funeral, one of his predecessors, Fr. Fitzpatrick, S.J., spoke of the support that Carey and Fr. John Corridan, S.J., had received from New York's Francis Cardinal Spellman during the 1951 New York dock strike. The New York Jesuit provincial thought the cardinal was going to tell the two priests to cease their involvement in the strike. Yet, despite great pressure on the cardinal from some employers, who were generous benefactors of the archdiocese, Spellman did not. Carey and Corridan convinced him that if the Church withheld its support for the strikers there was a great danger of a return of communist leadership. Spellman gave them his blessing and told Carey and Corridan to continue.[73] In February 1953, Carey was troubled by a persistent question raised by some people, "What did Father Corridan do that was

---

[72] Carey Folder, SAD File, Catholic University Archives, July 27, 1984, Carey to Higgins.

[73] Fitzpatrick's text, May 31, 1989, New York Jesuit Province Archives.

wrong?" Carey was startled because "I for one do not know that he did anything improper." In the face of a threat by a Catholic layman to cut off donations to the Jesuits, Carey said he appreciated the wholehearted support his superiors had given him. "What are we in business for," they said, "if it be not for the helping of men to save themselves in this world and the next."[74]

Religious Community Officials

Relations of religious labor priests with religious superiors were less confrontational than for diocesan labor priests with their dioc esan superiors. Perhaps this was due to diocesan labor priests being more involved with local labor–management controversies and greater pressure from economic and political operatives than for religious labor priests who were more involved in Labor Schools and Institutes of Industrial Relations, mostly on Catholic college and university campuses. Examples cited here of relationships of religious labor priests with their religious superiors were in the context of labor–management controversies, often complicated by the influence or fear of influence by diocesan authorities.

New York's Fr. Philip Carey, S.J., in August 1945, received a highly commendatory letter from Fr. Zacheus J. Maher, S.J., the Jesuit superior general's representative for the American Assistancy. Noting the difficulties, disappointments, and toil involved in the settlement of a New York City bus strike, Maher offered "sincere congratulations," saying "the spontaneous tributes" of the workers were testimony to the splendid service rendered to labor, management, the city, the Society, and the Church. Calling Labor Schools something designed to foster right order and be "one of our most potent weapons against Communism," Maher compared the Jesuits' Labor School to the pioneering work of earlier Jesuits—"Marquette and

---

[74] Donohue to Carey, February 18, 1953, New York Jesuit Province Archives.

the Missionaries [Who] will say that your field is easier of cultivation that was theirs?"[75]

In February 1952, Carey quoted an letter sent earlier to Fr. Thomas J. Murray, S.J., president of Baltimore's Loyola College, from Dick McGrath, a member of his brother John's stevedoring company in New York.[76] McGrath said the company's board of directors had initially opposed a contribution of any kind to a Jesuit cause, because "Fr. Corridan [whose] advice to labor, and his activities opposing management in the steamship and stevedoring industries, have been most unfair." McGrath also mentioned that "a great many of the prominent steamship men in the City of New York have taken from their list of charities, all Jesuit activities." He gave a token donation and desired to discuss the matter with Murray at some time.

Murray had no wish to criticize Corridan. In fact, he admitted that he was "doing a lot for labor, but in doing so, could he not refrain from damning management? Perhaps not...I merely write in the hope that the interests of the Society can be safeguarded." After making it clear to Murray that the problem was criminal collusion between the International Longshoremen's Association (ILA), gangsters, and some of the employers, Carey quoted the New York's John McGrath: "I'm in business to make money, let the priests take care of morality." Carey called such opposition an honor and the approval of Spellman and the provincial a great source of encouragement.

California Province Fr. Peter J. Dunne was well known for having been dismissed from Catholic institutions and being embroiled in frequent conflicts with Jesuit and Church authorities. In 1936 he was sent home from Jesuit missions in China for a well-intentioned, but mistaken, judgment. In 1945 he was dismissed from St. Louis

---

[75] Maher to Carey, August 13, 1945, New York Jesuit Provincial Archives.
[76] Murray to Carey, February 4, 1952, New York Jesuit Provincial Archives.

University for opposing its Jesuit president's efforts to reintroduce segregation on the campus. In 1947 he was reassigned from the Jesuits' Loyola University–Los Angeles and the Archdiocese of Los Angeles as a result of his involvement in a major studio strike in Hollywood and for plotting against major producers and a turncoat union leader, Ronald Reagan, who allegedly smeared the strikers as "commies or commie sympathizers."

Periodically, Jesuit and archdiocesan officials voiced strong suggestions and orders to silence and/or remove Dunne.[77] Prior to taking Jesuit final vows, Dunne was accused of having a penchant for trouble with his superiors because of his frank and challenging ways. In 1943, Dunne was told by Fr. Thomas King, S.J., that during a retreat to Jesuit seminarians, a few participants had said "they were forced to read into your remarks a certain spirit of independence and criticism.... Critical remarks about certain Superiors gave them the impression that you were slightly inclined to be against the government."

Dunne's account of troubles in St. Louis University was recounted in a 1945 letter to SAD's Higgins.[78] Dunne noted that also bearing on his dismissal from St. Louis University were social, political, and economic views of his that clashed radically with the views of a controlling clique. The clique centered on Fr. Bernard Dempsey, S.J., "who cleverly dispenses anti New Deal, bitterly anti-Roosevelt, Big Business philosophy under the guise of encyclical doctrine." Dunne noted that a few Jesuit and lay professor supporters were afraid to speak up against the clique. The issue had to do with the perceived impact of Dunne's views on students and Jesuit scholastics. Instead of confronting Dunne directly, "they plotted behind my back in connivance with the rector to ease me out at the end of the semester.

---

[77] Dunne Folder, California Jesuit Province Archives, Los Gatos, California.
[78] Dunne to Higgins, May 27, 1945, Catholic University Archives.

The Negro question simply served as a pretext to oust me without waiting until the end of the semester."

As distasteful as he found the lies concocted about him at St. Louis University, Dunne was most saddened by the repercussions for the Institute for Social Order.[79] Speaking at his parish in Santa Barbara, California, Dunne complained bitterly about the "misuses" of the Jesuit vow of obedience to serve the ends of the St. Louis group and the Missouri provincial administration.

Dunne's involvement in a Hollywood labor–management dispute in January 1947 led to his difficulties with the local hierarchy, Jesuit officials of Loyola University–Los Angeles, and the provincial offices.[80] The controversy involved the Conference of Studio Unions (CSU), on the one side, and movie producers and the International Association of Theater and Stage Employees (IATSE), on the other. Dunne characterized the labor dispute as "a vicious conspiracy that was being protected by the 'club wielding' Los Angeles Police Officers [and] if the CSU lost this strike, which [Dunne] didn't believe they would, it would be a blow to Democratic trade unionism all over the world." He decried the smearing of the CSU president as a "communist." His provincial told him that the Los Angeles Chancery Office was requesting prior notice of his talks, the purpose of any meetings he attended, the identity of the sponsoring committee, names of others on the platform, and copies of outlines of his radio talks on the controversy.

In the reply that the acting California provincial sent to the vice president of Loyola University–Los Angeles, where Dunne served as a professor, was a letter from Joseph Scott, a powerful L.A. lawyer and Loyola graduate, complaining of Dunne's involvement in

---

[79] Dunne to Carroll, June 4, 1945, Oregon Jesuit Province Archives, Gonzaga University, Seattle, Washington.

[80] Dunne Folder, California Jesuit Province Archives, Los Gatos, California.

the controversy. At the bottom of the letter the vice president scribbled, "The enclosed letter is sent for your information and guidance. I am getting it from all sides and it is making it very difficult to keep people interested in a financial way." The acting provincial labeled Scott's letter a "bombastic tirade and unsubstantiated accusations...an insult to a priest, the university, and to the Province." Asking to be excused for being so upset by the enclosed letter, Duce told Malone, "I don't intend to sell a fellow Jesuit down the river simply because Joe Scott doesn't agree with his idea, which I hope is the idea of the Popes on the reconstruction of the social order."

In June, the acting provincial apparently had inquired about a temporary assignment for Dunne in the Jesuit New York Province. The acting provincial told the president of Loyola University that the New York provincial had declined, saying "his own relations with the diocesan authorities are not the best, and he is fearful that Fr. Dunne's presence might complicate matters." Hoping no injustice would be done to Dunne, the acting provincial sent to Fr. Vincent McCormick, S.J., Jesuit assistant general in Rome, a letter from Daniel Marshall, member of a prestigious L.A. law firm. In the letter Marshall referred to a report sent to many priests by a Catholic executive accusing Dunne of disloyalty to the Church and preaching Communism. Marshall said Dunne's position was exactly the same as that of the priests whom Bishop Manning had appointed as investigators and that had been published in the archdiocesan newspaper. Marshall also noted that, when the Archbishop's endorsement of the Fair Employment Practices was publicly maligned, Dunne firmly defended it. Marshall was convinced that no bishop, priest, or layperson had done more to spread the Gospel of social justice than Dunne. The fact that other Church leaders had failed to do so, he said, "should not be a reason for interfering with the apostolate in which he is engaged."

To those who complained that Dunne associated with communists, Marshall paraphrased the bitter complaint of one communist who

131

had charged that Dunne was the leading Jesuit infiltrator of Communism in the United States, on direct orders from Rome. Marshall concluded, "If those outside the Society [of Jesus] who have power to dispose of him insist that such must be his lot, the responsibility would be placed squarely with them. They cannot in justice support that insistence." Duce replied to Marshall a month later, "Your eloquent and extremely touching letter has been kept as ammunition, should such a request be made for the removal of Father Dunne from Los Angeles."

In the September 22, 1951, issue of *The Nation* [pp. 236–39], freelance writer and correspondent Joseph Strocker, wrote a very complimentary article, entitled "Father Dunne: A Study in Faith," after Dunne had served as a parish assistant in Phoenix, Arizona. Noted were the several altercations Dunne had had with Church authorities and his defense of the Catholic Church in debates with the Protestant polemicist Paul Blanshard at Harvard University, which prompted great praise and even conversions. Strocker said that despite Dunne's forthright championing of liberal causes "he has yet to receive a single commendation for his efforts from his superiors. Nor has his own Jesuit province invited him to speak on the subject at one of its schools or colleges."

The writer quoted Dunne as saying, "It's a matter of faith.... Either I believe in the things the church stands for or I don't. If not, there is no sense in remaining a Catholic. If I do believe in these things, they don't cease to be true because of the action of the Catholic hierarchy." Strocker continued with Dunne's assertion that he and not the hierarchy represented "authentic Catholic thought." Dunne dismissed the hierarchy as "ministers of mediocrity who consistently sacrifice truth and justice to expediency." Regarding accusations by his superiors of Dunne's imprudence in his crusades, he was quoted as saying, "They mean anything that steps on the toes of someone who is important"

In the late 1980s, Dunne explained the demise of SODEPAX, of which he was general secretary, after three years of successful interfaith cooperation in assisting development in the third world and world peace.[81] Essentially, Vatican officials and Paul VI had no wish to continue such close cooperation with the World Council of Churches. Dunne was disappointed, but not bitter. By that time, he was inured to repeated "hierarchical machinations." Citing what is probably one of the major explanations of all the authority problems cited above, Dunne pointed to the censorship among the Jesuits and the Catholic Church, prior to Vatican II.

In the Foreword of *King's Pawn*, SAD's George Higgins stipulated that he was not competent to adjudicate all of Dunne's personal conflicts, but said that *King's Pawn* "promises to be the most controversial book of its kind published in recent years." Deeming Dunne above peevishness, rancor, and vindictiveness, as well as a person of solid faith with a very wry sense of humor, Higgins said that few U.S. priests of the twentieth century could match Dunne's mix of talents. With reference to Dunne's diverse assignments, taken up on short notice and with a readiness to take his licks and adapt, without self-pity or lasting anger, Higgins concluded that Dunne's behavior was evidence of "the depth of his lifetime commitment as a religious and his ability to carry [his assignments] out with professional competence of a high order" [p. xi].

For several years, Fr, Thomas Shortell, S.J., had tried to obtain permission of his Jesuit provincial to establish at Boston College the kind of Industrial Relations Institute, that Shortell had been instrumental in establishing several years earlier at the Jesuit College of the Holy Cross in Worchester, Massachusetts. In July 1948 he wrote a lengthy letter listing eight detailed reasons why his request should be honored, given his many years of persistent effort and deep discouragement. Very striking among arguments of support

---

[81] Dunne 1990.

from papal encyclicals and Jesuit superiors general, were two quotes. One was from CIO president Philip Murray, "[All] your speeches about the dignity of labor avail little unless you implement them in practice." The other was from street talk about the Jesuits, which Shortell disagreed with but could not deny: "They are 'lace curtain', only one step removed from workers but afraid to soil their hands with a labor union." There is no evidence of a response, positive or negative, from the provincial, but a few years later the Boston Archdiocesan Labor Guild was transferred under Jesuit direction.[82]

Fr. Louis Twomey, S.J., of New Orleans, became quite controversial in the late 1950s due to his involvement in racial and labor issues and as a recipient of some "tasteless and immoral" hate mail. Some of the mail came from fellow Jesuits—who were at odds with "the official mind of the Jesuit Order"—and some came from the Radical Right. "Even his out-of-town speaking engagements had been cut back by his religious superior, Fr. Patrick Walsh, S.J., president of Loyola University–Los Angeles.[83] Twomey was also called to Rome by the Jesuit superior general, Pedro Arrupe, to cooperate in drafting a major document on race. The statement complimented Jesuits in the United States for their activity among immigrants, but cited a poor record of service to Blacks.[84] American Assistant General Fr. Vincent O'Keefe wrote to Twomey: "The letter, as you know, was a tremendous success, and that letter owes more to you than any other individual."[85]

In late 1958, Twomey asked his provincial why the rector of the Loyola Jesuit Community was reluctant to include in the tenth anniversary issue of *Blueprint*, the Institute's regular publication, the Jesuit

---

[82] Shortell File, New England Jesuit Provincial Archives, Holy Cross College, Worchester, Massachusetts, July 20, 1948.
[83] Payne 1976, 162.
[84] Ibid., 259–261.
[85] Ibid., 272.

superior general's "norms for the proper deportment on controversial topics," which had been sent in a letter to all Jesuits. The provincial said the superior general's letter was "a high tribute to your ceaseless and self-sacrificing endeavor in the interests of the ISO [Institute of Social Order], [and] conveys a message well worth preserving and reprinting in your November issue of "Christ's Blueprint." The provincial could not see how "even a person wholly at variance with the policy and principles advocated by your publication, could take exception or find fault with the simple, clear, and just norms set down in His Paternity's [superior general's] letter in discussing controversial topics."[86]

Twomey died in October 8, 1969, after a long illness. The eulogist at his funeral, Loyola's vice president for academic affairs, pointed out some paradoxes in Twomey's life. Such a kind man was embroiled most of his life in controversy and such a humble man achieved secular greatness and became one of the most influential men of his time.

While working for the National Catholic Rural Life Conference, Fr. James Vizzard, S.J., wrote his provincial, in late November 1965, trying to level with him about his own feelings and behavior. At the time, Vizzard was suffering from serious personal depression.[87] A similar letter to a Pat Donohue (with no further identification) was dated in late March 1971, apparently after Vizzard had emerged from his depression and was motivated by a desire to respond to vocal observations made about him in a consultors' meeting (a regional executive body among Jesuits) about Vizzard.[88] These included allegations that he was a persona non grata, that he might

---

[86] Twomey File, Loyola University–New Orleans Archives, Twomey to O'Neill, October 18, 1958, and O'Neill to Twomey, October 28, 1958.

[87] Vizzard File, Stanford University Libraries, Department of Special Collections and University Archives, Vizzard to Connelly, November 22, 1965.

[88] Vizzard File, Stanford University Libraries, Department of Special Collections and University Archives, Vizzard to Donohue, March 29, 1971.

use his proposed assignment (Project Equality) as a platform for larger (and presumably inappropriate) involvement, that he was not very perceptive about people, that he was prevented by his enthusiasm from seeing what was happening under his nose, and that his health was precarious.

Vizzard's expansive response to these observations was that his style might be offensive, but his commitment to the Church, the Jesuits, the poor, truth, and honesty were beyond reproach. His ability to express his views clearly and forcefully was extolled. Project Equality was more than enough to engage time and energy. He was aware of two troubled Jesuits who lived with him. So he talked to them and hoped his enthusiasm and dedication would rub off on them. He saw potential in a young Jesuit when almost no one else did. The mental and emotional disturbance he so painfully suffered was a matter of past history. Doctors' examinations indicated no barriers to the Project Equality assignment. He cited his good relationship with Catholic and interfaith clergy and noted that his work was overseen by a national board. He also referenced a 1967 letter of the Jesuit general on the "Interracial Apostolate."

The president of the Jesuit School of Theology in Berkeley, California, in July 1971, replied to Vizzard's request to join that Jesuit community.[89] After consulting with several Jesuits "who know you and love you," the president told Vizzard that the those interviewed said that he caused dissension through "endless" criticism of policies and procedures; made it "more difficult to conciliate scholastics with the faculty"; his dissatisfaction with the rector was public knowledge among scholastics at Alma College and this "undermined his position with them"; his conversations "continually focused upon himself and projected achievements"; he showed "a loss of contact with reality [thus] making the fall much more serious

---

[89] Vizzard File, Stanford University Libraries, Department of Special Collections and University Archives, Buckley to Vizzard, July 31, 1971.

when facts and data finally come in"; assigning Vizzard to Berkeley would be psychologically a poor step for him and would "court serious conflict where none need take place, where complicated interrelationships are now beginning to take a positive and firm form."

Vizzard had already been rejected by three Jesuit communities—Georgetown, Alma College, and Berkeley. The president of Berkeley Theology Program admitted he did not know anything about Vizzard's Georgetown experience, but asserted "no one is asking you to leave the community at Santa Clara, as far as I know, no more than preventing you from moving into one of the houses in San Francisco." Yet, the president stated that no matter how painful such forthrightness might be to Vizzard, there was hope the rejection from Berkeley would not be read as a personal rejection. The president said, "There was universal agreement that your work is of critical importance for the Province [but] I don't think that anyone gains finally from covered motivations and double-talk." In concluding, he asked for prayers on behalf of the Berkley community and was sure Vizzard would find the community a friendly group to visit and his apostolate would always receive all possible attention and encouragement.

Vizzard's reply to the president in early August 1971 was filled with thanks for the president's candor, charity, clarity, and courage. Especially appreciated was "the first clear and comprehensive analysis I have ever received from anyone on how my personality and 'style' affects other people."[90] He disagreed, however, with the allegations that he exaggerated his accomplishments, overstated future achievements, or made inflated projections. In a report he sent on his involvements, he said he was open to receive from the province or assistancy any evidence and/or insights about "wild dreams, im-

---

[90] Vizzard File, Stanford University Libraries, Department of Special Collections and University Archives, Vizzard to Buckley, August 2, 1972.

possible dreams, pursuit of which can only lead to tragic disillusionment." Admitting he could be wrong, he would be "eternally grateful to whoever can demonstrate it to me," but admitted he was hurt by rejection by the Berkeley community. He would never voice criticism and rebuke anyone who might criticize the decision. In closing, he said he would gratefully accept an invitation to visit the Berkeley community.

Vizzard received a letter, in mid-August 1971, from Fr. Richard Vaughan, Jesuit provincial of the California Province, in which he stated that, on the grounds of psychological instability, he did not favor Vizzard's plans to assist the Equal Opportunity program.[91] "I could not assign you to such a project with the attitude you manifested toward the bishop. We cannot afford another failure in the Social Apostolate.... I am asking you to concentrate on your job in a consistent, calm way."

The same provincial sent Vizzard, at the end of May 1972, a letter of assignment to be chaplain, at the request of César Chávez, for migratory farm workers in the San Joaquin Valley.[92] He was reminded that assignments were based on the vow of obedience and understanding of Ignatian discernment, of which the "basic premise is indifference, something you have never had from the moment we began discussing your future last April." He was accused of being determined "to get exactly what you wanted and closed to any other possibility."

After noting that presenting three options was "completely foreign to the notion of obedience to our Constitutions," Vaughan suggested that, if he was unable to accept Jesuit obedience, "then you should be honest with yourself and the Society and consider a life

---

[91] Vizzard File, Stanford University Libraries, Department of Special Collections and University Archives, August 13, 1971, Vaughan to Vizzard.
[92] Vizzard File, Stanford University Libraries, Department of Special Collections and University Archives, May 31, 1972, Vaughan to Vizzard.

where you are no longer bound by such obedience because obviously you would no longer be living the Jesuit vocation." The enclosed summary of their meeting revealed a very stormy relationship. When the meeting ended and Vizzard stated he would not be quiet about what had transpired during the meeting, Vaughan retorted, "[There] you go again pushing, threatening again." Vizzard replied, "The case was already closed. I'm just telling you, out of a sense of decency, so you can be prepared to deal with it—if you can."

A week later, Vizzard sent four comments and a letter to Vaughan about the late May meeting.[93] First, Vizzard found very disconcerting Vaughan's persistence that Vizzard was emotionally and mentally imbalanced and especially Vaughan's continued refusal to confer with a professional who knows Vizzard. "Your own so-called 'clinical judgment' is not clinical and is, rather, an inexplicable prejudice." Second, Vaughan's remarks about early retirement and leaving the Jesuits were deemed "absolutely incredible." Such an option could not be authentic for Vizzard, but he hoped we would have the strength to live with difficulties entailed in serving as chaplain to the migratory farm workers. Third, rephrasing the maxim "God writes exceedingly straight with crooked lines," Vizzard accused Vaughan of having written very crooked lines with Vizzard's life." Fourth, remarking that their letters had crossed in the mail, Vizzard said that "after a painful period of prayer, consultation, and discernment," he was at peace in accepting God's new call. César Chávez offered the remaining twenty-two days of his fast for the intention that Vizzard would join him and the union and requested all the hundreds of participants in each night's liturgy to do the same. That "his personal sacrifice and their prayers were be

---

[93] Vizzard File, Stanford University Libraries, Department of Special Collections and University Archives, June 2, 1972, Vizzard to Vaughan.

ing answered," prompted Vizzard to close with the rhetorical question, "Is not that a sign that this is truly God's will for me."

Vizzard received a signed letter, in mid-November 1974, from eleven Jesuit province directors of social ministry, praising his work with the United Farm Workers (UFW) and the "Farm Labor Contractors Registration Act Amendments of 1947," as well as his appointment by the labor secretary to the Standards Advisory Committee on Agriculture of the Occupational Safety and Health Administration.[94] The directors said, "So we all thank you, with the hope that you can continue your good work, despite the serious effects of your last [back] operation."

In early April 1975 Vaughan said he wanted Vizzard to continue working for the Farm Labor Law, though he felt that the UFW might not have policies and directives prepared for challenges if the legislation were to be passed.[95] If it did not pass, any "showdown" with the union would be regrettable. Yet, Vaughan was quite supportive, asking Vizzard to put up with the frustration he experienced with the union and "to continue the important task of lobbying on their behalf.… I understand full well the need for recognition you desire from the top people in the Union.… I hope you find some consolation and strength in the knowledge that you have my backing." Vaughan closed, wishing Vizzard well in initiating a new community and for continued health improvement.

The last letter to come from Vaughan was at the end of November 1975, but this wasn't the last word about the continuing tension between the two Jesuits.[96] The handwritten letter was a reply to an

---

[94] Vizzard File, Stanford University Libraries, Department of Special Collections and University Archives, November 11, 1974, Social Ministry Directors to Vizzard.
[95] Vizzard File, Stanford University Libraries, Department of Special Collections and University Archives, April 9, 1975, Vaughan to Vizzard.
[96] Vizzard File, Stanford University Libraries, Department of Special Collections and University Archives, November 26, 1975, Vaughan to Vizzard.

earlier Vizzard complaint about Vaughan refusing to speak with him. Calling Vizzard's behavior childish, Vaughan thought it utterly useless to communicate with him because Vizzard seemed to have an insatiable need for approval and affection, no matter what the time or place. "I no longer intend to support your cause because I do not think Jesuit communities should be psychotherapy communities.... When you return to Washington, I urge you to see a psychiatrist and get involved in group therapy."

After visiting the Jesuit superior general in October 1975 concerning relations with Vaughan, Vizzard was told to discuss matters with Fr. Gerald Sheahan, U.S. assistant to the general, which he did by correspondence rather than in person.[97] Enclosed was Vaughan's last letter and Vizzard's account of frequent illnesses—an eye operation and five back surgeries, a two-year period of depression (successfully overcome) and sixty-three serious hospitalizations. Also recounted were affirmation from superior generals Jansens and Arrupe and previous provincials, as well as Vaughan's demands for additional monies while Vizzard assisted the cash-starved UFW and Vizzard's noncomplicity in his brother's cable to Arrupe about "a flagrant violation of the Society's and the Gospel's mandate of brotherly love." The letter closed with request for some relief and guidance about personal reform and repentance, modest financial assistance, and possible transfer to another provincial's authority.

Four months later, Sheahan had conversations with two Jesuits who lived with Vizzard and with Fr. Angelo D'Agostino, S.J., a psychiatrist in Tampa, Florida.[98] Noting that there were two sides to every controversy, Sheahan explained that he did not see his role as "one of a judge in a closed hearing but rather of a bridge." He drew two conclusions. First, despite Vizzard's assertion that he only attacked

[97] Vizzard File, Stanford University Libraries, Department of Special Collections and University Archives, Vizzard to Sheahan.
[98] Vizzard File, Stanford University Libraries, Department of Special Collections and University Archives, March 6, 1975, Sheahan to Vizzard.

institutions, others perceived his attacks on Jesuits who had devoted their lives to those institutions as *personal*. "Just as you feel yourself put down by Fr. Vaughan when he does not agree with the manner in which you serve the institution of the UFW." Second, Vizzard was said to place too many emotional demands upon other Jesuits for support "without offering any support in return." Sheahan offered four recommendations. First, request lodging from the two priests in the small community and discuss with the rector the points Sheahan had raised. Second, wait out the remaining time of Vaughan's term as provincial in order to forestall further aggravation and talk with Vaughan's successor. Third, use the financial assistance made available to Vizzard's family. Fourth, utilize available money for psychiatric assistance from Fr. D'Agostino, who promised to offer help at any level, even "at the Jesuit-buddy level."

Vizzard received from the new Jesuit provincial, in 1977, a report on his professional meeting with the psychiatrist, D'Agostino, in early 1976.[99] Prompted by Sheahan's advice and Vaughan's insistence, Vizzard issued a written waiver to allow D'Agostino to convey a professional opinion of Vizzard's mental/emotional status, deemed "necessary, useful and permissible." In D'Agostino's opinion, Vizzard was open and candid; has a clear grasp on reality, though defensive at times; harbors a deep sense of hurt and resentment, which "objective facts of his life seemed to give much justification for"; appears sometimes aggressive and not always prudent and diplomatic; occasionally over-sensitive; usually self-confident but obviously needing affirmation; feels rightly or wrongly not adequately received by others. After recounting Vizzard's history of illness, depression, and hospitalization, D'Agostino said, "One really has to wonder how over so many years he has been able to carry on an energetic, demanding and, by all accounts, highly successful ministry." Suggesting steps to reduce stress in Vizzard's life,

[99] Vizzard File, Stanford University Libraries, Department of Special Collections and University Archives, January 5, 1977, Mahan to Vizzard.

D'Agostino concluded he was free of any psychiatric disorder, but volunteered to meet him at any time. D'Agostino closed, "I believe that his file covering the last five and a half years should have this letter as a corrective to whatever in those files reflects Father Vaughan's bias."

One week later, the provincial thanked Vizzard for his two letters and said he agreed with him about how stressful the "limbo status" of his ministry must have been.[100] Enclosed was a check to pay off a Bank America debt and assurances that he would receive a generous monthly check for personal needs, as well as wonderful words of affirmation and appreciation. Quite pointedly, the new provincial admitted that the work with Chávez had reached an end, as evidenced by Chávez's refusal to answer mail and phone calls. So, César should judge Vizzard on his performance alone; hopefully, he would soon respond. If not, then Vizzard should know of the provincial's support. "You have given a great deal to the UFW and it seems a shame that the organization now refuses to communicate with you. Try to take care of your health."

Six year later in 1983, Vizzard received greetings from Rome on the occasion of his Golden Jubilee as a Jesuit and a priest. The letter from the vice provincial for education said that Vizzard was a dear friend and inspiration.[101] The vice provincial commended him for his courage in pursuing social justice, before it was popular or acclaimed, and he called Vizzard "a trail blazer" in the California Province's social ministries, laying a strong foundation by his blending of intellectual and social apostolates. Greetings were enclosed from the delegate of the Jesuit superior general. He praised Vizzard for service to the Jesuits and the Church, teaching economics and political science, undertaking the arduous task of research

[100] Vizzard File, Stanford University Libraries, Department of Speical Collections and University Archives January 11, 1977, Mahan to Vizzard.
[101] Vizzard File, Stanford University Libraries, Department of Special Collections and University Archives, August 14, 1983, Woods to Vizzard.

and publishing, and advocating on behalf of the poor. Stressing Vizzard's ten years of service with the National Catholic Rural Life Conference. the delegate thanked him in the name of the Society of Jesus for his Jesuit years. He concluded by saying that Vizzard's latest apostolate was one of suffering, which he bore with faith and obedience to the Lord, making Vizzard an instrument of God's love. Finally, on the occasion of Vizzard's Golden Jubilee, the president of San Francisco's St. Ignatius Prep thanked Vizzard for being a priestly model and personable friend to Jesuits, as well as to the people of God who had benefited so much from Vizzard's dedication and service.[102]

Non-Catholic Religious Leaders

The few contacts between labor priests and non-Catholic religious leaders indicated here can be attributed to a very insular attitude among Catholics prior to Vatican II. At Pope John XXIII's suggestion, however, Catholics leaders, scholars, and activists threw open church windows to concerns of the world and to cooperation with other religious groups. However, such groups were wary of extending the hand to Catholics until Vatican II's momentum.

Reginald Kennedy, executive secretary of the National Conference of Christians and Jews, on January 12, 1940, wrote to Detroit Archdiocese's Fr. Raymond Clancy, saying that many associates "were deeply impressed with the fine speech that you delivered at the CIO mass meeting during the Chrysler strike.[103] Five years later, Clancy was among 125 Catholic, Jewish, and Protestant clergy—many of

---

[102] Vizzard File, Stanford University Libraries, Department of Special Collections and University Archives, Sauer to Vizzard, no date given.

[103] Correspondence, Wayne State University Archives of Labor and Urban Affairs and University Archives, Clancy Collection, Box 2, Folder 13.

them listed in *Who's Who in Social Justice*—who signed an interfaith declaration entitled "Pattern for Economic Justice."[104]

In mid-1945 SAD's Higgins was invited to contribute an article about the Catholic position on labor for *Prophetic Religion* by David S. Burgess, chair of the Labor Commission of the Fellowship of Southern Churchmen (FSC).[105] Southern Protestant churches were very conservative. Burgess said, and the average Protestant can learn much from "the progressive views of Catholic priests and officials regarding organized labor." "[Because] of my lack of acquaintance with the Catholic leaders of the South I have been at a loss to find a man such as you who would be able to write on the subject." When Higgins officially retired in 1980 from the USCC (formerly the NCWC), several encomiums were voiced about his relations with the Jewish community.[106] Bishop John McCarthy of Austin, Texas, said of Higgins, "George was the only identifiable, national Roman Catholic with deep, deep ties to the Jewish communities." Joseph Rauh, prominent Jewish leader, long-time Washington lawyer, and director of Americans for Democratic Action (ADA), said, "No one person did more to bring the religious community into unity behind the civil rights bill than George." Rabbi Marc Tannenbaum of the American Jewish Committee said, "On every major issue of human welfare and on every major issue of Catholic-Jewish concern, George Higgins was always there."

San Antonio's Archbishop Robert Lucey, in 1957, was the recipient of the Distinguished Service Award of the Anti-Defamation League of B'nai B'rith. The speaker on the occasion was Senate majority leader Lyndon Johnson, who said, "There is no need for advertising to recognize a truly pure heart and a truly pure mind. The finest

---

[104] Wayne State University Archives of Labor and Urban Affairs and University Archives, Clancy Collection, Box 2, Folder 8.
[105] Higgins File, Catholic University Archives, Burgess to Higgins, June 15, 1945.
[106] Costello 1980, 242–246.

recommendation that can be made of any man is that he is Archbishop Lucey's friend."[107]

Fr. George Dunne, S.J., in 1969, was named general secretary of the Committee on Society, Development and Peace (SODEPAX), a joint ecumenical program devoted to arousing world consciousness to the problems of development and peace.[108]

In June 1944, Fathers Drolet, Reintjes, and O'Connell, S.M., formed a joint clergy committee for social action in New Orleans. The committee had good cooperation from Protestant ministers and Jewish rabbis.[109]

Fr. Carl J. Benecke, S.J., of Loyola-Marymount–Los Angeles, in 1984, received a citation from the National Conference of Christian and Jews for almost fifteen years of distinguished service to the interfaith communities of the Los Angeles area.[110]

A Congregational minister said of Fr. Siedenburg, S.J., Loyola University–Chicago administrator and scholar, that "having sat with him throughout the greater part of the winter on the Regional Labor Board I think that I have never met a man who had greater capacity for conciliating and arbitrating disputes among men."

---

[107] Bronder 1982, 41–64.
[108] Dunne Folder, California Jesuit Province Archives, Los Gatos, California.
[109] Drolet Folder, SAD File, Catholic University Archives, June 1, 1944, Higgins File.
[110] Benecke File, Oregon Jesuit Province Archives, Gonzaga University, Spokane, Washington.

7

CONCERNS REGARDING THE CHURCH

Complaints, Failings, & Worries

W hatever the amount or quality of Church support, labor priests still had concerns about the Church, including complaints, failings, and worries. Sometimes implied were differences and/or disagreements between those priests. Sometimes failure to differentiate between concerns, on the one hand, and differences and/or disagreements, on the other hand, led to serious misunderstandings of the "labor priests' movement" by some less discerning authors. Sometimes concerns also revealed firm agreements among labor priests.

Among the concerns were Catholic institutions' opposition to unionization of employees, indifference of workers to social reform, union leaders' corruption and indifference to Church teaching on labor–management relations, influence of rich and powerful on Church authorities, unreasonable expectations of priests' abilities and influence, exploitation of Church workers due to inadequate wages and benefits, excessive secrecy and dishonesty among Church leaders, excessive concentration on Communism by some Church leaders and pastors, recourse to racist attitudes and activi-

147

ties by some Church leaders, over-extension of the scope of authority by some Church leaders, inadequate and/or antiquated education for priests—especially with regard to social issues, uniformed outlook on Socialism, insensitivity toward anti-Semitism, and unreal expectations of Catholic and non-Catholic public officials and labor leaders.

New York Fr. Carey, S.J., encouraged his predecessor at Xavier Institute of Industrial Relations, Fr. Joseph Fitzpatrick, S.J., to focus on economic theories, especially Marxism, as he began his doctoral studies in sociology at Harvard University.[1] Carey said he was quite dissatisfied with the little written about "Vocational Society," especially some of the "brash manifestoes set out by certain Catholic writers on the matter." Near the end of 1945, he cited New York ACTU chaplain Fr. John Monaghan about so many workers thinking that the only place for the Church was Sunday Mass and that the Church was not interested in workers' problems.[2] Thus, efforts of labor priests were another way of reaching the masses through the things in which they were interested.

In April 1946 Carey also expounded on the subject of Church involvement and influence to Fr. Michael Mulcaire, C.S.C., a Portland University priest-economist.[3] He asked, do we want leaders who are Catholics, such as Tobin (Teamster president), Joe Ryan (International Longshoremen Association president), and others who were good Catholics in their personal lives, but had been infected with secularism, laicism, and liberalism, which separated them into compartments? Such were not the type of leaders Carey would want to develop. Citing items from Leo XIII and Pius XI, Carey

---

[1] Carey File, New York Province Jesuit Archives, June 11, 1945, Carey to Fitzpatrick.

[2] Carey Folder, SAD File, Catholic University Archives, November 13, 1945, Carey to Higgins.

[3] Carey Folder, SAD File, Catholic University Archives, April 1946, Carey to Mulcaire.

would seek workers imbued not merely with Catholic principles and their application, but who possessed technical, commercial, and social competence. He would not look to Catholic Action, which had no intention of displaying any strictly union or political activities. Rather, Pius XI would look to those whom Catholic Action had trained.

In July 1950 Carey noted that people often expected a priest "to be sort of a Tammany Hall captain who will take care of them when they are in trouble or need."[4] He agreed that if the people were too poor, ill, or broken down, the proper job would be to equip and alert them to their own responsibilities. Convinced the vast majority were passive, some potential for leadership still remained given the great sacrifices a few workers had made to attend Labor School sessions. Yet, most workers were not interested in social reform. After a particular gripe or problem was resolved they seldom returned to the Labor School. Replying to SAD's Higgins's questions in October 1950 about Malcolm Johnson's book, *Crime on the Waterfront*, Carey said his experience was that whenever there was a labor racketeer there were political and business counterparts and all profited at the expense of the rank-and-file and the public.[5]

Hartford's Fr. Joseph Donnelly told Archbishop O'Brien in early 1953 that "local educational programs are not satisfactory," due to failings of local directors, repetition of the same classes to a small nucleus, difficulty in getting people to meetings, and their interest only in getting professional knowledge, already attainable in the University of Connecticut, but not in Catholic Social Teaching.[6] Seeking some solutions from SAD's Higgins and other labor priests,

---

[4] Carey File, New York Jesuit Province Archives, July 28, 1950, Carey to McLeech.

[5] Carey File, New York Jesuit Province Archives, October 30, 1950,Carey to Higgins.

[6] Donnelly File, Hartford Archdiocesan Archives, March 16, 1953, Donnelly to O'Brien.

Donnelly was not optimistic. Other Labor Schools had faced a decline in educational programs and had been left to die. "That I hope we shall not do." For him, the solution lay in positive support for the Young Christian Workers (YCW) movement. He suggested that two or three younger priests be sent to YCW workshops, for he was convinced that YCW could train apostles to carry the social action teaching to workers and persuade them to put it to constructive purposes.

Fr. Jerome Drolet of New Orleans spoke about Church employees being exploited.[7] His pastor, for example, underpaid the janitor, who was "still struggling heroically on his thirteen bucks a week." He wrote about a proposed declaration aimed at the White Citizens' Council, but Archbishop Rummel seemed reluctant to make a statement on the issue.[8] The auxiliary bishop warned parishioners in rural areas about organizations, councils, associations, etc., that taught principles on race and other issues that were contrary to Catholic doctrine. Yet, when Drolet inquired of a minor Chancery official about the matter, he was told, "the question you raise is of political nature and the Archbishop refuses to become involved himself and refuses to allow his priests to become involved in it." What he meant was that labor policy on construction of private schools, colleges, hospitals, clinics, and similar institutions operated by religious communities was not covered by policy.

California's Fr. George Dunne, S.J., out of concern over excessive secrecy, had earlier asked for the identity of those who had accused him of certain defects in obedience, etc. Writing in August 1943, his provincial thanked him for his humility, frankness, and sincerity, but told him it was better that the identity of the consultors not be known.[9] In August 1944, Dunne wrote to complain about an item in

---

[7] Drolet File, Catholic University Archives, October 22, 1940, Drolet to Hayes.

[8] Drolet File, Catholic University Archives, July 26, 1956, Drolet to Higgins.

[9] Dunne File, California Jesuit Archives, Los Gatos, Calif., August 12, 1943, King to Dunne.

the *Province Review* concerning the election defeat of a layman, John Costello, who was esteemed as a friend and person of character. Dunne thought the defeat was deserved since Costello's public record responded to "the forces of reaction."[10] Costello had stirred up race prejudice toward Japanese-Americans and supported the interests of the wealthy and opponents of labor unions. Dunne was saddened that Costello was Jesuit-educated, because "he failed, despite his talents and virtues, to show himself a peerless, progressive leader inspired by genuine Catholic social ideals."

In April 1945, Dunne expressed concern over the St. Louis University president forbidding attendance of African-American students at dances on the campus. He told the provincial that the only way he could remain at the university would be "to publicly disassociate myself from it and relentlessly condemn it—as I should were the practice of sexual promiscuity [be] imposed on the students."[11] He deemed the policy a mockery of the Institute of Social Sciences (ISS) and Institute of Social Order (ISO). "The most grievous social problem in this country...with international implications...is the Negro problem, the problem of racism." Dunne was convinced that the "ISS can serve no useful purpose as long as it is connected with St. Louis University," and he did not hesitate to state such to the director of ISS, Fr. Leo Brown, S.J.

Around the same time, Dunne was called to task by Fr. Holloran, S.J., the university president, for a radio address on the St. Louis University–sponsored Sacred Heart Program.[12] The address was on racial prejudice, especially maintaining "separate schools for white and colored." Although St. Louis's archbishop, John Glennon, had

---

[10] Dunne File, California Jesuit Archives, Los Gatos, Calif., August 21, 1944, Dunne to Seeliger.

[11] Dunne File, California Jesuit Archives, Los Gatos, Calif., April 1, 1945, Dunne to Missouri Province Provincial.

[12] Dunne File, California Jesuit Archives, Los Gatos, Calif., April 14, 1945, Holloran to King.

ordered that absolutely no parochial schools, high schools, or colleges were to accept colored students along with whites, Holloran had opened admissions to colored students at the university. But he noted, "I have made many, many enemies, have taken untold abuse, and have lost for the University I do not know how many thousands of dollars." He claimed Dunne had said that those who even think of separate schools, whether they were in overalls or in purple, were nothing other than whitened sepulchers. Dunne was asked to refrain from sending any copies of the address to anyone who might have requested it and to refrain from discussing the topic in St. Louis in the future. However, Dunne sent a copy of the address to the Jesuit assistant general and asked that Holloran's order be rescinded. The Jesuit assistant general upheld Holloran after Holloran explained the restrictions. The assistant general also revealed allegations of personality and character defects of Dunne that Holloran and other Jesuits at St. Louis University had observed.

In a letter Dunne wrote later to SAD's George Higgins—in appreciation for "the lift of a little boost and a word of approbation"—he commented briefly on the situation.[13] Holloran was privately bitter that "splendid moral influence" of another Jesuit, Fr. Heithaus, was putting force on him, but he publicly took "full credit for it" and ordered the Student Conclave to pass a "secret" resolution excluding Negroes from all social functions at the university. Dunne cited Holloran's comments in a piece in the May 17, 1945, *St. Louis Post-Dispatch:* "We do not approve, nor shall we attempt to enforce, identity between white and colored students in the wider and less defined field of social relationships, contacts, and activities." Holloran was also cited on the same day in the *St. Louis Globe-Democrat.* "We do not attempt to ape the mistakes of communists who, after a futile

---

[13] Higgins File, Catholic University Archives, May 27, 1945, Higgins to Dunne.

venture in the field of utter leveling, have now reverted to a structure of society that human nature and common sense would have told them are requirements of civilized, harmonious, and prosperous relations." Dunne noted another Jesuit's recollection that Holloran publicly attempted to identify the Apostles, Pope, and Christ Himself with the vicious heresy of racism—"the Pope who recently stated bluntly and unequivocally, 'The only way to salvation is to repudiate definitely *all* pride of race or blood'."

Dunne related other activities at St. Louis University that he felt had led to his dismissal from the university, namely, that his social, political, and economic views clashed radically with the views of a controlling clique, which centered on Fr. Bernard Dempsey, S.J., "who cleverly dispenses anti–New Deal, bitterly anti-Roosevelt, Big Business philosophy under the guise of encyclical doctrine." The clique was quite upset by Dunne's popularity among students and Jesuit scholastics. "None of them had the courage or decency to challenge my views openly, but they plotted behind my back in connivance with the rector to ease me out at the end of the semester. The Negro question simply served as a pretext to oust me without waiting until the end of the semester."

He told a Jesuit priest-economist at Gonzaga University in June 1945 that he was saddened the Institute of Social Service would be used as an instrument for the further entrenchment of "the spirit of reactionism and to establish more solidly our alliance with the 'rich well born' rather than regain its original purpose to spread enlightened and progressive ideas."[14]

In July, he sent his provincial a manuscript on "anti-Semitism" for submission to Fr. Daniel Lord, S.J., of *America* for publication as a

---

[14] Carroll File, Jesuit Oregon Province Archives, Gonzaga University, June 4, 1945, Dunne to Carroll.

pamphlet.[15] The provincial was warned that things Dunne taught would disturb some people. "One of the charges lodged against Christ by ecclesiastical authorities of His time was that He went about stirring up the people. I have learned that this is still a crime." For future peace of conscience any decision to go or not go to China would be made by his superiors without any influence from him. "Then ... if things go wrong, if I am unhappy, if I seem to accomplish nothing, I shall at least be spared the scruple of constant fear that I have substituted my will for the will of God." The provincial replied that the article on anti-Semitism would be decided by the censors who would decide whether or not "it would be desirable to have the article published without correction and revision.[16] When you have taken care of this, as indicated in the reports, you may return that article for final revision."

In March 1942, SAD's Hayes spoke of Fr. Donovan, who stated that seminaries annually should try to turn out men "who are first men of tried virtue, then passably grounded in the sacred sciences, above all the science of dogmatic theology, able and willing to be reliable practitioners in dispensing the mysteries of God."[17] Other matters were to be left to the five-period of canonical examinations, pastoral internships, and post-seminary course work. Hayes said Donovan was slightly out of touch with the pope and actual seminary practice and added, "It would take no more time to create a right attitude, one of sympathy and awareness, toward social problems than it has taken in the past to build a wrong attitude.... Pius XI asked for more, with his customary amplitude where priestly learning was concerned."

[15] Dunne File, California Jesuit Archives, Los Gatos, Calif., July 9, 1945, Dunne to King.
[16] Dunne File, California Jesuit Archives, Los Gatos, Calif., August 6, 1945, King to Dunne.
[17] Hayes File, Catholic University Archives, March 17, 1942, Hayes to Ebner.

Hayes was severely criticized in summer 1942, over inclusion in an issue of *Social Action Notes for Priest* of an excerpt from a speech by Vice President Henry Wallace. Though labeled as secularist "drivel" because it contained no specific reference to Christ, the excerpt, Hayes proclaimed, was included simply as an example of what a leading government official had said about world arrangements and the role the United States ought to play in them.[18] Noting that Pius XII and his predecessors had asked Catholics to cooperate with anyone who believes in God, with people of goodwill, Hayes stated that the United States has the best record among big countries who take belief in God seriously. Although Wallace's theology left much to be desired, he was deeply aware of the Lord's test of practical charity toward others. "I would rate him above many Catholics in political life, perhaps above a few priests."

At that time, Hayes replied to a Brooklyn Confraternity of Christian Doctrine director about urging students to study "Catholic sociology."[19] Hayes mentioned the dispute over the existence of a "Catholic" philosophy, sociology, social ethics, social morality, etc. However, he opted for predominate—if not exclusive—teaching about the ethics and morality of socioeconomic life, rather than about social facts. For factual material was given in the public schools that the students attended. To Quinn's query about the reasons for spending precious time on such matters, Hayes listed three great departments of life: worship-prayer-sacraments, marriage-family, and economic-political community.

As a result of his work in SAD, Hayes would prioritize the economic-political community, even spending one-half a year on it. Furthermore, Hayes thought that in economic and political matters people had many opportunities to do either right or wrong, especially in light of obligations laid down by Leo XIII and Pius XI "to

---

[18] Hayes File, Catholic University Archives, July 24, 1942, Hayes to Gallick.
[19] Hayes File, Catholic University Archives, August 6, 1942, Hayes to Quinn.

help create right institutions in economic and political life—organizations of employers and employees, legislatures, government agencies.... Most of them know our teaching on divorces and birth control; they don't know our teaching on wages." Then, Hayes noted his failure to mention "Catholic Action...mainly discovering to the laity their apostolate." He did not know how this fit in a Confraternity of Christian Doctrine (CCD) program, but thought it would bolster a course on social principles as well as other things, "while remaining distinct (as several of the clergy have insisted to me)." He closed, "Emphasize for future workers the right aims and conduct of workers' organizations built on the right notion of work. I wouldn't suggest more sociology courses—not precisely Catholic sociology."

The main suggestion Hayes offered in September 1942 for a thesis on "Motivation in Catholic Labor Education" was explaining the failure of Church leaders to make the deeper spiritual and temporal motives operational.[20] Others included not suggesting new motives, emphases, and content for courses; limiting instruction to ethics or expanding it to all areas of Catholic teaching. Hayes thought that the conclusion would be the same as discovered in Catholic Action and Catholics in general, namely, that Catholics desired a job and reasonable comfort, but were not interested in being part of any crusade. He replied negatively to an inquiry about the possibilities of a labor education program in a wealthy suburb of Detroit.[21] He suggested YCW and YCS (Young Christian Students), two organizations he had been very involved in earlier in Chicago. Since he was unable to follow through after joining SAD, the inquirer was encouraged to call or visit a monthly meeting of such Jocists cells that several young priests had established in Chicago.

---

[20] Hayes File, Catholic University Archives, September 11, 1942, Hayes to McKay.
[21] Hayes File, Catholic University Archives, September 11, 1942, Hayes to Collins.

In March 1943 he replied to questions about theoretical and practical aspects of Catholic Action.[22] He noted that the cell-like structures of the Jocists (YCW and YCS) were used in ACTU. Small groups of members from the same shop formed to meet, plan, and act together. Both ACTU and Jocists were recruited by newspapers, personal contacts, breakfasts, and occasional Eucharists. Yet, there were handicaps. First, ACTU suffered more from Catholics losing a sense of social responsibility about social institutions than Jocists suffered from a loss of a sense of social responsibility for the Church as an institution and the Church's more obvious functions. Young Jocists more readily answered the call to personal morality and convert making than the call to rebuild economic and political reality. Second, ACTU suffered opposition from Catholic and other employers who were fighting and trying to squelch the organization, but they cared little about the vast majority of the Jocists cells that did not threaten the status quo of big business. Third, ACTU also received opposition from AFL, leftist, and corrupt union officials. In the face of similar opposition, Hayes thought "priests are just a little more helpful to CA [Catholic Action] than to ACTU chapters. Both take time to break down the clergy's skepticism, but there is less likely to be trouble with the former [YCS and YCW]."

SAD's Higgins was embroiled in a controversy over critical remarks he made in late 1945 about Brooklyn's Fr. Lodge Curran in a review of a Curran's book in Scranton University's *Best Sellers*.[23] The focus was Curran's persistent, strident attacks on socialists, communists, and anyone else who did not join in his outcries. Higgins told the editor of the review journal that Curran was being harmful to national unity and embarrassing to his fellow Catholics and priests. Also, he wrote, Curran had told some prominent members of the hierarchy that "if they neglect to investigate the matter fully, [they]

---

[22] Hayes File, Catholic University Archives, March 4, 1943, Hayes to Devine.

[23] Higgins File, Catholic University Archives, August 31, 1945, Higgins to Eugene P. Willgin.

will be led to believe from his remarks that I have been giving solace to the enemies of the Church, etc., etc. That's hardly manly procedure.... I do anticipate that I shall be called upon more than once to defend my own position."

In an early May 1955 article in "Yardstick" focused on corruption on the New York waterfront, Higgins compared the script of the movie *On the Waterfront* to Allen Raymond's book, *Waterfront Priest*.[24] His interest was not primarily on either, but on a syndicated review of the book in several U.S. Catholic newspapers. The review, which was sympathetic to the work of Fr. John Corridan, S.J., pointed out a double standard of morality in industrial relations. Higgins agreed the media had succeeded in leaving the impression that the corruption scandal was purely and simply a problem of union racketeering and union gangsterism.

Yet, he wrote, "the public has the right to expect that labor leaders, as professional, self-proclaimed champions of social justice, will exhibit a higher degree of honesty and integrity than almost any other group of men in public life. Noblesse oblige!" The book emphasized that "the unscrupulous greed of far too many waterfront employers" and Corridan thought the offending union, the International Longshoremen's Union (ILA), "was dominated by the employers more than by the men on its roster and was in no real sense of the word a labor union at all." The movie sensationally dramatized the sins of labor, but hardly hinted at management's sins.

For Higgins, it was regrettable that a syndicated review in the Catholic press favored the movie's tack rather than the book's tack on the waterfront scene. He asserted that extensive SAD files on the waterfront problem indicated that "the number of individual Catholics and...Catholic publications which have vigorously criticized

---

[24] Higgins File, Catholic University Archives, "The Yardstick," May 2, 1955.

the offending union…far exceeds the number of those who have in any way criticized the offending employers."

A mid-May 1955 "Yardstick" column also compared the movie to a book, in this case Budd Schuler's novel *Waterfront*.[25] Noting that the novel was more realistic and less dramatic than the movie, Higgins focused on the final scene in the novel, in which Fr. Barry (Corridan) took a lonely midnight stroll along the North River (Hudson) waterfront, wondering if he would ever find enough zealous laypeople to do the job of social reform. He thought, "As a priest, [I] can inspire them, teach them, encourage them, but after that, it is up to them to do the job on their own initiative and in their own fumbling way. Will there ever be enough of them?" Higgins closed by noting that the unanswered question pertained not only to the New York waterfront, but "wherever else there is work to be done in the field of social reform."

In late 1956, Higgins expressed to Fr. Louis Twomey, S.J., of New Orleans, surprise and shock at the news of the demise of the Catholic Committee of the South.[26] He hoped and prayed something could be done to save the organization or to establish something in its place.

In late 1970, Higgins reviewed John Laslett's *Labor and the Left: A Study of Socialist and Radical Influences in the American Labor Movement, 1881–1924*. He deemed the book "commendably factual and non-ideological," as were earlier works by Perlman, Taft, Shannon, Karson, Foner, Grob, Bell, and others.[27] Among the many facets of Laslett's work Higgins found intriguing were the findings on the influence of religious factors. Despite later Catholic leaders attempts to stall the growth of Socialism, the fact that "some of the

---

[25] Higgins File, Catholic University Archives, "The Yardstick," September 19, 1955.

[26] Higgins File, Catholic University Archives, November 26, 1956, Higgins to Twomey.

[27] Higgins File, Catholic University Archives, book review, November 30, 1970.

Massachusetts shoe workers were willing to embrace it in the early period suggests that Marc Karson's hypothesis—that the opposition of the Catholic Church precluded virtually all socialist influence among the Irish workingmen—is somewhat oversimplified. Stressing that Laslett was best equipped, Higgins called for further research into the role of Catholics—mainly Irish—in promoting and/or thwarting the rise of radical and socialist influences in the American labor movement.

In mid-1979, Higgins reported in *Commonweal* on a May 16–18 Washington, D.C., meeting of labor leaders and interfaith social activists.[28] He surmised some activists in the 1960s and 1970s were cynical about the importance of reviving the earlier cooperation between religion and labor, but thought the meeting was only a first step. From an interfaith perspective, he wrote, it was "one of the best meetings of its kind I have ever attended." Passed unanimously was an interim plan to broaden the base of local religious and labor communities, Blacks, Hispanics, women, and those from the Evangelical and Pentecostal traditions, especially in the Old South.

In a November 25, 1980, *America* article, Gerald Costello, one of Higgins's biographers, scanned some of the two thousand short "Yarsdtick" articles. He found that Higgins was cited about the necessity of prayer as priests became more involved in social action. He warned further about "politicizing the gospel message by converting the Sunday homily into a partisan, tub-thumping harangue." Sermons on the moral aspects of current social issues were suitable for church discussion groups, provided there was opportunity for "give and take." Such was applicable to the McCarthyism of the 1950s, the Vietnam War of the 1960s, and labor politics. Higgins also cautioned trade unionists and social reformers who were trying to substitute Church pronouncements for effective union and

---

[28] Higgins 1979, 356–358.

community organizing. In his "Yardstick" columns between 1982 and 1991 he challenged Catholic hospital administrators and their hired antiunion consultants by vigorously defending Catholic teaching, criticizing the inappropriateness of antiunion consultants, and praising the integrity of the labor movement.

In 1966 San Antonio's Archbishop Lucey urged all clergy and religious operating parishes, schools, and institutions to follow the federal minimum wage law of $1.25 an hour, which had recently been enacted.[29] He stressed the rights of workers to a living wage, good working conditions, health insurance, social security, workers' compensation, and time off for holidays and vacation. Instead of just shouting the gospel and words of hope about poverty disappearing, Lucey urged the clergy and religious to be leaders and examples. "In the next century," he said, "the Church will make or break Christian civilization in the field of human welfare. Dogma in the Church is safe—only the law of love is in peril."

In late 1966 Lucey sent a memo to priests, religious Brothers, and religious Sisters about paying union-scale wages on all archdiocesan construction projects. He attached a copy of the "Personnel Policy for Lay Workers in the Chancery Office Building" and a memo requesting specific information about wages paid and the source of the information.[30] Referring to Leo XIII and general Catholic Social Teaching, Lucey stated that some religious were not providing worker safeguards and were paying starvation wages. "It would be a tragedy," he declared, "if a Catholic building was constructed dishonorably on the blood and sweat of honest workmen.... God judges Religious more sternly...because their crimes against humanity are also a disgrace to the Church." He asked about the wages of Catholic hospitals, child care agencies, homes for the aged,

---

[29] Lucey File, San Antonio Archives, November 12, 1966, Lucey to clerical and religious administrators.
[30] Lucey File, San Antonio Archives, August 6, 1966, Lucey archdiocesan administrators.

as well as of parish janitors, housekeepers, sextons, bus drivers, gardeners, and choir directors: "[If] a person dedicated and consecrated to religion gets three meals a day, should a working man with a wife and children get less?"

He preferred the chancery deal with union contractors, "because of their intelligence, sense of honor, and proven integrity." He contrasted the nonunion worker as defenseless and alone one who "must shut his mouth or complain and be fired." At the end of the news release about Lucey's remarks and the policy, his secretary said that, while all archdiocesan parishes and institutions followed the union scale and paid their workers justly, it was tantamount to selfishness to expect others to be generous, while the Church was tightfisted. "The Church owes it to the community, even if non-Catholic institutions and private employers refuse to meet their obligations, to contribute her share of justice."

In early 1955, Fr. McKeon, S.J., of Philadelphia, congratulated New Orleans's Fr. Louis Twomey, S.J., on his newsletter, the *Blueprint*, especially in analyzing "the lack of social consciousness among Jesuits."[31] After twenty years in the Social Order work, McKeon was saddened that so few Jesuits, so pledged to obedience, had failed "to answer the explicit wishes of the Holy Father and Father General." Indeed, Twomey's remarks on the need for training echoed McKeon's stinging report to the Jesuit general several years earlier. Scandal was attributed to superiors who, because of their ignorance, could not interest Jesuits in the Social Order and Jesuits who talked ignorantly about unionism. While hoping recent efforts would eventually produce some good results, he closed, "It is for the few of us on the firing line to keep up the fight.... Yet how the indifference of those in authority can be reconciled to the principles and ideals of the Society is beyond me."

---

[31] McKeon File, St. Joseph College Archives, Philadelphia, January 11, 1955, McKeon to Twomey.

New York's Fr. John Monaghan, periodically wrote a column, entitled "Don Capelliano" for the parish bulletin.[32] One column contained one of Monaghan's many pithy phrases: there was little awareness of the real world and less awareness of the idealized world, he pointed out, if a priest "didn't often speak and work against the degradation of our slums, against the imperial tyranny of union-hating corporations, against the human belittlement of old workers, foreign workers, and unpaid workers." In early 1946 he told the *Wall Street Journal*'s Edward Lyman that the most recent conference about Holy Name Society Labor Schools revealed little more than a perfunctory response, especially in the absence of Holy Name Society moderators.[33] Due to ACTU's many obligations, it would not be able to recruit teachers to accommodate a single Holy Name Labor School, if parishes showed no interest and took no responsibility.

One of Monaghan's students in New York, Msgr. George Kelly, had compiled an informal collection of memories of Monaghan from priests in New York.[34] Kelly learned that Monaghan had once said, "My God, man no one under forty is entitled to be tired,.... The poor need you, and not just those in the parish." When Cardinal Spellman was outraged by the jailing of Archbishop Alois Stepinac by Yugoslavia's Marshal Tito, Monaghan told the cardinal that the spiritual life of the Church was never better than when bishops were jailed. Upon meeting his friend Bishop Bryan McEntegart during a trip to his new diocese of Ogdensburg, New York, Monaghan said that in six months McEntegart would be so surrounded by sycophants that he would never discover the truth about anything.

Kelly said Monaghan was known as the common people's "uncommon spokesman" and a "good pop psychologist." Aspirants to the

---

[32] Lynch 1997.
[33] Monaghan File, New York Jesuit Province Archives, January 30, 1946, Monaghan to Lyman.
[34] Kelly 1989, *in passim*.

priesthood were exposed to "a kind of poverty that they, as poor sons of poor immigrants, never had to face personally." He told them the most important thing in the world for a worker was his job, if he was poor. He insisted that workers' minds and brawn were no less important to economic prosperity than the investors' money and entrepreneurs. He was most concerned that workers' minds so seldom conformed to the mind of Christ.

For him the two enemies of the workers were Pragmatism and Marxism. The former was defined as "very pious looking and...frequently found at Communion Breakfasts." He never liked the term "labor priest," but saw the workers' wages as the Church's real wealth — not just novitiates, parishes, hospitals, and homes. He was disappointed that the Church's apostolate to workers was so immature that its record of involvement could be written on less than a page. Yet, appreciating that the hierarchy could not be expected to give blank checks to every untried or debatable organization, he also stressed the legitimate freedom of initiative for lay apostles when they perceived sound Catholic interests. Exercise of such Christian responsibility freed the hierarchy of blame for blunders or offensive actions by overly zealous or irresponsible lay activists. Such, however, was not the reaction of Spellman when ACTU supported the 1949 Calvary Cemetery strike, with the private backing of Kelly and Monaghan. So, Monaghan was very hurt when Spellman questioned his ecclesiastical loyalty at that time.

In 1994 a review of authors on the role of the Catholic Church in the labor movement in the 1930s, especially that of Fr. Rice,[35] said that Rice's effort to direct Pittsburgh's Catholic Radical Alliance (CRA) and ACTU away from anti-Semitism was not easy. Highlighted were the periodic failings of some Jews as union leaders, as well as their communist sympathies, opposition to Franco's side in the Spanish Revolutionary War, membership in the Communist Party,

---

[35] Heineman 1994, 364–394.

championing expansion of a secular state, clashing with some Catholic opposition to government advancement, and the obsession of the House Un-American Activities Committee (HUAC) with Jewish New Dealers and communists [pp. 389–90].

Rice used two strategies to circumvent an anti-Semitic backlash among Catholics. First, he placed ACTU firmly behind anticommunist Jewish CIO organizers and emphasized the battle between democracy and communism, rather than between Catholicism and Judaism. Second, in an August 1939 radio address, he stressed that the strongest fighters against Communism were Jews and that all people were responsible for the death of Christ—not simply Jews. Yet, despite all these steps and the Church's Social Teaching, labor priests and their labor union allies found themselves at odds with secular society, regardless of whether policy-makers were "conservative corporation executives or liberal government bureaucrats" [pp. 393–94].

In late 1995 the *St. Anthony Messenger* published "Msgr. Charles O. Rice," an interview by John Bookser Feister.[36] Rice was quoted as saying, "The work for justice is a fight. I don't believe that a priest has to be detached from everything. When you see an injustice, you have to fight it" [p. 23]. He counted his confrontation with and silencing by Archbishop John Dearden—one calling the Church to practice what it preaches with its own workers, among the most significant moments of his long career [p. 24]. Also interviewed by Feister was SAD's Higgins, who said, "Rice's column has been the best labor columns in the United States."

Fr. Sherrill Smith, in 1961, wrote "Speck of Hope" in San Antonio's AFL–CIO Labor Council's *Labor Reporter*, concerning discouraging news of unions in a local struggle.[37] He commented on the lot of the campesinos working in the valley who had been "blackballed"

---

[36] Feister 1955, 23–27.
[37] Smith 1966.

south of the Mexican–U.S. border and then "green-carded" north of the border. He thought the Church (unwittingly) opposed the migrant workers because it was not yet aware of any feudalism north of the border, part of its legacy. "It must be small consolation to the Mexican-American Catholics...that the Church's awareness—if that's what it be—may explain, at least in some measure, why she seems embarrassed by it all." He noted the grim symbolism of the hunger of *campesinos* as a sign of being hungry for justice. "The Lord of the poor promised those who hunger for justice would be filled. A number of us insist they need not wait till heaven."

In mid-1966, he replied to complaints about Smith by the public relations director of Santa Rosa Hospital. Whether out of ignorance or spite, the complaint declared, Smith had criticized the hospital's wages.[38] He found little to praise in claims that the hospital's wages were better than those in similar hospitals and institutions. "You make justice too relative when you make such comparisons. What kind of a claim is it to point out you are better than the worst?" Also criticized was the hospital's failure to recognize that fringe benefits are "no substitute for fair wages, you can't buy beans with a pension plan [and] holidays don't put kids in college."

To complaints that the Church, archdiocese, and hospital were being hurt by his criticism, Smith said that if the price of financial support is silence and looking the other way, then the price is too high. Catholic Charities without Catholic Justice implies that some have to suffer injustice while others thrive. To the charge that the Church was being subject to public taxation, he replied that, even if as part of the community the Church did contribute specifically and educationally, "Does this rule out any obligation whatever to pitch in financial help. I don't think so. It's certainly debatable." If the

---

[38] S. Smith File, San Antonio Archdiocesan Archives, April 25, 1966, S. Smith to Coughlin.

Church expected tax exemption, it should be the first to contribute to economic justice by paying adequate wages, etc.

In late 1959, New York's Fr. William Smith, S.J., discussed the right of employees to organize in Catholic charitable, educational, and religious institutions.[39] He granted that there were other means to obtain justice in Catholic institutions than collective bargaining and said that unions should not be forced on nonprofit organizations. New York State law exempted people in religious, educational, and charitable fields from labor–management statutes, he noted, but that exemption did not absolve employers "from providing proper measures of determining just wage scales, working conditions, grievance procedures, and adequate arbitration when necessary." He thought hospital employees had no right to strike to gain recognition, because "depriving patient services, primary or secondary is illicit." Although federal and state laws exempted hospital administrators from collective bargaining, implementation of the laws would have to be done "in such a way as to guarantee employees all the benefits and protections that would normally come to them from a collective bargaining contract." Although he thought it still debatable that faculty in high schools, colleges, and universities were free to exercise the right to collective bargaining—because personality, competency, and other imponderables might make a case for person-to-person relationships—there was no doubt about their right to seek counsel and to choose an outside attorney to be their spokesperson.

Although "this right had been denied to groups of teachers in some Catholic schools…a prosperous institution under Catholic auspices has the same obligation as a profit-making industry to its employees." Also, given the donations and functions of Catholic institutions, there should be a mutual agreement for adjusting the standards of both the institution and its employees. "In his letter on the

---

[39] Smith File, St. Peter's College Archives, November 14, 1959, Smith to Twomey.

Social Apostolate, Father General [of the Jesuits] notes that the standard of living of the members of the community should not be higher than the standard of living of the employees."

About confining collective bargaining to the employers and employees of Catholic institutions only, Smith replied "Yes" and "No." "No," if there was an obligation to enter into regional contracts, involving institutions of other denominations and secular institutions, or if such pacts would be advisable. Yes, if the other institutions similar to Catholic institutions are bound by the same obligations of social justice as Catholic institutions. To the question of Catholic institutions being obliged to recognize any union as a bargaining agent for their employees, he replied that a union has an obligation "to base its existence and proper aims and proper means" on social justice. Thus, there was no obligation to deal with "racketeers or communists who may represent the employees in name only." Catholic institutions have the right and duty to protect their name, purpose, and work, although dislike or discrimination toward the employees' representatives would be unjust. Nevertheless, employers would not be excused from prior obligation by the burden of collective bargaining or desire to conduct the institution in a paternalistic manner. The title for establishing just conditions for workers is social justice. The title for the omission of collective bargaining is prudence. To the question of what should be included in or excluded from in labor contracts, Smith thought there might be models of existing contracts. Local circumstances would dictate specific items in the contract, especially relating to the needs of employees and the finances of the institutions.

To the question of the status of Church teaching on the whole issue, Smith said he knew of no opinions in Catholic commentaries on the variable in the applications of the basic principles of social justice and social charity enunciated in the papal encyclicals. The best answers to practical questions would be *Social Principles* by Fr. John

Cronin, S.S. He closed saying that Catholic institutional administrators were reluctant to face the problem and "usually offer the same arguments put forth by employers in industry who seek ways and means of avoiding collective bargaining." So, the best way of teaching about and hoping for the applications of the Church's teaching by Catholic and non-Catholic industrialists would be "the practice of it by Catholics who are in a position to do so."

Smith's final concern about the Church was a lengthy defense of industrial relations degree programs in Jesuit colleges and universities, which critics labeled as "revolutionary."[10] To these critics he said: "Better a revolution on paper than riots in Brooklyn and bombs bursting in Manhattan." Granting that partial programs did exist in several Jesuit educational institutions, his approach was a more practical approach, as recommended by the Institute of Social Order's Committee on Industrial Relations, which had called for a full-time curriculum, with particular emphasis "upon the imperative need of developing leaders in trade union activity in the light of the social encyclicals of the Church."

In developing his rationale for the program, which several Jesuits had criticized, Smith said some very striking things, while complimenting the Jesuits' achievements in educating professional leaders. "Is there anyone who will dare defend the thesis that we have shown an equal initiative in providing the fifty million people who must toil for their daily bread with efficient, capable, well-informed leadership? They have a right to expect such help from Catholic educators." He concluded his rationale with reference to Leo XIII's proclaiming the condition of the working classes as the "burning question of the day" and a very high Jesuit superior's remark that if the Jesuits did not find a way of furnishing proper leadership in industrial relations, they might see the day when the Jesuits would have no schools or colleges.

---

[40] Smith 1944.

Fr. Louis Twomey, S.J., of New Orleans, complained that, while studying theology, formal study of Leo XIII's and Pius XI's social encyclicals was minimal.[41] In the 1940s, his provincial informed the Jesuit communities in the South of Twomey's plans to begin a Labor School, quoting the 1939 directive of the Jesuit General Congregation [worldwide highest legislative body of Jesuits] that each region and province begin concrete programs to implement the social reform articulated in papal encyclicals and explicitly listed social institutes and justice for racial minorities. In establishing the nonaccredited institute, Twomey was well received by otherwise reluctant faculty. By 1945, he was at St. Louis University Institute of Social Studies, where he completed his thesis deploring the failure of Catholic education, even seminaries, to develop social awareness.

In mid-1948 Twomey encouraged a Jesuit faculty member in Chicago's Mundelein Seminary to pursue group interest and involvement in social action.[42] "In the main," he said, "Catholic education has done a magnificent job" in teaching how to be good citizens of heaven and dutiful members of a future family, but "it has been tragically deficient" in teaching how to be dutiful members of society. Students have had "to formulate their own philosophy as best they can." His experience showed him that by not "pulling any punches" with men about the deficiencies of Catholic education he found deep understanding, satisfaction, and conciliation within the groups and for himself.

In late 1948, he thanked Hartford Fr. Joseph Donnelly for a section in his bulletin entitled "On the Fringe" concerning the opposition to and misunderstanding of priests like Donnelly and Twomey, who are "engaged in the vital work of spreading a knowledge and practice of Catholic social principles...utterly fantastic and yet so

---

[41] McNaspy 1978, *in passim*.
[42] Twomey File, Loyola University–New Orleans Archives, May 19, 1948, Twomey to Connery.

terribly realistic."[43] Noting it was not difficult to get discouraged or angry, he closed, "[There] is hope that even though our efforts may seem to have small present returns the future holds a magnificent payoff—or am I crazy?"

On one occasion in 1950 he expressed amazement that the biggest headaches "come from those who, if they had the slightest knowledge of Catholic social principles, would know better.[44] Amazed how little Catholics in prominent positions were aware of their contradictory attitudes, he added, "They may be fervent Catholics in their individual lives but in their rugged individualistic business relations they are confirmed Protestants." He surmised that Catholic education did not go beyond individual ethics to social ethics.

In mid-1952, Twomey congratulated Martin Work, executive secretary of the National Council of Catholic Men (NCCM), "for vitalizing the efforts of Catholic men in the United States."[45] He argued that clergy and laity were dragging their heels in implementing encyclicals. And in some instances they were allying themselves with the forces of exaggerated individualism. Such "has done more than any other factor to condition the soil in which Communism thrives…a dynamic negativism rushing to fill the void created in millions of men's souls as well as their stomachs by the collective spiritual, political, economic, and social failures." Martin Work, with the "enviable or unenviable" opportunity to activate the latent Catholic potential to implement significantly the principles of Catholic Social Teaching, could count on his fulsome cooperation.

---

[43] Twomey File, Loyola University–New Orleans Archives, October 21, 1948, Twomey to Donnelly.

[44] Twomey File, Loyola University–New Orleans Archives, April 28, 1950, Twomey to Schuyler.

[45] Twomey File, Loyola University–New Orleans Archives, June 21, 1952, Twomey to Work.

A month later, Twomey shared with Work the experience at the Summer School of Social Action in Dallas, a city with appalling reactionary Catholic thinking.[46] Rather than embracing Catholic social and economic teaching, wealthy people were fighting it. He was convinced there had to be some way to have well-to-do Catholics become involved in the popes' plans for the reconstructing of the social order, however slow or late the efforts. In closing, he bemoaned the fact that such people were missing an opportunity to bring "their non-Catholic Colleagues the only solution that makes sense."

In mid-1953, he repeated to SAD's McGowan earlier observation that interest in the social apostolate was the exception instead of being the rule and that adequate response should be even greater than response to the "Protestant Revolt" in the time of Ignatius. Again, he said Communism was an effect rather than a cause.[47]

In early 1954, Twomey was shocked by a diocesan seminarian's request to direct "seminarians to a real liberal movement within the American Church," especially with severe criticism of *Commonweal* and *America*, which Twomey characterized as "doing a top-flight Catholic job and represents…the best expression of genuine Catholic liberal thought in America."[48] Twomey offered a broad insight into his own conviction on the "real liberal movement within the American Church." To criticism of "priests interested in bringing Christian principles into union members," he cited the "magnificent zeal and Christ-like devotion of American priests, diocesan and regular, who have gotten into the field of industrial relations." Granting the Church had done so "altogether too slow," he said

[46] Twomey File, Loyola University–New Orleans Archives, July 6, 1952, Twomey to Work.
[47] Twomey File, Loyola University–New Orleans Archives, May 25, 1953, Twomey to McGowan.
[48] Twomey File, Loyola University–New Orleans Archives, February 24, 1954, Twomey to Creel.

such priests' personal sacrifice "challenged the complacency of Catholics in general by their work with laboring men and scarcely deserved the epithet of being labeled 'Johnny-come-latelys'." He was convinced that the "greatest difficulties from reactionary Catholics both in the clergy and laity...especially in the South, is a two-headed affair coming as it does from prominent Catholics with vested interest in anti-unionism as well as racial segregation." He offered to give all possible help, "provided that after you read this you still think that I am the kind of priest from whom you like to get direction."

He expressed shock about a letter by Fr. Robert Hartnett, S.J., editor of *America*, concerning "the attitude of the Provincials."[49] What the attitude was is not clear from the letter, but Twomey's comments give some insight. From his nationwide travels Twomey learned that there would be little chance of the Jesuits getting where they belonged on the issue "until there is a complete and brutally frank review of the whole Jesuit educational effort in the United States." He saw it as a movement to save the Church in America from the ultra-reactionary elements of McCarthyism. He was confident that the articles in *America* would provide the Church with a rallying ground for solid, progressive thinking, which "is developing among our younger men, despite the lack of social orientation in our scholastics." Also, "we will not lose the tenuous hold we now have with those outside the Church, and how, though they may be 'decent Godless pagans', are looking for just such leadership as Catholics could give if only they had the knowledge and will to take Catholicism and make it whole."

Referring to an August 17, 1954, article in *America* entitled "Compartmentalized Catholicism," Twomey told Hartnett that the more he understood the theological and philosophical implications of

---

[49] Twomey File, Loyola University–New Orleans Archives, November 20, 1954, Twomey to Hartnett.

Catholic Social Teaching the less he could understand clergy and laity who were simply not Catholic in their social and economic thinking and acting. Quite aware of such people, he found it "frightening as well as maddening," as well as "fascinating but plenty tough." With God's strength, as well as the "cooperation, if not always the understanding of my superiors, including the archbishop," Twomey thought that in ten years others would come along and profit from what he had been desperately trying to do.

He reminded Hartnett of the type of Jesuit whose contacts were largely with the well-to-do and who had imbibed their opinions and culture. "They don't know the Social Teaching of the Church and yet they pass apodictic appraisals of it anyway. And they are calculated, I fear, to fit in with what they know their friends want to hear." For example, a few indiscreet Jesuits broke ranks during the Louisiana right-to-work battle. Such an attitude—"the Church should stick to the sanctuary, etc."—created a serious and dangerous cleavage in the Catholic community at large, but was not peculiar to the New Orleans bourbons. That the bishop of Dallas had supported the Texas right-to-work law made many in New Orleans hopping mad. Hartnett was encouraged to pay close attention to the October and November issues of *Blueprint,* which tried to break through "the 'hush-hush' curtain that has stymied constructive criticism of our Jesuit failure to do a well-rounded job in education." Despite some slight trepidation, Twomey thought he could "use an uninhibited pen" for some time. Yet, he was encouraged by the growing number of "the younger set" who are fed up with all this white-supremacy bluster and antiunion bias. They are still inarticulate, but their day will come. When it does the picture will quickly change."

Responses to the *Blueprint* indicated the majority of the Jesuits emerging from tertianships, at least in the Southern Province, are "ready for a whirl at knocking down some of the encrusted prejudices, which our schools are only beginning to tackle." Sent to every province in the North American Assistancy and fifteen foreign countries, *Blueprint* had a circulation of about 1,200. Twomey would have loved to send some of the very encouraging letters to the provincials. Some might not have been oblivious of the ever-increasing number of subjects, who "are taking the General's 'De Apostolatu Sociali' in utmost seriousness and chafing under the lack of systematic training in social matters in our philosophates and theologates."

At the end of 1954, he asked for further comments in a letter, seeming to imply that *Blueprint* stressed industrial and race relations too much, along with "a sort of mixed impertinence for scholastics."[50] He was quite willing to adjust if *Blueprint* was missing the larger perspective, but "the general attitudes down here are far from those that should be formed according to the Social Teaching of the Church. Anti-Negro and Anti-unionism still are the great road blocks to realizing the kind of South you and I are praying for." He suggested that seminar reading material on philosophy and theology be related to the Social Teaching of the Church.[51] Agreeing both were invaluable, he added, "there must be an effort made to take principles out of the realm of pure theory and apply them to the concrete circumstances of political, economic, and social issues."

In early 1955, Twomey replied to another Jesuit seminarian in St. Mary's College, Kansas, Thomas Madden, S.J., and insisted that, however delicate, a social issue had to be faced "if we ever hope to remedy the situation that is presently a drag on our efforts to implement the Social Apostolate,"[52] Cited for special commendation was Kansas City's Fr. Friedl, S.J., as "one of the early pioneers in

---

[50] Twomey File, Loyola University–New Orleans Archives, November 20, 1954, Twomey to Bernard.

[51] Twomey File, Loyola University–New Orleans Archives, December 7, 1954, Twomey to Welsh.

[52] Twomey File, Loyola University–New Orleans Archives, February 8, 1955, Twomey to Madden.

this difficult but fascinating work." Twomey agreed with Madden's insistence on experience "combined with formal training in the principles as well as the practice of Catholic social doctrine."

In late 1955, Twomey warned Fr. Anthony Achee, S.J., of Albuquerque, New Mexico, against prematurely labeling any group he was cooperating with as red, pink, or fellow travelers.[53] Some authors did not talk in terms of the natural law or might be described as "muddle-headed liberals." Yet, he hesitated to label them "communist" or "communist sympathizers." Many were "decent godless pagans," looking for satisfying answers, and Catholics must find ways to give them our answers. Such entailed joining groups and movements not so attractive to Catholics. Avoiding them meant little or no Christian influence. "We must learn how to influence our environment and we can do this only by getting into the environment and by word and example prove to good-willed people that what we have is what they need."

In mid-1959 Twomey reminded the executive director of the Madison, WI, National Institute of Labor Education that Loyola University–New Orleans was the only southern higher educational institution tackling the twin explosive social issues of antiunionism and racism.[54] Loyola had great potential in trying to solve such problems. Absolutely necessary was financial support of agencies interested in "promoting right order and human decency in labor and race relations," especially Wisconsin's agency.

In early 1961 Twomey informed LeMoyne College Labor School director Fr. Richard McKeon, S.J., about the racial strife in New Orleans around the time Archbishop Rummel had banned segregated

---

[53] Twomey File, Loyola University–New Orleans Archives, Octoer 22, 1955, Twomey to Achee.
[54] Twomey File, Loyola University–New Orleans Archives, April 27, 1959, Twomey to Mire.

parishes and schools.[55] Describing as tragic the failure of clerical and lay leadership, Twomey called the situation of the Church there "pathetic," but with some hope of a concerted Catholic plan of action on race. "In other words, we are in the process of establishing a Catholic Council on Human Relations. If this succeeds, as we hope and pray it will, there is some chance that we can rebuild the image of Church in this area."

In late 1961 Twomey wrote to Higgins about a clipping from the very conservative Catholic newspaper *The Wanderer* and about the racial scene in New Orleans.[56] Although the newspaper had caused Twomey trouble in the past and he would find it easy to defend the positions that the editor attacked, he was convinced it would be "a waste of time to try to have a discussion with such people." He also expressed great disappointment that it took the NCWC so long to issue a copy of *Mater et Magistra*, so that the advantage of great publicity given the encyclical, upon its issuance from Rome, was lost. In regard to the New Orleans racial scene, Twomey said, "There is no hope at all for any real move in the racial field until the coadjutor [Bishop John Cody of St. Louis, Missouri] comes." However, Twomey was more confident about the South in general and believed "we have gotten over the hump. In the future...that progress will be really swift and meaningful." Deeming it rather tragic that the leadership had come entirely from secular sources, such as the NAACP and federal courts, Twomey said, "Surely...as far as the Church is concerned, this era will be looked upon as one in which we failed to take advantage of the magnificent opportunities which were ours."

---

[55] Twomey File, Loyola University–New Orleans Archives, March 8, 1961, Twomey to McKeon.

[56] Higgins File, Catholic University Archives, October 4, 1961, Twomey to Higgins.

8

DISAGREEMENT *AD INTRA ECCLESIA*

The "Problem" of Father Coughlin

C hapter 7 described concerns labor priests had about the Catholic Church that might have led to disagreements among the labor priests. Here, we focus on concerns about the Church *ad intra ecclesia*. Later volumes will examine disagreements about unions, Labor Schools/Institutes of Industrial Relations, and economics/politics –

that is, *ad extra ecclesia*. Examples of *ad intra ecclesia* issues involved priest-orator Fr. Charles Coughlin of Royal Oak, Michigan; Fr. William Smith, S.J., of Crown Heights, Brooklyn; ACTU's methods and goals; New York dockworkers; and failings in seminary education. This chapter addresses the Coughlin experience. The next chapter will address the other above-mentioned conflicts.

Fr. Charles Coughlin

Some have the mistaken belief that Charles Coughlin was a labor priest in the U.S. Church, but the contentious relations he had with his ordinary, Archbishop Edward Mooney of Detroit, is hardly characteristic of labor priests![1] Indeed, because of Coughlin's antics, Mooney's support of the worker movement in Detroit received wider import. The "Coughlin problem" was a very complicated, painful, and prolonged one, according to Leslie Tentler, whose treatment is summarized here, before the account revealed in Mooney's and others' correspondence. Under Mooney's predecessor, Bishop Gallagher, Coughlin was his own man. Both were alike in economic views, political theory, temperament, and reaction to unions and Communism. Before Mooney's arrival in Detroit, efforts by some U.S. bishops, the NCWC, the apostolic delegate, and the Vatican to temper the actions of Coughlin and Gallagher were futile [pp. 314–29]. Despite Mooney's cautious temperament, an eventual clash was bound to ensue, even if he had not been sent to temper and/or curb Coughlin's utterances and actions. Until 1942, Coughlin's political involvement and continued testing of the Chancery Office's authority had met with restrained response, before Mooney told New York Archbishop Francis Spellman, "[the] situation cannot be cleared up without some injury to the Church one way or another."

For example, as early as 1938, Mooney tried in various ways to clear up the situation without too much fallout for the Church. He appointed ecclesiastical censors for Coughlin's radio speeches and weekly column in the newspaper *Social Justice*, which Coughlin founded in 1936. Mooney refused his imprimatur on three articles that Coughlin intended to publish in the booklet *Can Christians Join the CIO?* Deeply alarmed by Mooney's policies, cited in an October 4, 1938, press interview, Coughlin referred to the "personal stupidity" of President Roosevelt and asserted that no Catholic could in conscience be a member of the CIO. Coughlin was promptly and publicly chastised by Mooney for failure to utilize "the prudent counsel of a friendly critic," the aim of "the Church's legislation to

[1] Tentler 1990, *in passim.*

provide." Mooney went further, "No Catholic authority has ever asserted that the CIO is incompatible with Catholicity on the basis of its publicly stated principles." As for remarks about Roosevelt, Coughlin was reminded that priests always and everywhere were required "to impose upon themselves a fine sense of restraint in the language they use."

Prior to the publication of Mooney's statement in the *Michigan Catholic*, the archdiocesan newspaper, Coughlin assured Mooney that he accepted the gently worded rebuke, but publicly announced that he was preparing a statement of his own. Mooney told the apostolic delegate, Archbishop Ameleto Cicognani, that Coughlin was earnestly advised not to do so. Coughlin, then, informed the press that Mooney had refused to allow the public rebuttal. So Coughlin announced he was canceling his 1937–1938 radio broadcasts. Coughlin's lawyer told the press, "It was quite apparent that Father Coughlin would be permitted only to talk in platitudes...[and] that he could not say what he thinks, but only what the Archbishop thinks" [pp. 332–33].

As Mooney feared, Coughlin's followers reacted bitterly through letters and rallies in Chicago, Cleveland, and New York, as well as in the pages of *Social Justice*, the ownership of which Coughlin transferred to a Toledo business leader, Walter Baertschi. As outcries increased in scope and intensity, Mooney wrote to Cicognani on October 29, 1938. If the situation was prolonged due to distortions among Catholics and ignorance among Protestants, Coughlin might find it impossible to submit to Church leaders. Yet, "One word from the Holy See now will count for a great deal."

Cicognani asked Mooney to compose a statement to be issued by the Holy See. When the statement was made public on November 20, 1938, Cicognani told the press that Mooney's criticisms had been "just and timely...every bishop has not only the right but the duty to supervise Catholic teaching in his own Diocese. [An aggrieved priest] has the duty of using his influence to keep the matter from becoming the occasion of public agitation." Also, the priest can appeal a bishop's actions to the Vatican. Prior to Cicognani's public intervention, Coughlin had negotiated a return to the air and tried to void Mooney's censorship guidelines. Mooney stood firm, however, hoping Coughlin would quit, although Coughlin twice visited Cicognani seeking support for a return to broadcasting. Coughlin proposed three of his assistant pastors for Mooney to appoint as censor, instead of Msgr. William Murphy.

Coughlin's version of events differed from Cicognani's. He alleged that Cicognani thought the confusion could be dispelled best by Coughlin's return to the airways and Mooney would allow such, once Coughlin accepted Murphy as censor. Yet in an early December 1937 exchange with Cicognani, Mooney got the mark of his troublesome priest, when Coughlin was characterized as "a more mysterious combination of self-willed impetuosity and strategic cleverness in putting 'one on the spot'." Coughlin was recognized, even by those who disagreed with him, as quite charming. He was also "a duplicitous man, uncannily alert to the vulnerabilities of those around him. Coupled with his essentially paranoid view of the world and his penchant for impulsive action, these qualities made him a formidable opponent."

True to form, Coughlin forced Mooney to allow control of *Social Justice* back in Coughlin's hands, by telling the press on December 7, 1937, that he would be "Editorial Counsel...provided this met with the approval of his superior." Mooney then told Cicognani, it was proper to ignore any discourtesies and allow Coughlin to re-associate with *Social Justice*, but with accountability for its "content and policy." Indeed, Coughlin had come to Mooney for such permission, which he received with the required conditions.

Coughlin's return to broadcasting was relatively noncontroversial. Yet, in March 1938 he proposed a corporate form of government for the United States, revealing "an alarming indifference to demo-cratic values." *Social Justice* was preoccupied with American neu-tralists, apologies for the excesses of Germany's and Italy's regimes, and identifying Great Britain as a major culprit. Summer 1938 showed a deeply anti-Semitic tone by serial publication of *Protocols of the Elders of Zion* under his byline in his weekly column, "From the Tower." He sprinkled in some disclaimers, but his prefatory re-marks were deeply anti-Semitic. Admitting the *Protocols* were prob-ably a forgery, he insisted on their "factuality"—the remarkable correspondence between the plans of the perhaps-fictitious "el-ders" and events that currently menaced the future of Christian civ-ilization.

Thus, Jews were responsible for the Russian revolution and for most of the spread of Communism. Nazism was only "a defense mechanism against the incursions of Communism." He had re-vealed his anti-Semitism earlier, but publication of the *Protocols* ex-hibited a virulent anti-Semitism, which alarmed Mooney, who was neither anti-Semitic nor a supporter of Fascism. In several issues of the *Michigan Catholic*, Mooney condemned anti-Semitism and urged Catholics to heed only official spokespersons of the Church for au-thentic teaching. Yet, each of Coughlin's 1938 radio speeches were approved by the censor, with only minor changes, as well as his *Social Justice* columns. The principal censor was Fr. Sebastian Er-bacher, O.F.M., a widely known supporter of the labor movement and the Catholic Worker Movement—no more anti-Semitic than Mooney [pp. 335–36].

Mooney's apparent tolerance of Coughlin's increasingly extremist rhetoric did raise questions. Coughlin's fans were informed that, while permission was given Coughlin to speak and write, there was no implication of approval of what he said. Mooney told NCWC general secretary Msgr. Michael Ready that, without clear grounds in Canon Law to apply, the problem was political. So, there was almost no chance of stirring up reactionaries by seeming to muzzle

Coughlin. For, "Father Coughlin's articles on Jewish matters are...so cleverly gotten up and so contrived to say and unsay a thing in almost the same breath that it is impossible for a censor to do much deleting.... I have no advisory influence with Fr. Coughlin" [p. 337]. Coughlin displayed mere token cooperation, it was thought, and often submitted a copy of his speech only at the very last minute. Mooney argued that Jewish groups had added to the uproar. Unfortunately, instead of simply ignoring Coughlin or accepting equal time to offer factual and calmly reasoned refutations of perceived mistakes or gullible impressions, "they did neither...they set up a terrific howl and then ran" [pp. 337–38].

Mooney's complaints about Jewish reaction were not surprising. The sophistication and international experience he developed in his earlier assignments as apostolic delegate to India and Japan gave him few—and always formal—contacts with Jews and Protestants. And at that time neither Jews nor Protestants were notably interfaith visionaries or activists. Tentler remarked, "American society in the 1930's, for all its apparent secularity, was a good deal more tribal than it is today. It took the horrors of the Second World War to breach the walls that kept the tribes apart" [p. 338]. With publication of new diocesan regulations, Coughlin had to stay out of partisan politics and was forbidden to endorse or disapprove of candidates for political office, "except in rare cases where the judgment of the ordinary has authorized them to do so in defense of the essential interests of religion" [p. 339]. If Coughlin planned to test archdiocesan regulations, he had few options. For most of the stations that formerly carried his program were not willing to renew contracts with him. Hence, the cancellation of his 1940–1941 broadcast season.

Coughlin's days as the radio priest were thus formally ended, but *Social Justice* still caused Mooney some concern. In June 1939 Mooney twice complained to Coughlin about the magazine's anti-Semitic tone and "abusive language," with little success. In August

1939 Coughlin was told that the magazine had to be declared a Catholic publication and placed under Mooney's authority or Coughlin had to sever all connection with it.

Coughlin pretended to disconnect from the magazine, but as Mooney told Al Smith in December 1939, "In my heart I fear that the dissociation is more formal than real. The magazine is largely a promotional sheet for his activities. He contributes occasional supervised articles—under a permission that was given in order to avoid the danger of even greater scandal" [p. 339]. Both knew the limits of Canon Law, but the increasingly "scurrilous content" of the magazine and Coughlin's obvious ties to it prompted Mooney to try again. In February 1940 Coughlin was ordered to sever all ties with *Social Justice* or to place it under full Church authority. He agreed fatalistically and by May 27 there was no article signed or directly attributed to him. Rome belatedly had inquired about harsher action, but Mooney demurred for fear of causing greater harm, especially during the 1940 political campaign.

Yet, the Pearl Harbor attack did invoke harsher action, because *Social Justice* continued bitterly to criticize Roosevelt and his advisors about Britain's war aims, as well as the purposes and later conduct of World War II. In March 1942 Mooney learned that the federal government was planning to bring sedition charges against the magazine's editors and publishers. On April 2 Coughlin announced that he alone was responsible for the contents of the magazine because of his "effective moral and spiritual influence over the editor, publishers, and owners," baiting Attorney General Biddle to indict him.

Mooney moved quickly and publicly ordered Coughlin to admit publicly his disobedience and announce his surrender of all responsibility for *Social Justice*, saying "I shall be obliged to proceed, however, reluctantly, to canonical measures designed for the priesthood to enforce clerical obedience" [p. 341]. A heated April 28 meeting with Coughlin was followed by Mooney's agreement to meet with Coughlin's lawyer on April 30. To avoid Coughlin's indictment, there was agreement that *Social Justice* should cease publication immediately.

In early May, the legal case was dropped quietly and Mooney wrote a profuse thank you letter to Roosevelt for his help in solving "a problem embarrassing alike to civil and ecclesiastical authority [which] would have been impossible but for your own magnanimous attitude." Coughlin agreed, knowing failure to honor his pledge would mean automatic suspension of his priestly faculties [p. 341]. Very relieved, Mooney told Cicognani the sorry mess was finished and the numbers of complaints were negligible and mostly from Coughlin's fanatic fans. "Apparently he has alienated the major portion of the simple Catholics who followed him so blindly. For that, at least, it may have been worthwhile to be patient" [p. 342].

Until retirement in 1966, Coughlin was pastor of the Shrine of the Little Flower in Royal Oak, Michigan. After World War II, he occasionally gave vent to his extreme views on domestic and international politics, although denied permission to speak outside his parish. He also had to submit most of his public speeches for vetting even into the 1950s. He maintained a following in Detroit and elsewhere after the war. Many of his diehard followers later became partisans in the anticommunist crusades of Wisconsin Senator Joe McCarthy [p. 342].

Tentler stressed that the "Coughlin problem" was related to Mooney's "labor problem." As early as 1937, as indicated above, Coughlin insisted that Catholics were obliged to oppose the "communist-dominated CIO." Although concerned about communists and inroads by sectarian leftists into the CIO, Mooney was convinced that Coughlin's assaults were dangerous, because they created the impression among Catholic workers that the Church was an ally of the employers. Convinced that these Catholics were potentially a powerful force for moderation in the labor force, Mooney gave full rein to Fr. Clancy and the Archdiocesan Labor Institute, as well as to Fr. Hubble and Mr. Paul Weber in Detroit ACTU.

Whatever one makes of Tentler's final estimation of the Mooney–Coughlin battles, the work provides an excellent background for understanding correspondence on the conflict contained in several other archives. As indicated above, Coughlin began broadcasting as an electrifying speaker and friend to labor, but as time passed he became controversial over his interpreting the causes of the Great Depression of the 1930s, as well as being anti–CIO.

Another member of the hierarchy, concerned early about Coughlin, was Cleveland Bishop Joseph Schrembs, who noted that some of his recent mail contained complaints about some of Coughlin's sermons and Fr. Cox's presidential interests.[2] Schrembs told Msgr. Ready, NCWC secretary general, "These letters, I fear, represent a very large bulk of the opinion outside the Catholic Church and are, I believe, deserving of an honest, straight-forward, yet measured answer over the radio by Father Daly [host of the NCWC's "Question Box"]."

A recent convert from and critic of Protestantism wondered why the hierarchy did not silence Coughlin, in view of his bitter criticism of Hoover's administration and the Versailles Treaty. The convert regarded such comments as "political," ones unbecoming a priest and harmful to the Church. Schrembs quoted from the letter, "There is no priest or layman anywhere whose talks provoked as much bitterness and religious hatred and bigotry as these so-called sermons of Father Coughlin." Cox's interest in being a candidate for the presidency was said also to have provided an excuse for widespread unfavorable comment and "rekindled the fires of religious bigotry

---

[2] Schrembs File, Cleveland Diocesan Archives, February 11, 1932, Schrembs to Ready.

and intolerance." The convert requested to be informed, if Fr. Daly were to respond to the question, "Have the Bishops and the Catholic Church the power to silence a priest who runs wild as these two have?"

An answer may have been given privately by Amarillo, Texas, Robert Lucey.[3] An early supporter of the CIO, its president John L. Lewis and the New Deal, Lucey had been criticized in Coughlin's *Social Justice*. Coughlin, Lucey said, "represents no one but himself.... Least of all...[does he] reflect the sane constructive Social Teaching of Pope Pius XI."

One of the earliest labor priest critics of Coughlin's economic ideas was Georgetown and Catholic University professor and editor of *America* Fr. Parsons, S.J., especially in his mid-1930s articles drafted for publication.[4] The first draft, "Father Coughlin and the Banks," focused one of the key planks in Coughlin's platform. The role of the bankers and the banking system, Parsons claimed, helped to make Coughlin famous and was a topic rarely missing from his speeches. To search out Coughlin's principles, Parsons made a distinction between what was said about the bankers and their system. "It cannot be said that Father Coughlin, in the heat of his oratory, always makes this separation and this may make his proposals to abolish the system seem more valid than they are" [p. 1]. Currency became the prime object of Coughlin's reforms and private banking the focus of his arguments, since he alleged that bankers deliberately created depressions and that the sole purpose of modern banking was to create money scarcity. He called for the nationalization of banking and credit, which was the principal function of banks. Despite claims that private banking was unconstitutional and Coughlin's support for the Nye–Sweeney Bill in Congress, there was no support for his constitutional argument and there was

[3] Bronder 1982.
[4] Parsons File, Georgetown University Archives, "Father Coughlin and the Banks," "Father Coughlin's Ideas on Money," 1935.

no chance of that legislation being passed and enacted, either in Congress or in the forum of popular opinion.

Parsons would agree with Coughlin that private bankers were often guilty of ignorance, greed, and a gambling spirit, but asserted that the real power in the nation was "among those who pay the campaign funds of the parties...the big industrialists." So, even if the power to grant or withhold credit were in the control of the government, the campaign contributors would be the beneficiaries. Parsons concluded that such was also the practice in totalitarian nations and the first plank in socialist governments. Conceding that proper government supervision of banks and others who controlled currency was less dangerous than giving government actual ownership and control of credit, Parsons cited Ryan.

"What business needs," Ryan said, "is not more credit but more sales, and this is an industrial not a monetary problem" [p. 7]. Schemes for government control of currency and credit to remedy U.S. unemployment had never been intelligently explained. He cited Pius XI, who deemed the depression fundamentally and almost entirely industrial, i.e., maladjustment between production, distribution, and consumption of wealth. Parsons cited sociologist and economist, Msgr. A.J. Muench of the Milwaukee Archdiocesan St. Francis Seminary: by becoming involved in partisan politics, Coughlin had put Catholic Social Teaching in peril. "If it fails in politics, as fail it must with untenable proposals, people will have their confidence shaken in it to such an extent that the laborious work which Catholic sociologists have done in its behalf will not recover for many years to come."

Parsons' second article, "Father Coughlin's Ideas on Money," discussed the other key and popularly acclaimed plank in Coughlin's platform. Acknowledging Coughlin as a dedicated champion of the poor, Parsons insisted that theories had to be based on more than a love for the poor. For Coughlin it was once again the story of the bankers and not the industrialists. Governmental financing schemes were confused and unreal. Support for the Nye–Sweeney banking bill was neither forthcoming nor necessary, given the Roosevelt administration's lifting of price controls and commitment to a stabilized dollar. It was Coughlin's and not the Church's ideas, as Pius XI cautioned. Muench's caution expanded: "[If] the practical matters of money and banking are not matters of technique, then nothing in the whole field of economics is technique." Parsons ended by complimenting and admiring Coughlin's incomparable service in making the nation aware of evils in the U.S. economic system and his almost dire warning in light of changing times. Besides offering untried theories, there was danger of distracting people from the need to reform industrial life. "If people begin to look for prosperity and justice in some easy magic of monetary reform, the long hard job of social justice in the factory will be overlooked [which] will be tragic."

In 1935 Cardinal Mundelein of Chicago indirectly criticized Coughlin during the bestowal of an honorary degree on Roosevelt by the University of Notre Dame.[5] The message was quite pointed, "No individual Catholic bishop or priest, no organization of laymen or Catholic newspaper has the right to speak for twenty million Catholics in this country in the matter of politics." More direct criticism of Coughlin would have put Mundelein in a dilemma between his desire to support Roosevelt, president and friend, and interfering with the prerogatives of Coughlin's superior and friend, Bishop Gallagher of Detroit. So Bishop Sheil, Chicago's chancellor and auxiliary, was asked "to 'go public' with disdain for Coughlin which they both shared" [p. 326]. Publicly, Sheil's statements would appear authoritative, but among the hierarchy, an auxiliary bishop's statements would generate less conflict.

---

[5] Sorvillo 1990.

190

Also, on December 12, 1938, coinciding with the termination of Coughlin's regular Sunday afternoon broadcast, Sheil read a statement on the NBC Radio Network to a nationwide audience. Prepared in consultation with Mundelein, the statement criticized Coughlin for presuming to speak for American Catholics on political issues and for accusing Jewish bankers, money lenders, and speculators for the economic malaise of the times. The message was repeated for the next two years before Catholic and Jewish audiences. The culmination came in Sheil's speech on the day of Mundelein's death, after Coughlin had criticized Roosevelt's Lend-Lease proposal as a dangerous intervention in foreign affairs. "The devising of a course of action is not something to be divined by emotional charlatans who have become statesmen overnight and whose unctuous voices betray a first urge to hear themselves talk, no matter what they convey. You know who I mean" [p. 328].

In late 1938, Coughlin asked Schrembs if the priests and bishops of Cleveland would like to hear about the controversy in the United Automobile Workers (UAW) ranks from Homer Martin.[6] Coughlin had done the same on two earlier occasions for the priests of the Detroit Archdiocese, gathered at Coughlin's Little Flower shrine, as well as for the priests of the Fort Wayne (Indiana) Diocese and the faculty of Notre Dame University. However, in a September 14 response to Coughlin, Schrembs said, after consultation with several priests, well-informed about industrial relations in the Cleveland Diocese, it was decided that such a talk by Homer Martin would be unwise, given the conditions of high tension between the AFL and CIO.

Sometime in the late 1930s Catholic University Fr. Francis Haas sent a telegram to Coughlin, calling his program "excellent." Yet, he

---

[6] Schrembs File, Cleveland Diocesan Archives, September 7, 1938, Coughlin to Schrembs.

added, Coughlin's program needed some clarifications from the encyclicals about wages and salaries, high enough to insure maximum employment, the rise of nonowners to ownership, and the promotion of industry councils.[7] That is, the formation of an economic order that would consist of each industry collaboratively cooperating to handle employer associations and employee–unions problems directed to benefit the common good. Such would also include agriculture and government supervision when necessary.

On September 3, 1937, Cincinnati's Fr. Edward A. Freking, secretary-treasurer of the Catholic Students' Mission Crusade, reported to Mooney six startling highlights of a meeting with Coughlin, very early in his public career.[8] First, Coughlin planned to hand over his National Union of Social Justice to diocesan directors, appointed by the ordinaries of each diocese, but insisted the director have absolute authority in the dioceses they represented. Coughlin, as national director, would provide all necessary material and information, train the directors, pay their expenses for a one-week training course in Detroit, and put one million dollars a year in the organization. Second, in expressing opposition to Msgr. John A. Ryan, Coughlin accused Ryan of belonging to communist societies and of being coeditor of a book denying the divinity of Christ. Freking told Coughlin he should feel conscious-bound to make such charges known to the proper Church authorities. Third, Coughlin thought that the Summer Schools of Social Action in Toledo, Milwaukee, and elsewhere were simply approvals of the Democratic Party under President Roosevelt's leadership. Freking said, "Father Coughlin's attitude seems to be that he, and he alone, has sources of information that are not available to others. Yet "Coughlin revealed no 'secrets' about the CIO or the Communist Party which were not common knowledge." Fourth, most of the priests at the meeting

---

[7] Haas File, Catholic University Archvies, late 1930s, Haas to Coughlin.

[8] Mooney File, Detroit Archdiocesan Archives, September 3, 1937, Freking to Mooney.

were unwilling to question Coughlin, holding him to be an infallible authority. When asked about the details of the plans, Coughlin gave little or nothing in reply. When asked if the meeting was held with the knowledge and approval of Mooney, Coughlin replied that he had not informed Mooney about the meeting. Fifth, while insisting that the National Union was being kept out of politics, Coughlin said its social justice aims would be achieved by the referendum and initiative. Six, he expressed or implied that "the hierarchy was either asleep or else ignorant of the problems of social justice." In a desperate effort to empower or lionize the National Union, he said "he was working under expressed orders from Rome, but should that be become unnecessary to the success of the movement, he would be willing to step out at any time."

On September 15, 1938, Fort Wayne's Bishop Noll wrote to Mooney to make it clear that whatever Coughlin's behavior Noll was playing fair with Mooney.[9] In doing so, Noll made several points. Noll never exchanged correspondence with Coughlin, except about a ceremony at which he was invited to speak. When Reardon, managing editor of *Social Justice*, wrote to Noll about an anticommunist sermon being proposed for the Feast of Christ the King, Noll told Reardon to contact Mooney, as chair of the NCWC Administrative Board. Coughlin and another Detroit priest drove to Notre Dame University, where Coughlin addressed the audience, although he had not been on the program. The only conversation Noll had with Coughlin was during a walk from Notre Dame's auditorium to the administration building. Then, Noll told Coughlin that Mooney had called Noll and, among other things, said Mooney was willing to see "Coughlin or anyone else upon application for an appointment at any time." Noll was quite anxious to disabuse any of the NCWC Board and members of the hierarchy that he was friendly with Coughlin. While Bishop Gallagher was active in Detroit, Noll said

[9] Mooney File, Detroit Archdiocesan Archives, September 15, 1938, Noll to Mooney.

there had been no critic of Coughlin like himself. Noll's paper never referred to Coughlin's radio talks, so as not "to disedify [*sic*] one group by criticizing him nor to give encouragement to the other group by seeming commendation." A request to write an article for *Social Justice* came from Reardon, not Coughlin. Noll refused the offer, but would write such an article for *Our Sunday Visitor*, which *Social Justice* was at liberty to copy. Noll did not know whether Reardon or Coughlin was to blame for sending the copies of *Social Justice* to the U.S. bishops.

Although Noll had no objections to bringing the recent matters before the NCWC Administrative Board, he would not want any discussion of Reardon's overtures on behalf of Coughlin, unless Noll could speak for himself. In light of the exchange about Coughlin, Noll felt it important to clarify relations with the NCWC and its staff. Concerning whatever Reardon told Mooney, Noll was not certain. Yet, the incident is "only one instance of my being the Goat innocently, and the accumulation of such instances is what I had in mind when I wrote to you two days ago, at which time I referred to the 'pressure' brought on me from all sides'." Noll strove to be ultra-loyal to the NCWC, even when Noll had information that suggested some differences in attitude with the NCWC. Noll had no personal ill feeling toward Ryan, precisely because he worked for the NCWC. Noll's acting editor was told to publicize practically everything about the NCWC, but even after Ryan had criticized the newspaper for quoting John L. Lewis's negative assessment of CIO official John Brophy. Noll liked McGowan greatly, but said, "I believe that he also lacks considerable knowledge of the 'other side'." Noll claimed that he had never been accused of being duplicitous or insincere. He felt that most of his difficulties flowed from his great sincerity and frank expression of convictions for the good of the Catholic cause.

Also embroiled in Mooney's troubles with Coughlin, in October 1938, was Fr. Edward Lodge Curran, a priest of the Brooklyn Diocese and president of the International Catholic Truth Society, who had written some articles in Coughlin's *Social Justice*.[10] The information came in a letter from Brooklyn's Thomas Molloy to Mooney, attempting to explain that Curran bore Mooney no ill will, "because he understands sympathetically at least some of the exacting problems that you have been called upon to solve." Willing to meet with Mooney and give respectful attention in future writings and speeches to any suggestions or requirements that Mooney might seek, Curran was under the impression, said Molloy, "that since the *Social Justice* magazine is provided some form of ecclesiastical censorship that no objectionable writings will ever be approved for publication." Molloy assured Mooney he and Curran would offer their full interest and cooperation in Mooney's prudent and tactful efforts to convey Church Social Teaching on current economic, political, and social issues.

In late November 1938, Mooney replied to a November 16 letter from apostolic delegate Cicognani, who thought it would have been better if the *Protocols of the Elders of Zion* had not been published.[11] Mooney recalled his earlier discussions about problems with Coughlin. Stating that neither *Social Justice* nor the radio broadcasts were "productive of real good for the Church," Mooney starkly related the dilemma Coughlin placed the Church in. Either make it clear that Coughlin did not speak for the Church and censoring any evidently wrong statements or stop Coughlin from writing and speaking by use of authority, which was bound to be misinterpreted. In very frank language, Mooney voiced his real assessment of Coughlin: he could not be counted on to choose the interests of

---

[10] Mooney File, Detroit Archdiocesan Archives, October 7, 1938, Molloy to Mooney.
[11] Mooney File, Detroit Archdiocesan Archives, November 26, 1938, Mooney to Cicognani.

the Church before his own personal interests or follow Mooney's advice. Indeed, Mooney thought Coughlin almost by nature was vindictive, suspicious, and given to inaccurate thinking and broad oratorical statements. In fact, years of great popular acclaim and the support of noisy followers had inflated Coughlin's sense of self-importance. Mooney said some restraints on Coughlin's nationwide broadcasting would soon have to be enacted. "The difficulty...is that the bishops who happily have no local problem are a bit too disposed, perhaps out of delicacy, to leave it up entirely to one most directly concerned and thus by their negative attitude aggravate, in a certain sense, the general problem."

Another labor priest who disagreed with Coughlin, as early as 1939, was Baltimore Fr. John Cronin, S.S.[12] His article discussed concentration of power in corporate America and, unlike the Populists and Coughlin, rejected the idea of currency reform. Rather, Cronin insisted on democratizing industry, according to Pius XI's plan in which industries would be compelled to base decisions in part on the rights of labor and the public interest. Indeed, if concentration of economic power were "cut off at its source," banking influence would be diminished.

A major disagreement with Coughlin surfaced in Detroit's Fr. Clancy's November 15, 1939, response to a radio address by Coughlin, which was said to have played a decisive role in the failure of the back-to-work movement of Chrysler automotive workers.[13] The public dispute and rebuke arose from Coughlin's erroneous citation of a papal encyclical as a basis for urging the United Automobile Union (UAW) to return to work during the Chrysler strike.[14] The talk on Detroit radio station WMBC, paid for by UAW and sponsored by Detroit Association of Catholic Trade Unionists of which

---

[12] Cronin 1939.

[13] Riesel and Levenstein 1949.

[14] Clancy Collection, Wayne State University Archives of Labor and Urban Affairs and University Archives, Box 1, Folder 14.1.

Clancy was chaplain, began with assurances that Clancy was interested in the well-being of all Americans and Detroiters and, as a Catholic priest, he was solicitous as well for the achievement and persistence of justice. Quoting Leo XIII and Pius XI about industrial relations, as moral and religious issues and not just economic and social issues, he felt that the task of correcting Coughlin was unpleasant but necessary.

Agreeing with Coughlin over the distress of thousands of the victims of the dispute, Clancy challenged Coughlin's arguments: some of his factual statements, his interpretation of the National Labor Relations Act (Wagner Act), and his exposition of Catholic Social Teaching. With regard to facts, the company, not the union refused to enter into arbitration of grievances. The strike was about higher wages and other issues. With regard to the Wagner Act interpretation, the act allowed workers to strike, except in the case of achieving the right to organize and bargain collectively through freely chosen representatives. The act did not provide machinery for mediation or conciliation, although such disputes on occasion gave rise to lockouts or strikes. As to misinterpretations of *Quadragesimo Anno* regarding the obligations of ownership, the encyclical did not refer to nonowning workers, but to the propertied classes only and the preceding paragraphs discussed inheritance and taxes. Clancy said that had Coughlin applied the encyclical citation to Chrysler rather than to the union-organizing workers, he would have been more accurate.

In reference to the workers' suffering and the ugly reactions to the misuse of Pius XI's text, Coughlin also misquoted and used his own words, because Pius XI was speaking of the fascist system. By substituting the word "state" for "it," Coughlin claimed that Pius had said, "The state alone can conclude labor contracts and labor agreements." In other words, Coughlin "would make the Holy Father appear to be the advocate of a fascist control of both management and labor." Clancy ended his response with three hopes. One,

Coughlin would not advise the workers to join the back-to-work movement, which would be very injurious to unionism and make the workers' sacrifices useless. Two, Coughlin would join Clancy in prayers for a speedy and just solution to the dispute for both the company and the union. Three, Detroit would lead the United States "to the enjoyment of prosperity in peace and justice."

In mid-1941 Msgr. Ryan became indirectly involved with Coughlin, when Ryan received a letter from Fr. Edward Lodge Curran, editor of the *Brooklyn Tablet* and president of the International Catholic Truth Society, with copies to Coughlin, Mooney, NCWC general secretary Msgr. Ready, SAD moderator Bishop Gerald O'Hara, McGowan, and Hayes.[15] Ryan's letter in the April 28 edition of *Social Justice* was characterized by Curran as "one of the most uncharitable documents ever written and signed by a member of the Catholic clergy." Since Ryan's letter was on SAD letterhead, Curran thought Ryan was guilty of "all the resentment that may be aroused against the Conference, its Departments of Social Action, and the bishops and priests whose names appeared on the letterhead." Curran charged Ryan with violating "the virtue [charity] and stooped to false speech and insulting language about a fellow priest and about an official diocesan newspaper produced in the Diocese of Brooklyn." Ryan was said to owe Coughlin and the newspaper an immediate apology: "The only restitution you can make to the bishops and priests connected with the National Catholic Welfare Conference is to resign immediately as director of the Department of Social Action." Curran concluded with the hope that any future statements or writings would "be imbued with justice and charity."

A month later, Mooney wrote to Baltimore–Washington's Archbishop Michael Curley.[16] The occasion was the publication of the Msgr. Ryan piece in the *Brooklyn Tablet*. Coughlin and Curley were

---

[15] Mooney File, Detroit Archdiocesan Archives, April 29, 1941, Curran to Ryan.
[16] Mooney File, Detroit Archdiocesan Archives, May 29, 1941, Mooney to Curley.

told that Bishops O'Hara, Molloy, and Ready, as well as Mooney, did not excuse "the Monsignor's imprudent statements in question [and O'Hara] already reproved Ryan. O'Hara sent a letter of apology to Molloy, which he graciously accepted. Mooney and Ready apologized to Scanlan, the newspaper's editor. Mooney did not understand one aspect of the whole controversy, namely, that the people who resented Ryan's letter were the very ones who publicized it. They first should have written to O'Hara. Ryan would have apologized and the issue would have been resolved. Mooney closed, "If one had a suspicious mind he would be inclined to look for ulterior motives behind the publicizing of an offensive private letter."

In September 1945 an assistant to Mooney, Fr. John Donovan exchanged correspondence with Higgins. Donovan needled Higgins—with an indirect reference to the flap with Fr. Curran—over comments about Coughlin and the *Brooklyn Tablet*.[17] "How are you and Father Lodge Curran getting along? I hope you appreciated that *Social Justice* is not being published at the present time?" Two weeks later, Higgins remarked, "I judge that the budget of the Catholic Truth Society [of which Curran was the leader] has a rather unpleasant habit of sending copies of his correspondence to members of the hierarchy." In 1982, clarification of the dispute appeared.[18] Ryan said he regretted the remark and, despite Coughlin's mistakes, Ryan thought Coughlin was on the side of the angels and Ryan did not want to divide the forces of change.

In mid-1966, Pittsburgh Fr. Rice reflected on Coughlin's activities and impact.[19] Rice was asked on April 30, 1966, by Helen Clark for advice on a master's thesis on Coughlin and his relationship to the Church. She asked if the five questions asked of Rice were the same

---

[17] Higgins File, Catholic University Archives, September 6, 1945, Donovan to Higgins.
[18] Curran 1982.
[19] Rice File, Hillman Library, Pittsburgh University Archives, May 12, 1966, Rice to Clark.

ones asked during interviews with several priests, only one of whom knew Coughlin and Mooney personally. To the first question, why the only member of the hierarchy to publicly support Coughlin was Dubuque (Iowa)'s Archbishop Beckman, despite a proportionately larger support from priests, Rice replied that the clergy and people supported Coughlin and loved his criticism of the status quo, with which they themselves were very displeased. The majority of the people and clergy were still pleased with Roosevelt, and Coughlin had as much support from the hierarchy as from the clergy. However, "Many bishops did not speak out because they didn't speak out on anything." To the second question, that of the six Catholic newspapers researched only the *Pittsburgh Catholic* had consistently criticized Coughlin. Examination of the editorials of the other five indicated that the majority probably supported Coughlin throughout his career. Rice's response was biting. "The level of stupidity was very high in the Diocesan Press and indeed in all the Catholic Press." To the third question about Coughlin helping or hurting the Church's crusade for social justice, Rice replied, "He hurt the crusade because he diverted many good people into the sort of nonsense that he was advocating." The fourth question asked if the Church was hurt by Coughlin's economic teaching before 1935, his involvement in the 1936 presidential election, his stand on neutrality after 1938, and his controversial speeches regarding Jews. Rice said, "Of course, he hurt the Church. I'm not so much concerned here with his tarnishing the image of the Church. But I am concerned with his leading astray some good people. Narrowness always hurts the image of the Church, so he hurt it." The fifth question alluded to Mooney's publicly questioning Coughlin's speeches in 1937 concerning the CIO and Roosevelt, but failed to caution Coughlin publicly when he became more "vitriolic." Rice replied that Mooney was taking his time, so as to move at the right time. Coughlin was then perceived as a good, but misguided and intemperate priest, his influence was diminishing, and he had become more sour, but to a limited listening audience. Yet, Rice disagreed with Mooney's decision to silence Coughlin for the rest of his life.

In late 1994, Rice, like the NCWC, was said to have viewed Coughlin as anti–New Deal and anti-Semitic.[20] In 1938 Rice told Coughlin he was doing a disservice to America's Jews and Catholics, as well as providing radicals with the charge of anti-Semitism, to use as a weapon "to attack the Church and to discredit Murray's anticommunist efforts within SWOC and the CIO" [p. 387]. For, Jews were well represented in regional Communist Party ranks.

---

[20] Heineman 1994, 364–394, *in passim.*

9

MORE DISAGREEMENT *AD INTRA ECCLESIA*

Smith, Dockworkers, Dietz,

& Seminary Education

Fr. William Smith, S.J.

F r. William Smith, S.J., served in two Jesuit Institutes for Industrial Relations (IIRs)—Brooklyn Crown Heights and Jersey City St. Peter's College. Eventually, he became controversial in labor priests' circles. In late 1942 SAD's Hayes wrote to Smith, complaining about an issue of the *Crown Heights Comment*.[1] Vice president Henry Wallace had defects in his philosophy, Hayes thought, but he said Smith's reaction was more friendly "than the attitude of many priests and lay Catholics whom I have heard speak of Him." Also criticized in the same issue was Smith's assertion that a U.S. bishops' remarks about South America were a whack at the U.S. State Department. The bishops and many South American Catholics deplored Protestant missionaries traveling to Latin America with plenty of cash, but Hayes claimed that the State Department connection was very indirect. "The Bishops have no intentions of

---

[1] Hayes File, Catholic University Archives, November 25, 1942, Hayes to W. Smith.

blasting the State Department, nor the United States Government, in any case. Outside of this point you give the Bishops' statement a fine notice."

Smith replied at the end of November 1942 that the parts of Wallace's speech critiqued in the *Crown Heights Comment* were those that caught the fancy of the *Daily Worker* and were meant by Smith as cracks at current trends and not at Wallace himself.[2] Whether or not the bishops' statement was a criticism of the State Department or not, Smith thought that *that* "is where the criticism belongs." A friend of Smith insisted the State Department was largely to blame for the progress of Protestant missionaries in Brazil. The YMCA and other groups received help as well.

In late 1943, Ed Scully, editor of New York ACTU's *Labor Leader*, made unfortunate remarks about CIO vice president James Carey being fired by CIO president Philip Murray because of contacts with the Socialists and Social Democrats. Hayes invited Scully to a meeting of clergy and laity to create a little more unity and cooperation among those in the East who were trying "to do something with workers' schools."[3] Hayes told about Phil Murray being attacked by Smith in the *Crown Heights Bulletin*. New York Fr. Carey, S.J., rebuked Smith in a letter without harmful publicity. Yet, Murray was "hurt deeply because any priest's understanding and sympathy were important to his type of real Catholicity."

On June 11, 1945, New York's Fr. Carey, S.J., wrote to a "Father Joe" who—judging from the context—was Fr. Joseph Fitzpatrick, S.J.[4] Among other comments, Carey mentioned that because of strained relations with Smith any cooperation with him seemed hopeless. Smith deemed the CIO to be completely dominated by communists. Carey completely disagreed, because the CIO was such a fact of life

---

[2] Hayes File, Catholic University Archives, November 30, 1942, Smith to Hayes.
[3] Hayes File, Catholic University Archives, November 5, 1943, Hayes to Scully.
[4] Carey File, New York Jesuit Province Archives, June 11, 1945, Carey to "Fr Joe."

that such arguments from people like Smith had no power over the people "to dissuade them from it," and CIO president Murray was sincerely interested in ousting communists. Yet, Carey said priests and their co-workers must understand better the exigencies and demands of the labor movement and provide Murray with constructive aid. Carey quoted an unidentified priest, who may have been given to exaggerations, saying, "Unless we priests have actually helped to form a labor movement, we have no right to talk about Communism." Carey realized that repetition of such a quote would not place him in the category of a "rabid anticommunist, especially in the context of his soulful confession to and hopes for "Joe."

Also in December 1945, there was exchange of correspondence between Miller and Higgins, focused mostly on the Spanish Civil War. On December 10, Miller stated his preference for Smith's approach in the *Crown Heights Comment*: "Withdraw recognition from Franco and Communism enters Spain [and] any Catholic who falls for it has allowed the party to make a sucker of him."[5] Miller was especially upset that CIO president Murray, as labor leader, had no business barging into Spanish politics. "[As] a Catholic," he said, "he was guilty of a kind of sacrilege (as Fr. Smith said) to give a hand to the persecutors of his fellow Catholics in Spain." Admitting that he did not know enough about Franco, Miller asked Higgins for arguments against Franco.

About a week later Higgins admitted he did not know enough about the Spanish controversy "to carry on our friendly discussion any further."[6] Yet, he felt very strongly that it was unfair to Murray and other Catholics in public life to make their stand on Spain a test of religious loyalty and orthodoxy, particularly since the saintly and scholarly priest Don Struzo continued to criticize Franco even more

---

[5] Higgins File, Catholic University Archives, December 10, 1945, Miller to Higgins.

[6] Higgins File, Catholic University Archives, December 18, 1945, Higgins to Miller.

vehemently than "the phony liberals who are connected with *PM*, the *New Republic*, and the *Nation*." Higgins added that Struzo might have been wrong in his analysis of the Spanish Civil War, but the point is "we can hardly question his orthodoxy." Higgins agreed that as a labor leader Murray had no business barging into Spanish politics, but neither did Smith and Patrick Scanlon, editor of the *Brooklyn Tablet*, have the right to attack George Meany, Matt Woll, and Bob Watt of the AFL for some of their comments on the Russian situation. Higgins feared that Smith and Scanlon were determined that there was an "official Catholic" position on every political issue. Yet, some members of the hierarchy stubbornly refused to get in line. For example, Chicago Bishop Bernard Sheil agreed wholeheartedly with *PM's* position on Spain. Higgins's guiding principle was, "With regard to political issues which do not directly concern the integrity of the faith and morals, we have no choice but to allow individual Catholics to make their mistakes." The only alternative Higgins saw was to require Murray and other trade union officials to clear their statement through an ecclesiastical censor.

On March 25 and 29, 1953, Smith had written to Frank Folsom, president of RCA. On June 4, Folsom telephoned Smith's provincial, Fr. John McMahon, S.J., to complain about Smith's "very presumptuous and inappropriate letters."[7] McMahon had appointed Xavier Industrial Relations Institute's Fr. Philip Carey to investigate the situation and Carey delivered an oral report, which stressed the "tactless, impolite and discourteous tone of Father Smith's two letters." Although Smith's case about the RCA Harrison, New York, plant was solid, he ruined it by his bullying tactics. Smith had been mistaken in contacting the president, when there was already a good relationship between Smith and the personnel manager, McGrady, who had very accurate knowledge and experience concerning papal encyclicals. Smith's suggested settlement was deplored by

---

[7] Smith File, St. Peter's College Archives, June 7, 1953, Folsom to McMahon.

Carey. For, Jersey City St. Peter' Institute should have defended its students in a nonpublic manner, he believed. In fact, Carey continued, Smith should have requested another union to investigate the Harrison situation and offer suggestions. Smith's bullying tactics amounted also to a blasting at a Communion Breakfast, if he did not get his way. After hearing Carey's report, McMahon left a message for Folsom, who was attending a board of directors meeting: "Please tell Mr. Folsom, *I Deeply Regret the Impolite Tone of Father Smith's Letters.* I shall be glad to talk to Mr. Folsom when he comes in, if he wishes to call." McMahon's memo ended, "He did not call."

New York Dockworkers

There were disagreements among labor priests on the docks over their effectiveness, ecclesiastical support, etc. In March 1999, Professor James Fisher of St. Louis University and later of Fordham University presented a preliminary paper at Notre Dame University's Cushwa Center, entitled "Covering the Waterfront Culture and Ideology in the Catholic Metropolis, 1936–1960."[8] Fisher mentioned Msgr. John O'Donnell, chaplain of the Port of New York and known as "Taxi John," who was praised by Joe Ryan, president of the corrupt International Longshoremen's Association. Ryan was supposed to have said that O'Donnell refused to interfere "in the internal disputes in the Family of Labor [and stuck] exclusively to his business...the Spiritual." O'Donnell was said to have reciprocated with, "He [Ryan] keeps his hands off the spiritual things of my Church, Guardian Angel Parish, and I keep my hands out of his business."

So, when Corridan supported the wildcat strike among the dockworkers, O'Donnell was said to have complained to the New York

---

[8] Corridan File, Fordham University Archives, March 1999, Fisher, James, "Covering the Waterfront Culture and Ideology in the Catholic Metropolis, 1936–1960."

Archdiocesan Chancery Office that Corridan actually was working on the docks and had initiated the strike. Although it has been shown above that Spellman did not censure Corridan, Fisher added a questionable and curious judgment about Corridan and his work: "Though he [Corridan] won a temporary reprieve, the event signaled the beginning of the end of his waterfront apostolate."

In late 1984 a former Jesuit J. McGrail answered an inquiry about Corridan from playwright Fr. Neil Hurley, S.J.[9] McGrail had lived at New York Xavier Labor School with Corridan during the labor dispute and filming of *On the Waterfront*, which featured Corridan, and he offered insights about Corridan and Carey. McGrail tried to imagine who was responsible for Corridan being called on the carpet by the Chancery Office—big donors or others fearing loss of control and profits, if Corridan were not silenced. The "apostolate had received the approval of two of Pete's [Corridan's nickname] superiors, who, it is piously believed, did not back down when pressure was applied." McGrail closed, mentioning O'Donnell, the New Port chaplain and vaguely recalled that he may have turned in a report to the Chancery Office. "Was he in the back pocket of the Ship Owners? I seem to recall that he had a very nice life, with a lot of expenses paid for him (a car? an apartment?] by a person or persons unknown. Pete never had it that good. For transportation he and only the bus or his own two feet."

Fr. Peter Dietz

In 1953 Sr. M. Harrita Fox, the most extensive biographer of Milwaukee's Fr. Peter Dietz, elaborated on his disagreements with Msgr. John A. Ryan and others in the beginnings of the NCWC.[10]

---

[9] Corridan File, New York Jesuit Province Archives, August 15, 1984, McGrail to Hurley.
[10] Fox 1953, 223–229.

After tracing Dietz's life and career, Fox evaluated Dietz's accomplishments and difficulties relative to other Catholics interested in the labor movement in the early part of the twentieth century. Mentioned were his efforts to overcome the inertia, conservatism, and opposition he met in the Roman Catholic Central Verein, the American Federation of Catholic Societies, NCWC, etc. She insisted that had Dietz been listened to by the bishops, the Catholic Church labor movement in the United States would have antedated that of NCWC and SAD. Yet, Dietz did play a significant role in having labor as a part of their agenda. Fox insisted, "Dietz exerted a greater influence directly on the labor movement than any priest before or since." He was said to have presented the Catholic Church in the United States as an ally, preventing "the labor movement from splitting over the religious issue as it had done in Europe and Canada." He had the precedent for the Association of Catholic Trade Unionists. Likewise, Dietz prevented the AFL's affiliation with Socialist International groups and encouraged its closer relations with the International Federation of Christian Trade Unions. His failures were attributed to employer groups opposed to unions; his own personality revealed in many ways, especially in disagreements with "fellow priests who were not yet educated to the plans he advocated"; his being many years ahead of times "when few bishops or priests had the courage to brave the implications of his programs."

In her Preface [pp. vii-ix] Fox admitted Dietz was not the first American priest to take an interest in workers, but he was "the first to take literally the exhortation of the Holy Father to devote 'all the energy of his mind and all the strength of his endurance' to implementing the papal program. He resigned his pastorate to become writer, editor, lecturer, and organizer in the cause of trade unionism." Fox's dissertation director, Notre Dame's Professor Abell, added more in his Foreword [pp. v–vi], calling Dietz "the key figure" in the U.S. Catholic social movement during the first quarter of the twentieth century. Dietz was said to have foreseen the direction of the U.S. labor movement. Unlike Ryan and others, Dietz did not stress cooperatives and copartnerships as the more desirable solutions to the wave of strikes. He viewed these as "panaceas of reform" and insisted that real widespread change would only come from the labor movement. He was on more intimate terms with labor leaders than the rest of the Catholic clergy. Fox said labor history has been witness to the accuracy of Dietz's insights.

In a letter written to Fix in 1953, SAD's director, Fr. McGowan, took exception to some of the evaluative comments about Dietz.[11] Congratulating Fox for a detailed and readable book on Dietz, McGowan agreed that Dietz was "a great pioneer who had all but been forgotten until your book appeared.... But I think you made him too much of a person." He thought the real story came through, but Fox had made serious mistakes. First, many bishops and priests who defended labor at the time were taken up with other responsibilities. Second, "the times" militated against both the American Federation of Catholic Societies and Dietz's specific proposals. As a federation largely of fraternal insurance and ethnic societies after World War I, it produced only a plan of financing by the U.S. bishops in 1917. The Federation "thought the Bishops were now sufficiently interested in it, but it was not itself much interested." Third, it was not true that Bishop Muldoon thought Dietz had no place in the NCWC because of "pronounced stand on labor unions." By 1919, Dietz was opposed to the very minimum of social legislation, but the U.S. bishops' *Pastoral Letter of 1919* favored much social legislation. By that time, Dietz was said by Bishop Schrembs to be "apart and alone." So, why get Dietz involved in something with which he did not agree? Fourth, Ryan's view of unions as the chief agency for promoting workers' private ownership would resonate with Dietz's "growth and progressive development of unionism,"

---

[11] McGowan File, Catholic University Archives, August 7, 1953, McGowan to Fox.

but Fox, Abel, and Dietz missed the connection. Fifth, in discussing Dietz's dismissal from the Archdiocese of Cincinnati, Fox was said to have failed to stress sufficiently the role of Dietz's October anti–League of Nations and pro-Harding articles. The argument that the League of Nations could not use force was deemed "very ignorant." Dietz's November 1920 letter to the Chamber of Commerce opposing the open shop was preceded in March 1920 by SAD's denunciation of the Chamber of Commerce program as antiunion. Sixth, in November 1922, Schrembs and a not-so-reactionary Cincinnati archbishop defended the NCWC in Rome. McGowan thought the reasons for Dietz's dismissal from Cincinnati were not the ones Fox had alleged, namely that the archbishop was too reactionary. Seventh, too much was made of the NCWC's original Committee on Social Action, which died for lack of money, and it was SAD that called the Chicago meeting, where the Conference on Industrial Problems, as a membership organization, was inaugurated. It was assumed that the Conference would pay for itself and would receive only limited assistance from the NCWC.

Failings in Seminary Education

There were disagreements about the adequacy of seminary training to prepare seminarians for social justice work after ordination. In the late 1930s, St. Louis Fr. Leo Brown, S.J., a doctoral student in economics at Harvard University, made an indirect reference to such deficiency in seminary training.[12] Bemoaning the uninvited in terference of some priests in strike situations, Brown stressed, "It would be better if they stayed out of things. Instead they become a kind of disruptive influence and show their ignorance of the facts of life in industrial relations." Mentioned already was Fr. Louis Twomey, S.J., of New Orleans, a very vocal critic of Jesuit seminary education. In early 1942, SAD's Fr. John Hayes replied to Fr. Mark

---

[12] Brown File, Midwest Jesuit Province Archives, St. Louis, Missouri.

Ebner of the Cathedral Latin School in St. Louis, Missouri, concerning a comment made at a Catholic Educational Association Convention by Fr. Joseph Donovan, C.M., about seminary education.[13] Deeming the seminary a good undergraduate program, he said if more is attempted, what the Church expects from the program would be diminished. Donovan seemed quite satisfied with what was known as the curriculum or regime of most seminaries at that time—training in virtue, dogmatic theology, administration of the sacraments, preparations for canonical examinations, and internships with judicious and zealous pastors. An admitted need was an integral post-seminary program for priests "who are good but might be made infinitely better." Ebner's own experience was that internships in Catholic Action, as well as involvement in the Legion of Mary, Confraternity of Christian Doctrine, etc. "all too often seem to be working in reverse." Ebner's references were to comments that Hayes had made at a 1941 Conferences on Industrial Problems about social action classes and clubs in seminaries. Hayes agreed with Ebner's assessments. Donovan a great man, Hayes said, but he's slightly out of touch with the pope and actual seminary practice. "It would take more time to create a right attitude, one of sympathy and awareness of social problems, than it has taken in the past to build on a wrong attitude. Of course Pius XI asked for more, with his customary amplitude where priestly learning was concerned."

In mid-1945, New York's Fr. Philip Carey, S.J., wrote to Fr. Joseph Fitzpatrick, S.J., his predecessor as director of the Xavier Institute of Industrial Relations, encouraging him as he began a doctoral program in sociology at Harvard University.[14] Carey was convinced of the necessity of having people prepared to tell "authoritatively just what our Catholic program should be." Carey was certain that such

[13] Hayes File, Catholic University Archives, March 17, 1942, Hayes to Ebner.
[14] Carey File, New York Jesuit Provincial Archives, June 11, 1945, Carey to Fitzpatrick.

could be done only by "thorough study of the opposite philosophies, their well springs, their reasoning, their understanding of the facts of modern society, and the conclusions and programs that they then deduce." Admitting that he was utterly dissatisfied with the exposure to Catholic Social Teaching received in his days at Woodstock, the Jesuit theological training center, Carey confessed how very uncertain he was of himself, "because I do not know where I am going."

10

ASSOCIATION OF CATHOLIC TRADE UNIONISTS

Controversial Support for Labor

I n the late 1930s, as a Harvard doctoral student in economics, St Louis Fr. Leo Brown, S.J., objected to the strong public positions taken by SAD and ACTU in support of labor on almost every issue.[1] "Too much fervor for workers' rights at the expense of management results only in labeling you as pro-labor, thereby, diminishing your ability to gain a true perspective which might lead to more creative solutions to their problems." By 1942 when Brown was on the faculty of St. Louis University with Fr. Bernard Dempsey, S.J., Brown was predominantly associated with labor, due to his interest in establishing a Labor School. Dempsey, on the other hand, was close to business leaders, due to his expertise in fiscal and monetary policy.

Between late December 1944 and early January 1945 there was an exchange of correspondence between Higgins and Detroit ACTU's Paul Weber. On December 30, 1944, Weber was alarmed by the use of the name "Associated Catholic Union" in the Gary, Indiana, deanery council of the National Council of Catholic Women, as

---

[1] Brown File, Midwest Jesuit Provincial Archives, St. Louis, Mo.

mentioned in the October 1944 issue of Higgins's *Social Action Notes for Priests*.[2] Weber deemed that name as dangerous and an infringement upon the name of ACTU. Also, reference to "taking over union leadership" was judged to be dynamite. "If nothing else, I think we must take immediate steps to see that we are not confused with these people. They will break up all our operations if they approach the subject this way." Weber asked Higgins whom to contact in Gary to clear up the issue.

On January 2, 1945, Higgins, too, expressed alarm and said that the insertion in *Social Action Notes for Priests* was "an embarrassing accident."[3] Weber was advised to confer with Detroit's Archbishop Mooney to seek permission to make a formal statement in Detroit ACTU's *Wage Earner*, of which Weber was the editor. The statement should completely disassociate ACTU "from the new and very dangerous movement. I warn you that you will have to proceed cautiously for, as I understand it, Bishop Noll of Fort Wayne [Indiana], is actively encouraging and supporting the new venture." In closing, Higgins promised to seek further advice from Ryan and McGowan upon their return to SAD.

On January 3, 1945, Higgins wrote Weber (with copies to New York ACTU's Roger Larkin, Chicago Catholic Labor Alliance's Ed Marciniak, Fr. William Smith, S.J., and Fr. Benjamin Masse, S.J.) about President Tobin's editorial in the January issue of the *International Teamster*, entitled "Keep Religion Out, Tobin Orders."[4] For Higgins, the editorial was an "all-out blast at such comments as the ACTU, The Catholic Labor Alliance, etc." He asked Weber to delay any editorial until he could contact Tobin personally. He had already asked Tobin for a more complete expression, as well as a personal interview. Higgins suspected that Tobin's rather undignified

---

[2] Higgins File, Catholic University Archives, December 30, 1944, Weber to Higgins.

[3] Higgins File, Catholic University Archives, January 2, 1945, Higgins to Weber.

[4] Higgins File, Catholic University Archives, January 3, 1945, Higgins to Weber.

outburst was only done on an impulse. If a cat-and-dog fight started, Tobin would undoubtedly "be able to line up support from other labor leaders who may not at the moment share his extreme views."

On January 9, 1945, Higgins informed Weber that Ryan suggested ignoring the Gary affair: "If it has more success than he [Ryan] now feels that it will have, you could then, with perfect propriety, issue a public statement disassociating your own group from the Associated Catholic Union." There were also disagreements among labor priests over ACTU's effectiveness, relations with CIO unions, organization, methods, etc.

In March 1945 Higgins told Fr. William Kelly of the considerable confusion of Higgins, McGowan, and Miss Bresette of SAD found in Kelly's "friendly letter" of March 16, 1945.[5] In the most recent issue of *Social Action Notes for Priests* they could find only one reference that could be interpreted as "sniping from the rear" at the New York ACTU. That possible reference was a summary of the thinking of Midwesterners in Chicago and not merely Higgins's own thinking. The emphasis was on the Detroit ACTU, which was concerned about the establishment of an ACTU in Gary, Indiana, "a group which apparently is hell-bent on reforming the labor movement overnight." Long before that meeting in Chicago, Detroit Paul Weber had written SAD several times, expressing fears about the Fort Wayne ACTU. Higgins emphasized, "I trust that this background material will make it crystal clear that it was Weber and not Father Higgins who first raised the question."

Higgins was disturbed that Kelly suggested "patronizing the New York ACTU" and said, "God forgive me if I haven't the horse sense to appreciate the splendid work this group has done. Please advise what further steps I can take to apologize to the group for any false impression I may have left." With irony and needling, Higgins

---

[5] Higgins File, Catholic University Archives, March 19, 1945, Higgins to Kelly.

hoped Kelly was exaggerating when he implied the SAD was setting itself as a little pope to enforce "uniformity in everything affecting the social apostolate." He did not seek the job, he insisted,
but as long as he held it, Kelly would agree he could only call the
curves as he saw them. Would Kelly have Higgins strive for "uniformity in everything affecting the social apostolate? Apologizing
for any false impressions and insisting he was only reporting on the
Chicago meeting, he requested details on specific grievances about
the matter raised by the people Kelly had consulted.

On March 19, 1945, Higgins wrote New York ACTU's chaplain, Father John Monaghan, about the exchange with Kelly over the New
York ACTU.[6] Higgins enclosed Kelly's letter, but the only comment
made was, "I assure you that I would much prefer to resign my position at the NCWC rather than engage in an open controversy with
a group which was doing splendid work when I was still in the
seminary." Monaghan responded the next day in a handwritten
note.[7] Roger Larkin would write Higgins for the ACTU executive
board and represent their viewpoint entirely without being influenced by Monaghan. While training ACTU members to assume responsibility for Catholic lay action in the field of trade unionism,
Monaghan deliberately refrained from formulating ACTU policies.
Carefully avoiding clerical domination, as inimical to the lay apostolate, he was pleased to note that ACTU, in a large measure, justi-
fied the faith Church authorities had placed in it, but he was irri-
tated by the very foolish oracular judgments on ACTU emanating
from priests who only know 'about' ACTU."

Monaghan was fond of stressing the legitimate freedom of initiative
for lay apostles when they perceived sound Catholic interests to be
at stake. Yet New York's Fr. Kelly did not think such respect had

---

[6] Higgins File, Catholic University Archives, March 19, 1945, Higgins to Monaghan.
[7] Higgins File, Catholic University Archives, March 20, 1945, Monaghan to Higgins.

been extended by SAD's Cronin, Haas, Higgins, and McGowan.[8] They were said to be "friendly with ACTU leaders in many places [but] they were closer to their Washington labor circle." Some criticized ACTU as interfering and dividing unions along religious lines, either bluntly or slyly, by raising questions worth pondering, but never with any strong defense of ACTU. Kelly said Higgins [just out of graduate school] had said as much in *Commonweal* in 1944. Monaghan complained to Ryan, who said New York priests to disregard what came out of the SAD staff. Monaghan said, "We send priests to Washington to represent the Church and they end up representing Washington to the Church."

When Cronin repeated doubts about ACTU in *Catholic Social Action*, Monaghan persuaded *Commonweal*'s editors to print Kelly's response, "ACTU and Its Critics." Cronin and Higgins considered the New York ACTU leaders overly sensitive. So both repeated their view that the real source of complaints about ACTU leaders were activists in other cities. Both resented the New York ACTU allegations that both SAD members were more in tune with national labor leaders than with the rank-and-file members of crooked and Red-dominated unions. Kelly's rejoinder was, "New Yorkers stand on their judgment to this very day." Support for the New York ACTU came from Catholic University Fr. Paul Hanley Furfey, radical and pacifist, who, according to Kelly, referred to "ideologues in academia and vested bureaucrats, whose reference center was always removed from that field of workers."

Despite George Kelly's strong condemnation of Cronin and Higgins, Monaghan's own reactions were more measured with regard to Higgins, but very stern about Cronin.[9] Higgins was congratulated on his doctoral dissertation, evaluated as "informative and interesting—and very fair—good work." He was asked to send a copy

---

[8] Kelly 1989, *in passim*.

[9] Higgins File, Catholic University Archives, 1945 Monaghan to Higgins.

to New York's Dunwoodie Seminary, where it would be appreciated. Cronin was called the *l'enfant terrible* of Catholic social action. His latest articles in *Commonweal*, "The Communist Complex," his bewildering letter to New York ACTU Roger Larkin, his megalomania, and his "taking John Ryan's mantle" all led Monaghan to deem Cronin "very dangerous."

On March 24, 1945, Higgins apologized to New York ACTU's Roger Larkin "for whatever disservice I may have done to the ACTU in the latest issue of *Social Action Notes for Priests*. I assure you that I will make full amends in the next issue.[10] Referring to "our most recent misunderstanding growing out of my brief report on the Chicago priests' 'meeting'," Higgins offered eight points not as defenses, but as explanations. First, as he had already told Weber, Higgins's reference was to the situation in ACTU in Gary, Indiana, and not New York. As Kelly and Monaghan were told, it was Weber, not the NCWC, who first started talking about techniques. Higgins hoped Larkin would appreciate that Higgins was caught in the middle. Although he sometimes made mistakes, they were "not necessarily prompted by a perverse and juvenile bias against ACTU." Second, although New York ACTU was not present at the Chicago meeting, Clancy and other Detroit priests attended the entire meeting. They were said to be "100 percent pro–ACTU [and] this group (all of these dear friends of mine) expounded upon ACTU's position brilliantly and convincingly." The group agreed that all new ACTU units should not be established without considerable preparation. Furthermore, there was a very convivial exchange, with the Detroit ACTU playing a leading role. Third, if there was a disagreement about whether or not there was a national ACTU office, Higgins did not want to get involved in a family disagreement. Even if it was Higgins's clear understanding that "the Detroit ACTU would not at all be prepared to admit that there was a national office of the

---

[10] Higgins File, Catholic University Archives, January 9, 1945, Higgins to Larkin.

ACTU," he was prepared to be subject to correction. Fourth, as far as he could discern all participants at the meeting spoke as private individuals and not representatives of their respective groups. He would make that clear in the next issue of *Social Action Notes for Priests*. Fifth, Larkin was advised to contact Clancy for elaboration of his position and, if Larkin approved, Higgins would forward Larkin's correspondence to Clancy ahead of time. Sixth, the Chicago group did not try to spell out the meaning of "well prepared" with reference to beginning an ACTU group, with anything more than a completely "academic and unjustified" basis. The members of the Chicago meeting had a feeling that "groups might spring up in communities where the local personnel had merely a whiff of the Encyclicals [and] would appropriate the good name of the ACTU, purposes that "might later prove embarrassing to the ACTU itself." Higgins thought such was the feeling of Weber, who first raised the issue." Seventh, if a disservice was done to ACTU by his incompetent and superficial treatment of the problem, Higgins said, "I regret the mistake sincerely and will do whatever I can to correct it. Eighth, he thought it would be advisable for him to cease writing on the subject, which had begun with a friendly academic discussion, but ended up in needless friction and disharmony. With warm personal regards and admiration of the pioneer work of New York ACTU, he added, "As a matter of fact, I can't help but think that the whole thing has only been taken too seriously."

On December 1, 1950, Higgins sent Detroit ACTU's chaplain, Fr. Hubble, items about the recent controversy over Detroit ACTU, much talked about privately at the Chicago CIO convention.[11] Without criticism of Detroit ACTU, he preferred to avoid any public controversy, because attacks and counterattacks go on almost endlessly. With specific reference to attacks on CIO leaders "allegedly

---

[11] Higgins File, Catholic University Archives, December 1, 1950, Higgins to Hubble.

socialists," he preferred the language of Chicago Catholic Labor Alliance Edward Marciniak: "Liberals" rather than authentic "Socialists."

While there is no available record of George Kelly's response to Higgins's request for detailed charges about Higgins's 1945 remarks on the New York ACTU, other than Kelly's *Commonweal* article, there are details of a 1952 disagreement over CIO leadership and Socialism between Higgins and the Brooklyn Social Action director Fr. William Kelly, and his assistant directors, Fr. Joseph Hammond and Fr. Richard Hanley.[12] The dispute, focusing on a column Higgins had written about CIO president Walter Reuther's political views was laid out by Kelly and his assistants in four points. First, Higgins should have given qualification or proof that Reuther had abandoned his "Socialist Faith" much earlier. Second, about Reuther not being doctrinaire, there should have been added, "if the last x years (5,10,15) are any indication he will not be doctrinaire." Third, corrections were necessary because Higgins might have been quoted out of context and, as an authority, his statements might be used to convince many Catholics in the CIO in the event any problem arose in the future. "The effect of this would probably confuse rather than enlighten the people whom you so ably defend." Fourth, available evidence was needed that Reuther has irrevocably abandoned all the essential facets of Socialism. Only solid contrary evidence could convince a large number of doubtful people in light of strong and concurring rumors that Reuther still might be a "Blanshardite." Kelly closed by thanking Higgins for the compliment of his request and in the hope that Kelly and his assistants had not been too blunt.

A day later, Higgins thanked Kelly for his "characteristically gracious, prompt, and incisive reply to my request for comments on

---

[12] Higgins File, Detroit Archdiocesan Archives, December 11, 1952, Kelly to Higgins.

the Reuther column."[13] He explained his failure to send the proposed column earlier to the Brooklyn Diocesan Social Action team and a dozen other priests and expressed substantial agreement with the criticism. There was the probability that he would have occasion to incorporate the criticisms, anonymously, in a later column on the subject. He had some misgivings about Reuther and even more about some of his staff, but he was willing to give Reuther the benefit of the doubt (for strategic reasons). However, he would let Reuther know that "we will be watching him rather carefully in the near future." Although some Catholics in the CIO headquarters strongly urged him not to raise the socialist issue at all, he thought it was necessary to raise the issue courteously, in order to encourage Reuther to keep his distance from "the long hairs."

That strategy was discussed confidentially with McGowan and some of Reuther's ACTU associates in the UAW when they were in Atlantic City. To accuse Reuther personally would have been a strategic mistake and possible injustice. However, Reuther needed to be needled occasionally about some of his associates, "just to let him know he is being watched." Having put Reuther on his guard, Higgins felt perfectly free to attack him personally, if Reuther indicated any sympathy for the socialist cause. Kelly's timely and gracious letter to Reuther was "just the sort of thing the doctor ordered [and] I hope many other priests throughout the United States will send him similar messages of congratulations." McGowan and Higgins requested a meeting at Reuther's convenience. By that time, Reuther would have read Higgins's column. "I am reasonably certain he will not be very happy about it, for I am advised by some of his Catholic associates in UAW that he is very sensitive about the socialist issue." Higgins wanted to be informed if any of Reuther's friends in the New York area misinterpreted or misrepresented the column, so that the record could be corrected. In closing, he said,

---

[13] Higgins File, Detroit Archdiocesan Archives, December 12, 1952, Higgins to W. Kelly.

223

"Bill, please accept my renewed thanks for your very great kindness in sending me such an intelligent analysis of the column. Kindest regards to Joe and Dick."

In the early 1950s the Detroit ACTU's chaplain, Fr. Hubble, sent a memorandum to Edward Cardinal Mooney of Detroit about the necessity and functions of ACTU parish conferences.[14] While the articles of the ACTU Constitution defined ACTU's purpose in terms of ultimate ends, the cardinal defined ACTU's purposes in terms of its effects on its members. Hubble noted that any differences among ACTU chapters in various cities, even New York, were about means and methods, never about goals or purposes. All agreed ACTU's basic method and activity was education. Mooney's view of ACTU methods was to select members, indoctrinate them in Christian principles, train them to apply the same in daily work life, and send them back to their unions. All was aimed at enabling them to inculcate, formulate, and implement Christian and American basic values in the policy and programs of their unions.

In reply to Mooney, Hubble said such functions were already being fulfilled in New York ACTU Labor Schools and in Detroit's Archdiocesan Labor Institute (ALI) under Clancy, composed of priest directors and teachers, as well as Detroit ACTU's president, Paul Weber, serving on the ALI Board and ACTU members assisting parish priest-directors of the parish Labor Schools. While several people thought such education was not sufficient and ACTU should be involved in organized activity within unions, Mooney thought that the ALI should teach the principles and ACTU should put them into effect. Hubble was said to have thought that, perhaps, what Mooney meant was, "The prime purpose [of ACTU] is to make the Catholic membership in the unions an organized force for sound unionism." However, the Constitution of Detroit ACTU said, "ACTU shall assist it members in applying Christian principles to

---

[14] Mooney File, Detroit Archdiocesan Archives 1950, Hubble to Mooney.

the problems of their respective unions, and shall formulate and recommend policies to this end." Hubble added that in Detroit the "conference" method was originally adopted as an anticommunist tactic. Conferences were described as "permanent counter-minorities...permanent core of leadership to give successful opposition to the [Communist Party]."

Admitting that the full story of these conferences still remained to be told, Hubble maintained that the failure of some conferences was due to personal and policy disagreements. He said very directly that it was impossible for some conferences not to become targets for criticism by unions and others because of a political-religious caucus and the inherent weaknesses of groups. For five years, save for the Teachers' Conference, which was involved in the University of Detroit–Guild controversy, there were practically no activities of the conferences. ACTU did fulfill its educational function through lectures, discussion forums, talks to nonmembers, and the Detroit ACTU newspaper, the *Wage Earner*, etc. Yet, even before attendance fell off, the conferences reached very few Catholic union members.

Convinced that ACTU faced a crossroad and "the only salvation lies in reorganization on the basis of the parish or inter-parish units or conferences," Hubble thought it necessary to understand the factors that caused the parish Labor Schools to vanish: too much work for the parish priest-director to do, superficial training, limited time, and other pressing demands. "At the time we tried to persuade ACTU members that their organization would have to take over the responsibility of the Labor Schools if they were to last. We still do." He thought ACTU parish conferences gave hope of more permanent effects, but did not view them as Labor Schools. The term "school" suggested a temporary process of learning and the goals were too ambitious in "plunging the students into the middle of the woods of encyclical doctrine and economic problems without sustained emphasis on fundamental attitudes of mind for motivating and directing Catholics into and in union activity."

In Hubble's mind, the inculcation and development of such attitudes, convictions, and principles "should be the fundamental task of ACTU." Pulpit sermons and inspirational talks were no substitutes for close association with people sharing those attitudes and principles, namely, those in parishes. Unlike preachers or speakers, small groups of fellow union members can appreciate the "headaches, heartaches, grief, frustration, discouragement, enmities, bewilderment, time-away-from-home, sacrifice, and weariness" unionists are asked to undergo. ACTU can prepare material to be discussed in the context of basic attitudes and principles. Maximizing the benefits of the parish conferences would entail periodic and well-publicized open forums made attractive by well-known and respected speakers, usually from ACTU. Hubble pointed to the successes of such attitudes and principles being utilized. The people who worked hardest in the ACTU educational program became most influential in their own unions. "New members have become full-fledged Actists. Several have begun to be active in their unions. New support has been found for the *Wage Earner*. ACTU in convention action has focused the principal activity for this year on the extension of parish units."

In late 1956 a memorandum to Mooney, presumably drafted by Hubble, pertained to Detroit ACTU leaving the national ACTU.[15] It was a story of tension between ACTU in Detroit and Chicago and ACTU in New York, especially its president Donahue's efforts to establish a national ACTU office, with himself as director and a national ACTU newspaper. Such steps were beyond the original ACTU constitution, which called for a director to establish and maintain liaison among the chapters and to promote new chapters in dioceses where none existed. A 1950 amendment added the director's duties "to publicize the work of ACTU as widely as possible and conduct fund-raising drives in cooperation with local chapters

---

[15] Mooney File, Detroit Archdiocesan Archives, November 3, 1956, Hubble to Mooney.

and directly to the end of maintaining a financially independent national office." By 1952 Donahue had failed to raise enough to support his activities as national director, and he was out of office.

Also reported was the split in the New York ACTU, with the resignation of Fr. Monaghan and his successor as chaplain. With Higgins's off-the-record statement about ACTU considered all but "dead" nationally, other chapters following the direction of Detroit ACTU. Detroit's disaffiliation would lead to the disappearance of a national ACTU. If such ensued, there was the need to change the name to the "Detroit Catholic Labor Conference," but most importantly the strengthening of ACTU's educational functions at various levels and through various types of media. The memorandum concluded that informal unity would be much more effective in influencing unions than any more formalized discipline, such as "organized conferences" within each group. Such an informal unity might enable AFL–CIO unity on state and county levels, Catholics in the UAW to evaluate and mitigate the materialistic humanism of its educational program, and Catholics in the Teamsters and Building Trades to understand selfish, narrow-minded, bread and butter unionism and Catholic pork-choppers.

11

LABOR PRIESTS' SELF-IDENTITY

Yorke, Monaghan, Corridan, McGowan, & Vizzard

Another key aspect of the labor priests' movement was the self-identity or changes in the self-identity of participants in the movement. Because labor priests have been neglected for the most part in earlier research, little can be said of changes in these priests' self-identity. Some glimpses into their self-identity appear here—even at a time in the Catholic Church when little attention was being given to such psychological dimensions of one's vocation and ministry and when the labor priests' activities were rather untraditional and controversial. Insights into priestly identity sometimes came from the priests' own statements and sometimes from the statements of others who came to know them personally. Revelations about the labor priests' self-identity as priests most often surfaced in their exchanges with other priests, public tributes, or eulogies. Often such expressions revealed cries of the heart in the midst of a difficulty, especially in relation to bishops or religious superiors, whose actions labor priests often challenged. These were typically phrased in terms of scriptural or papal texts. Descriptions by others of labor priests' self-identity as priests were usually in terms of their actions or teaching, often with reference to religious texts. Caution is necessary, however, in that much that others might infer is not necessarily always be within parameters of the labor priests' own self-image. Yet, such speculation is better than nothing at all!

San Francisco's Fr. Yorke had years of active, successful, and controversial ministry. In the late 1890s he was considered to be "a suitable candidate for the dignity and responsibility of the Episcopacy" four times. Each time his habit of conveying that "what he felt ought to be said was more dear...than Episcopal purple" drew negative reactions [pp. 41–42].[1] After various "suspect" charges were lodged against him, he resigned as editor of the archdiocesan newspaper and chancellor, saying, "I reserve to myself the right of making public all my reasons for my action at such time and in such manner as I shall judge best to protect my name and the integrity of my motives" [p. 43]. In March 1899 he had a warm audience with Leo XIII, who seemed impressed with Yorke [pp. 52–53].

Upon returning to San Francisco, Yorke was feted by laity, nuns, and priests. However, he met with chilly indifference from Archbishop Riordan. Yorke endured humiliations and was deemed an ecclesiastical "has-been" at thirty-four years of age. Some called him puffed up, but Brushser thought that "if ever a priest practices humility and accepted humiliation without calling a press conference to denounce 'unfeeling bishops', it was Yorke at this time" [p. 5]. By the 1901 Seamen's strike and other labor strife, Yorke was once again praised. The *Seamen's Journal* in May 1925 spoke of labor's assurance that Yorke never counted the cost of helping all suffering from need or injustice [p. 69]. With reference to Yorke's championing Catholic schools, the *Baltimore Catechism*, religious textbooks, scripture, and liturgy, Brusher said Yorke was a man with the common sense and energy "to have the genius to transcend the limitations of their own time and to realize the essential." Yet,

---

[1] Brusher 1971.

despite many achievements, "It is probable that the fiery priest's most effective influence was as an educator" [pp. 84–96].

When Archbishop Hanna came to San Francisco, he and Yorke seemed to get along. In April 1925 Hanna preached Yorke's eulogy. After reviewing Yorke's work, Hanna said, "A man of marked distinction among his fellow men, a constant, loyal friend, a faithful earnest priest, a mighty teacher, Christ's champion of the ramparts of Israel has passed from life to his reward" [pp. 250–54]. Brusher added his own assessment of Yorke's life as orator and person, but especially his moral courage. "When he believed in a principle whether it was tolerance, social justice, or nationality he did not hesitate to go from belief to action, from speculation to the rough reality of application." Brusher thought that without moral courage, Yorke might have been popular, been a bishop and enjoyed a smoother life. However, he also would not have been able to offset bigotry, support workers' rights, or mobilize American opinion behind Ireland's freedom from Great Britain. "He might have accomplished a great deal but he would not have been San Francisco's "Consecrated Thunderbolt" [pp. 296–71].

An earlier evaluation of Yorke appeared in 1943: Most laborers at that time revered Yorke as the father of the labor movement in San Francisco[2] [pp. 219–21]. Cronin felt that a lack of social vision and sense of civic responsibility was the reason for Yorke's harsh attacks on civil authorities and industrial leaders. Such was "a threat to peace and order, and afforded radicals an excuse to introduce their programs. Conversely, industrial progress and the general social well-being were, in his opinion, dependent on the prosperity and degree of industrial democracy enjoyed by wage earners" [p. 228]. Despite allegations that Yorke was using workers for his own personal gains, he insisted that his warranty for speaking on the labor

---

[2] Cronin 1943.

question was Church teaching, especially Leo XIII's [p. 95]. He argued that the first step to offset any control of unions by incompetent labor leaders and crafty politicians was personal morality. "[Your] power of character, standing by the great truths, the great powers of religion will determine for you what shall be the future of the labor party." He also cited Leo XIII in condemning false notions concerning human nature and destiny, such as "maximum satisfaction with the least possible expenditure of energy" [p. 123].

A more recent evaluation of Yorke, which appeared in 1987, contains interesting comments on Yorke's relationship to the Irish community of San Francisco.[3] Noting that some characterized Yorke as kind of a "Peck's bad boy," a single-minded Irish nationalist and militant in misleading his people, Lyons acknowledged that Yorke was one of the founders and leaders of the San Francisco labor movement, but demurred on his leadership role for the Irish. Instead of rallying the Irish community for economic progress and political leadership, Yorke "offered isolation rather than assimilation, frugality rather than prosperity, and political timidity rather than leadership." Yorke's sin was to use his preaching, speaking, and writing to oppose "Americanization" of the San Francisco Irish — opposing the melting pot theory, in favor of pluralism — long before the terms were in vogue, long before the former was cast aside and the latter embraced by most reputable social scientists.

In addition to biographical material on Yorke, several reflective pieces are noteworthy. The earliest of these appeared sometime in the 1970s, prompted by priests involved in Chavez's farm workers' strikes in the late 1960s.[4] To people who cast doubts on the validity of Yorke's use of *Rerum Novarum*, Bergman replied that when an employer asked Archbishop Riordan to silence Yorke during one

---

[3] Lyons 1987.
[4] Bergman 1970.

strike, Riordan replied that Yorke was merely explaining the encyclical. Bergman concluded that Fr. Keith Kenny and Fr. James Vizzard, S.J., legitimated their involvement in the Delano strike very much as Yorke had more than sixty years earlier [pp. 39–40]. In November 1978 Bergman published another article, a critique of Brusher's treatment of Yorke, using Brusher's and others' source material.[5] With a general approval of Brusher's account, Bergman detected a failure to "to bring out the full fascination of Yorke's career, and to define it in the context of Church history" [p. 37]. When the Church was institutionally conservative, Yorke was a precursor of Vatican II's view that the Church should actively "grapple with the questions troubling the minds of men" [p. 37]. Both Yorke and the priest Roncalli, later Pope John XXIII, between 1906 and 1907, used *Rerum Novarum* and "represented a progressive trend in the Church, then submerged, even suppressed" [p. 37]. Bergman thought Brusher was not aware of or had not reflected on efforts of Riordan, during his rift with Yorke, to raise funds from wealthy Catholics for construction of a cathedral and seminary [pp. 40–41]. Also, Bergman likened Yorke's failure to be a conciliator, as "father of all" in *Rerum Novarum*, to Archbishop Helder Camara of Recife, Brazil, who had urged the Church to set aside its "preoccupations with prestige…[and] become an effective servant of the poor." Also cited was Camara's saying that by conniving with or retreating before economic power, the Church "inculcates in believers fatalism as to poverty, serves as the opiate of the people" [pp. 43–44]. Brusher was congratulated for citing Yorke's condemnation of the heresy of the "superior race" in the Spanish-American War, Jewish pogroms in Russia as a crime against humanity and Christianity, eviction of American Indians from southern California, and the Ku Klux Klan.

---

[5] Bergman 1978.

Yet, Brusher was criticized for failing to note Yorke's support for the Chinese Exclusion Act, since he feared the continuance of Chinese immigration would undercut wages and costs jobs as scapegoats of the economic depression. His "Irish tribalism seems to have gotten in the way of his sense of 'racial heresy', of social justice, and of Catholic universalism" [pp. 45–46]. Referring to outspoken support of Irish nationalism, Bergman called him the Martin Luther King Jr. and Malcolm X of the Irish. "His dramatic style sacrificed accuracy for effect. The effect often was true to reality, just as an artist's brush strokes often bring out character better than does a photograph" [p. 51]. Bergman said that whatever Yorke's words or deeds, the Church should hail Yorke not as the "Surpliced Blackguard" but as the "Matchless Warrior" [pp. 51–52].

An evaluation of Yorke in 1973 by James P. Walsh focused on his failure to integrate Irish Catholics into the mainstream of American political and intellectual life.[6] After an overview of Yorke's early life, the American Protestant Association (APA) controversy, political and labor involvements, and support of the Irish-Americans, Walsh said, "Obsessed by the need to right every fancied slight to Irish and Catholics, Yorke became a permanent embarrassment and irritant to the hierarchy and a sheer delight to his working-class admirers" [pp. 19–21, 25–32]. In 1973 Walsh concluded that as well-meaning as Yorke was, he failed to chip the ghetto mentality and refused to further the dialogue between Irish Catholic labor and non-Catholic American culture. Two years later, Walsh wrote another article about Yorke that focused on the relationship of the progressives in academia, business, and professional life to the Irish-American community as represented by Yorke.[7] Extolling Yorke's contributions to the Irish-Catholic and labor causes, especially by fortifying turn-of-the-century Catholic organizers who would have advanced apprehensively without some form of Church sanction,

---

6 Walsh 1973, 19–21, 25–32.
7 Walsh 1975, 73–81.

Walsh pointed out another Yorke blind spot. Irish-Americans, thanks especially to Yorke, were convinced that government was so complicated that only politicians could make it work. Thus, with San Francisco Irish, "Yorke rejected the bold progressive assertion that the politician was a roadblock between the people and the government."

The most recent reflective piece on Yorke—written in 1981 by Timothy Sarbaugh—focused on his failure to give consistent and sincere support to striking workers in favor of support for the case of the Irish Catholics.[8] Specific reference was made to the 1916 longshoremen's strike, which he assisted only much later after others had approached him, in contrast to the 1901 strike that embraced so many Irish-Americans. After presenting many signs of his lukewarm interest, Sarbaugh concluded that Yorke was not as great a champion of labor in San Francisco as Brusher's and others' "historiographical assessment" had led many to believe.

When Chicago Fr. Reynold Hillenbrand was a seminarian at Mundelein Seminary he was known to have "developed [a] personal attachment to the papacy and papal teaching that would be the leitmotiv of his life." His dissertation on the indwelling of the Holy Spirit predated the papal encyclical on the Mystical Body. Avella added, "The renewed emphasis on the immanence of God and the power of God's activity in the heart of the believer would be an important back-drop for Hillenbrand's later work in liturgical and social reform and his encouragement of lay activism." As rector of Mundelein Seminary, the core of Hillenbrand's vision was "the goal of social reconstruction according to the corporatist or organized vision of society adumbrated in the social encyclicals. Clearly, this version of society was at the heart of his liturgical and social reform interests." At the 1945 National Liturgical Week, he spoke of "peo-

---

[8] Sarbaugh 1981.

ple worldwide being sick of individualistic, subjective piety because it lacks depth and vision." He argued that reaction to the sordid and stinking individualism in political and economic, industrial, and international life, which has "left the world in shambles." Indeed, as seminary rector, Hillenbrand had a lasting imprint on many labor priests, as Msgr. Jack Egan and Msgr. George Higgins often proclaimed privately and publicly.

New York Fr. John P. Monaghan was extolled with the title "the benign agitator."[9] Such was the fitting epitaph that Monaghan foreshadowed in the column of his bulletins, entitled "Don Capelliano." He was saddened by priests failing to speak and work against slums, "against the impersonal tyranny of union-hating corporations, against the human belittlement of old workers, foreign workers, and underpaid workers, and had little awareness of the world he lived in and less awareness of the world he was trying to reach." One of Monaghan's former students at New York's Cathedral College recalled a likely Monaghan yell, "My God, man, no one under forty is entitled to be tired.... The poor need you, and not just those in the parish."[10] When New York's Francis Cardinal Spellman expressed outrage over the jailing of Archbishop Alois Stepinac by Yugoslavia's Marshall Tito, Monaghan told Spellman that the spiritual life of the Church was never better than when bishops were jailed.

In early 1953, New York's Fr. Philip Carey, S.J., expressed thanks for the wholehearted support from religious superiors during his and Fr. John Corridan, S.J.'s efforts in assisting New York dockworkers and others.[11] Reacting to talk about the threats to cut off donations to the Jesuits, Carey said, "What are we in this business for if it be not for helping men to save themselves in this world and

---

[9] Avella 1994.
[10] Lynch 1997.
[11] Kelly 1989.

the next." With a request for prayers, Carey confessed, "[For] there is nothing in all this work except headaches and worry. Our only reward will be the fact that good men like you [a layman named Murray] will be able to lead decent Christian lives while doing the heavy labor and honest work on the docks."

During the eulogy for Carey, his predecessor, Fordham University sociologist Fr. Joseph Fitzpatrick, S.J., quoted excerpts from a letter he had received from Carey with a long list of sinful and corrupt situations in the ranks of labor and management.[12] Enclosed in the letter was a copy of the homily Carey gave on the fiftieth anniversary of his ordination to the priesthood. Fitzpatrick said, "Tears came to my eyes as I read it.... No words of mine can compare with Phil's own statement of the meaning of his life." Referring to Old Testament priests, Carey cited their lack of inheritance, with only the Lord as their portion, residing in cities scattered through the tribes, being isolated and lonely, holding their hands up to God so that they might bring God down to the hearts of His Chosen people. Referring to New Testament disciples, Carey said Christ demanded that they leave everything and follow Him. Carey then exclaimed, "And really, isn't that what it's all about! To spend one's life for God, to pour it out for brothers and sisters!" He told of once hearing his father tell him, "Don't waste your priesthood on God's holy ladies.... They are God's devout ones. It's the grizzly guys like me who need you." Despite his heartaches and anxieties, people gave him support and joy. Very conscious of his own failings and limitations as a priest, he had the joy of "helping his fellow travelers along the dusty road to eternity." He then spoke about his priesthood being with teamsters, sand hogs, and dockworkers. "[Men] who think and pray, not with the twisting of the philosophers, but who come to God with ideas and goals they can squeeze in their fists.... [The] gnarled and deeply holy people God has sent my way."

---

[12] Corridan File, New York Jesuit Province Archives, January or February 1953.

Fitzpatrick characterized Carey as deeply spiritual, unpretentious, generous, dutiful, an almost scrupulous and humble priest. Such was the core of Carey's life and priesthood, dedicated almost entirely to workers and their families, mostly in the New York Metropolitan area. His focus would always be workers' material and spiritual interests, striving to train leaders with the vision and skills racketeers and communist leaders pretended to offer, but always with tactful and indirect challenges. Frequently frustrated, downplaying or doubting both his ability and perseverance, and unable to get all the help he needed, Carey was always quite frank with diocesan and religious superiors.

In 1955, near the end of Allen Raymond's and the Henry Holt Company's publication *Waterfront Priest*, its prototype, New York Fr. John Corridan, reflected on his mission in the Church: "I certainly didn't come to this place as a knight in shining armor. I came as a priest, and a lot of people asked what business a priest had doing the kind of thing I've been doing. A lot of priests have gone before me and a great many more will follow, long after I'm gone."[13] He quoted from Luke's Gospel story of Jesus telling the apostles to launch out into the deep and telling the humbled Peter that henceforth he would catch others. "That's part of the job of any priest. He is looking for men—and women, too—who will truly serve God. That's been one of my great rewards in working with longshoremen around the docks. I've found some." He told of men who stood up and resisted evil, risked their lives in fighting tyranny, and went home each night with a clean conscience. "I'm looking for more." Discouraged when men lost jobs or were killed, he sighed that many people would have things better off, "because these men lived and made the fight.... A good many people have to sow seed in their lives and be content if they never see the harvest."

---

[13] Carey File, New York Jesuit Province Archives, *in passim.*

Yet, Raymond also found a happier, lighter, and pious side to Corridan. Using slang and chain-smoking, balanced by formal diction and "pushing the book" [finishing before midnight a priest's required prayers for the day by reading from a collection of Scriptural and Church Fathers' texts]. Corridan took an almost childish delight. "Some of the priests that are coming along now are ex–GIs. They know now that there's plenty of room in the church for priests who do more that swing a smoke pot.... There's nothing new to realize you can serve God by helping people." Corridan's eyes lit up talking about longshoremen, living and dead, who became friends and helped him. Raymond said Corridan "really loved them and loves his work." When conversation turned to cleaning up New York's waterfront, Corridan was sad but frank. "The rank-and-file dockworkers have lost this fight, and they won't make another fight for a long time to come. I've lost. I believe the city and people of New York [have] lost. The mobsters won .... The more unscrupulous elements within the shipping industry won." Raymond also said Corridan showed great concern about the city's spiritual harm by citing Pius XI's "[The] issue of our time is *for or against God*," as well as Corridan's own striking words, "Not until we can bring the spirit of Almighty God into our daily economic, political, and social lives can our city prosper. We have a longer and harder fight here than the fight against Communism. Communism is just the Russian version of materialism. On the waterfront we've got the American version."

In March 1999, at a University of Notre Dame Cushwa Center conference, Professor James Fisher of St. Louis University gave a paper on Corridan.[14] Of interest here were some comments Fisher made during the discussion period. Corridan, Fisher said, told Bud Schulzberg, director of the film *On the Waterfront*, "Bud, you can make a 'Going My Way' with substance." Also, Karl Malden, who played

---

[14] Corridan File, New York Jesuit Province Archives, excerpts from *Waterfront Priest*.

Corridan in the film, spoke lines said to be Corridan's—"This is my parish"—as well as the sermon on the crucifixion over the hold of the ship where a dissident had been murdered. Similar lines were supposed to have been voiced in 1948 when Corridan addressed the Knights of Columbus in New York.

In the summer of 1984 a former Jesuit, J. McGrail, answered an inquiry about Corridan from a Jesuit playwright, Fr. Neil Hurley, S.J.[15] While living in the Jesuit residence at Xavier from 1953 to 1963, McGrail had made efforts to gain some insights into Corridan and Carey. Both were said to be "enigmatic" characters McGrail were never able to understand. Attempts to draw out Corridan and to interest him in Xavier High School found Corridan not very communicative. "Though devoted to his job and diligent at it, he did not appear to me to be a thoroughly happy and joyful soul." McGrail thought it was due to Corridan's falling into the "Short Course," for Jesuits who manifested "outside interests," rather than attending classes and studying theology. "Such a 'fall' used to cause a stifling of all intellectual ambition, even in cases of some possessing a magnificent mind and great intelligence." McGrail did not know if Corridan had any friends, even Carey. "They seemed to have been walking down separate, parallel tracks, even during the time of Pete's [nickname] trouble—if one may fairly call standing up for longshoremen's rights and standing against their being victimized by the system, trouble." McGrail deemed Corridan "a kind of hero," who did battle in a segment of the real world, "in which there was an element of danger about which my knowledge, as opposed to his, was almost nil, and about which no serious effort was made to make us cognizant." McGrail encouraged Hurley in his efforts "to perpetuate Pete's memory in a movie that would do justice to him as a true apostle in a cause that was not always popular, as a fighter

---

[15] Corridan File, Fisher, James, "Covering the Waterfront: Culture and Ideology in the Catholic Metropolis, 1936–1960," a preliminary paper, New York Jesuit Province Archives.

for justice and as one who gave large proof of his devotion to his fellow man."

In mid-2003 Peter Steinfels wrote in his *New York Times* "Beliefs" column about Budd Schulberg, 1954 Oscar Award winner for the best story and screenplay, *On the Waterfront*."[16] The piece was occasioned by Schulberg's talk about Corridan at Fordham University. Schulberg said that Corridan—model for the film's Fr. Barry, the waterfront priest played by Karl Malden—was the moving spirit behind the whole film. Initially, Corridan was not receptive to the movie-making and was quoted by Schulberg as saying, "We're doing tough stuff down here and don't need a Hollywood movie." While making the film, Schulberg and the director, Elia Kazan, argued about including in the movie an entire sermon Corridan had actually given many times about the crucifixion happening wherever injustice was done to workers. Eventually Kazan agreed. In closing, Steinfels said there were now plenty of Corridans—clerical and lay   of many creeds giving hope and expertise to workers, migrants, homeless, battered women, ex-cons…. The question is, How many Budd Schulbergs are there?

In 2003 a New York archdiocesan seminarian [now a priest] cited one of Corridan's undated Labor Day sermons.[17] In it, Corridan described how the life of a worker was related to the work and life of Christ, how Catholic Social Teaching (especially from papal encyclicals) stressed the dignity and God-like quality of work and how one's final judgment by God depended not on one's annual income, but by respect for the God-like dignity in ourselves and others while earning one's income. He quoted from Corridan's sermon in the hold of the ship, reminding workers of Jesus' words that what we do to others we do to him, Corridan spoke of Christ realizing what it meant to provide food and shelter, stand in the shape-up to be

---

[16] Corridan File, New York Jesuit Province Archives, August 15, 1984, McGrail to Hurley.

[17] Steinfels 2003.

hired for that shift. Comparing the injustices of working on the docks to the crucifixion of Christ, Corridan spoke of Christ's aching back, aware of the racket-runners who took 20 percent of the long-shoremen's wages and aware of the silence and indifference at union meetings.

In a late 2003 interview, based partially on the research of Fordham Professor James Fisher, some Jesuits who knew Corridan gave brief assessments of him and his ministry.[18] Fr. William Reilly, S.J., re-membered Corridan as "popular, very friendly, and mixed in very well." Fr. Anthony LaBau, S.J., recalled Corridan's reaction when he made enemies for helping dockworkers against corrupt union officials. "Pete walked right past it. He really was courageous. No-body could threaten him, no one could demand he desist.... He stuck right to it."

When Corridan died in 1984, Fr. Joseph Fitzpatrick, S.J., wrote in *Catholic New York*, "It was sad to see so few people at his Mass of Christian Burial [at Fordham University Church]. Had it occurred 30 years ago, his Mass would have needed the cathedral [St. Pat-rick's]. There would have been thousands...the world then was ready to stand up and shout: 'Here was a man'."

In late 1951, Joseph Stocker, a freelance writer studying social prob-lems in southwestern United States, wrote "Father Dunne: A Study in Faith."[19] To explain the article's title, Stocker quoted Dunne: "It's a matter of faith.... Either I believe in the things the Church stands for or I don't. If not, there is no sense in remaining a Catholic. If I do believe in these things, they don't cease to be true because of the actions of the hierarchy." Stocker asserted that Dunne believed he represented "authentic Catholic thought" and not the hierarchy,

---

[18] McCarthy 2003.
[19] McDonnell 2003.

dismissing them as "ministers of mediocrity who consistently sacrifice truth and justice to expediency."

In late 1962 SAD's Cronin extolled Fr. McGowan, during a eulogy
in Kansas City, as possessing "a delicate and wonderful sense of
humor and the warm charm of those who see God in every person
and every creature that God has made."[20] Praising McGowan's absolute integrity, Cronin said "Father McGowan was tenacious and
unbelievably stubborn in holding for what he considered to be the
correct application of Catholic social principles. Arguments could
not budge him, nor induce him to compromise."

During a Month's Mind Mass in Washington, D.C., SAD's Higgins
characterized McGowan's distinctive qualities.[21] First, imaginative
vision coupled with a rare degree of daring and initiative! Second,
stubborn and unyielding courage, never dramatic or self-conscious!
Third, contagiously cheerful and good-natured patience springing
from a hidden life of prayer! Four, a disinterested and self-effacing
modesty and humility! In a February 8, 2001, "Yardstick" article,
Higgins also mentioned a major disappointment for him. How little
had been written or survived in archives about McGowan—a decent priest who made such a difference on the Church and society,
long before others even dreamed of such. In late 1962 *America* editors extolled McGowan's achievements, calling him "a great-souled
priest and tireless apostle of Catholic social action."[22]

In mid-1957, to a rousing ovation, Hartford Fr. Joseph Donnelly addressed Connecticut State Labor Council's first convention by praising the support of labor unions by Leo XIII, England's Cardinal
Manning, and Baltimore's Cardinal Gibbons.[23] Such was deemed

---

[20] Stocker 1951.

[21] McGowan File, Catholic University Archives, after November 17, 1962.

[22] Higgins File, Social Action Notes for Priests, December 1962.

[23] Editorial, *America*, 1962, 1167.

only fitting because, the priest represented Jesus, who as a trades-man with hammer and saw, gave new honor and dignity to work-ers. When the first labor priests gave strong support to workers, they may have sounded like revolutionaries, but they were simply proclaiming "that while the priest and the prelate [are] dedicated to all men equally, he must have a special interest in the problems and the welfare of the men who labor."

In mid-1965 SAD's Higgins preached at Donnelly's ordination as a bishop.[24] Donnelly was said to have fulfilled the ideal expressed by Pope Paul VI when he was archbishop of Milan. The priest must move to the people by hearing in factory sirens the technical source for the world's living and breathing. "It is for the priest to make himself a missionary if he would Christianity abide and become a new living leaven of civilization." Donnelly's coat of arms—invari-ably the bishop's attempt to portray his ministry—was described and explained. The episcopal motto was *Opus justitia pax*, a refer-ence to Donnelly's dedication to the truth that "peace can come only from the application of justice." Donnelly was said to be par excel-lence the type of apostle Pius XI had in mind, when toward the end of his encyclical *On Reconstructing the Social Order*, he instructed the bishops of the world "to assign specially qualified priests to the so-cial apostolate." Finally, with reference to the mound of green earth supporting a cross that signified Donnelly's work as director of the Hartford Archdiocese's cemeteries and testified to his heeding the instruction of Pius XI's *Atheistic Communism*. Higgins added, "A priest...who has the duty of administering temporal goods must bear in mind that he is obliged not only to observe the laws of justice and charity, but also that he must make a particular effort to show himself a real father to the poor."

---

[24] Donnelly File, Hartford Archdiocesan Archives, June 26, 1957, Donnelly to Hackett.

In 1979 Harry Browne—historian, sociologist, husband, and father, as well as resigned priest of the New York Archdiocese, tape-recorded his reflections on Chicago and Notre Dame Msgr. Jack Egan.[25] Egan's humor "wasn't an ego trip of special savior priests but boring from within for new institutional direction." His rhetoric and manipulative ways were "leading you down the primrose path with questions about how you were different from a social worker.... But then it all became a blur of Jack's presence like a great sun over the shoulder of my ministry." Browne referred to Egan as "the underground Eminence of the American Church." His many ways of connecting the boondocks and love-bureaucracy of social justice caring-ones around the country demonstrated that position. His hierarchical connections always intrigued me." Browne was amazed that the agenda of the Catholic Committee on Urban Ministry (CCUM) had become the national Church's agenda because of the role played by CCUM people in the 1976 "Call to Action" Convention in Detroit. "I think [it was] a great tribute to Jack and those of us who had been his aides and abettors, and co-conspirators." Realizing it was extreme to compare anyone to the sunshine in one's life, Browne said Egan had a warming glow, with his constant presence, encouraging calls, or notes. He "never missed a chance to back a faltering brother or sister.... I have come to think of him as the great connector...that divine work of putting people in contact with others."

He said it was not easy to place Egan in U.S. Church history, since he was so unique. Browne, author of the history of the Knights of Labor, mentioned several who had made their mark. There was New York's Fr. John Powers, who had intrigued d'Tocqueville in the 1880s; Paterson's Fr. James McNulty, from the 1880s to the 1920s; San Francisco's late–nineteenth-century Fr. Peter Yorke; Washington's Msgr. John A Ryan and Msgr. John O'Grady;

---

[25]Donnelly File, Hartford Archdiocese and Catholic University Archives, January 28, 1956.

Church–State relations expert Fr. John Courtney Murray, S.J.; conservative media giants like Fr. Charles Coughlin and Bishop Fulton J. Sheen.

Yet, Browne said Egan had done such things mildly different, because "the power-broker background of Chicago certainly affected his ecclesiastical style. He couldn't without technology, such as a phone and a plane, become the Jack Egan we know and love." Browne highlighted Egan's role as "a pioneer in the involvement of the laity as well as the clergy" and added that his continued honing of organizing skills helped Egan's "efforts to catch up with the women's movement [and found him]...as gracious as most of us...have been able to become in fact of that sometimes strident movement." Browne also thought that Egan's contribution in "bridging the gap between scholarship and using it for pastorally good influences" had been forgotten.

In the late nineteenth century, Italy, France, and Germany had clerical networks, "the movements of change within the Church" often saw developing political concerns with the industrialized society, the plight of the poor and workers, connected with scholarship. But "Jack certainly has done it in the United States." Browne compared Egan's movement to those of U.S. clerics in the 1880s and 1890s, which were "loosely headed by Dr. Edward McGlynn" in New York. Egan was loyal to the Church structure and even the hierarchy and Rome by "entertaining a sense of respect without kissing the sacred purple and other exercises of devotion which destroys one's integrity." So, Egan never exhibited the "we-are-outsiders" posturing "of the so-called contemporary American Catholic left."

In Margery Frisbie's biography, president emeritus of Notre Dame University, Fr. Theodore M. Hesburgh, C.S.C., described his friend Egan: When the image of the priesthood had been tarnished, with ordinary talents, hard work, and the Holy Spirit, Egan was extraordinary—close to thousands, served unstintingly, inspired many, always beyond the call of duty and answering "the higher call of love, justice, and social concern." In knowing Egan, people will be better Christians and humans "after learning of the broad sweep of his humanity."[26]

During the 1960s and 1970s Milwaukee Fr. Francis Eschweiller became very involved in social justice issues. He once spoke of the impact the Second Vatican Council had had on him.[27] While other priests were intimidated by Vatican II, the Council had made updating easier for him. When embroiled in controversies that were acceptable after Vatican II, Eschweiller realized that he easily could have left the priesthood. But he thought otherwise because the Church was "the people business at the highest, deepest, most profound level, where men and God meet, and I'm the coordinator of that. I create a condition whereby the two can come together, where people can experience the 'Good news' and realize the fullness of God." For him, the Church, without needless baggage, was his frame of reference and "the simple structure that Jesus instituted did not include." He had misgivings about some priests who quit too soon. Some, he felt were less than honest in their reasons for embarking upon some new and more productive "ministry out there"—free from the inhibiting and stifling roadblocks that the institutional Church had put in their way. "I haven't seen any significant exciting new ministries that have emerged in the promised land," he said.

Eschweiller was interviewed by Paul Wilkes for his book-length overview of Eschweiller's involvements during the Great Depression: labor issues, Labor Schools, and dealings with ecclesiastical and business institutions.[28] Eschweiller thought the Church, like

---

[26]Egan File, University of Notre Dame Archives, January 23, 1980.
[27] Frisbie 1991.
[28] No author, *Milwaukee Herald Sentinel*, 1974.

corporations, was not out front on respecting the rights of workers, to whom Christ would never be known, unless a priest was available to show compassion and understanding of their problems. Reaffirming his commitment to the priesthood, despite troubles with chancery officials, he said, the priesthood could persuade and influence, not manipulate and suffocate people. It provided so many opportunities to free people "from their inadequacies, fears, and hang-ups, and bring out their best potential." Trying to keep his eye on Jesus, Eschweiller tried to draw people out and keep them returning, bearing in mind the parable of the seed that germinated in people who were open. Despite about three years with Jesus, the apostles were not that faithful. In fact, Jesus relied on the Father and friends, although He was so strong and human. "I admit to my own lack of faith...always wanting things to germinate overnight.... But if you are true to yourself you really cannot lose. You look like a loser for ten or more years, but ultimately the day of vindication comes" [pp. 24–25].

In 1988, during his retirement, Eschweiller's interviews with Daryl Powers and Randy Johnson were written up by Connie Knight.[29] Eschweiller felt that Vatican II had aroused the "sleeping giant — the laity." For him, "all" are Church and authoritarianism tended to breed apathy. Eschweiller periodically printed *Bread of Life* for his friends with ideas of a pastoral or spiritual nature.[30] In 1996, he found writing his will had become a moment of truth, "a time to practice distributive justice as I bequeath the bulk of my estate to those who never had the luxury of leaving anything behind. For, very simply they have no 'estate'. It is sad that our sense of stewardship has to come so late in life."

---

[29]Wilkes date unknown.
[30] Eschweiller File, Milwaukee Archdiocese Archives.

In 1998 there were many testimonials to Eschweiller in *Bread of Life*.[31] Gerard Memmel, the former associate pastor in Good Shepherd Parish (Eschweiller's last assignment) said. "Fran was fearless in the vision of his own conscience. When the hierarchy of the church seemed wrong in his eyes, he cleared his own road doing what his faith dictated, no matter what he was told by others." Friends Tom and Marian Stump said, "He was a visionary and a prophet.... He impacted many persons by his forthright homilies on social and moral issues, unflinchingly taking unpopular stands from the pulpit,... And even after his death, still lingers...an individual who ignited a 'glow' which we as his friends must never allow to be extinguished." Then archbishop Rembert Weakland said, "Fr. Fran was Vatican II, and his death is the end of an institution."

In late 1980 there was a retirement dinner in Washington, D.C., in honor of Higgins, where speakers gave encomiums about him, "the priest."[32] Stephen Schlossberg, former director of Government and Public Affairs for the United States, said, "The labor movement is like his parish. I've gone to him with personal problems myself. I don't think it would be irreverent for me to refer to him as 'my priest'." Arthur Goldberg, former secretary of labor, Supreme Court justice, and U.N. ambassador, mentioned Higgins's "discreet spirituality, "To me he represented the body of the church's vast attitude involved in the issues." AFL–CIO secretary-treasurer Thomas Donahue called Higgins the sustainer, nurturer, and shaper of labor priests. At Notre Dame University's May 2001 commencement, when Higgins received the Laetare Medal, Notre Dame's president, Fr. Edward Malloy, C.S.C., said, "We honor him for following Jesus, a carpenter's son, and heeding a vocation to serve his Lord in the workers of the world."

---

[31] Ibid.
[32] Frisbie 1991.

Shortly after Higgins's death on May 2, 2002, Fr. Bryan Hehir, who had served in the Bishops' Conference with Higgins for several years, delivered a eulogy in Chicago's Holy Name Cathedral. The eulogy was divided into three aspects of Higgins's life: the person, the priest, the public man. Praising Higgins's intellect and courage, erudition, and humility, Hehir said, "His was a disciplined prophecy, carefully developed, stringently argued and consistently held.... You could always count on George to say what had to be said, to stand where it made a difference and to stay with an issue until resolution." Higgins was said to treasure the "heart of his priesthood" in the social ministry of the Church. "The very center of his commitment to the Social Teaching was what Leo XIII called the rights of workers...The labor movement was community second only to his Church." With a nod to the clergy sex abuse scandal then raging throughout the nation, Hehir said, "[By] the actions of some and the inaction of others George's death allowed us to see a different image of both the priesthood and church." With a nod to media announcements about Higgins's death, Hehir concluded, "We could read those tributes and say this is how it should be and how it can be."

Despite a rather successful career assisting César Chávez, the National Catholic Rural Life Conference (NCRLC), Project Equality, NCWC, and Jesuit Social Ministry, there were some very stormy moments for Fr. James Vizzard, S.J., especially with some religious superiors. In late 1965 he wrote to his provincial about some reported difficulties and behavior, since he had "a right to know my deepest feelings and problems.... The hours of depression have passed.... I have no intention of quitting.... I can and will continue to pay the price for this opportunity to serve the church...All I've done is to reveal to you, and perhaps more clearly to myself, what my cross is, 'Take up your cross and follow me'. I am confident...that with His help I can."

From August 1971 to November 1975 was a time of stormy relations between Vizzard and his provincial, Fr. Richard Vaughan, S.J., about some of Vizzard's past, present, and proposed ministries and community living. In October 1975 Vaughan labeled Vizzard a "manic depressive," even before meeting him, and asserted he had an excessive need for affirmation, approbation, and affection. The tug-of-war ended in January 1977 when Vizzard received a copy of a report by Fr. Angelo D'Agonstino, S.J., a psychiatrist with whom Vizzard had been seeing for almost one year.

As mentioned above, D'Agostino found Vizzard to be open and candid; to have a firm and clear grip on reality, even though at times defensive; to harbor a deep sense of hurt and resentment, which "objective facts of his life seemed to give much justification; to be sometimes aggressive; to be not always prudent and diplomatic; to be overly sensitive occasionally; to be unusually self-confident; to be obviously strongly in need of affirmation; to feel, rightly or wrongly, not adequately received by others." After an overview of Vizzard's history of illness, hospitalization, and depression, D'Agostino said, "One really has to wonder how over so many years he has been able to carry on an energetic, demanding and, by all accounts, highly successful ministry." With a few feasible suggestions aimed to reduce stress in Vizzard's life, D'Agostino concluded, "Still it is my considered judgment that he is free of any psychiatric disorder at this time.... I believe that his file covering the last five and a half years should have this letter as a corrective to whatever in those files reflects Father Vaughan's bias."

By January 1977 a new provincial, Fr. Terrence L. Mahan, S.J., discussed Vizzard's troubles over César Chávez and said, "You have given a great deal to the UFW and it seems a shame that the organization now refuses to communicate with you.... God bless you, Jim, and your work for His people." On August 14, 1983, Vizzard received congratulations for fifty years as a Jesuit priest from Fr. William J. Wood, S.J., vice-provincial for education. Singled out was "the lonely years of putting your neck on the line for social justice before it was fashionable and in circumstances that did not bring applause." Vizzard's intellectual and social apostolates had shown the way for very successful social ministries in his province. Similar plaudits came from Fr. Paolo Dezza, S.J., delegate of the Jesuit superior general: "I am told you have accepted this cross with great faith and obedience to God's will, letting your suffering bring you in to close union with our crucified Lord, and thus forge you into a more effective instrument of His redemptive love."

Fr. Anthony Sauer, S.J., president of San Francisco's St. Ignatius Prep, thanked him for being a priestly model and friend to Jesuits. "I pray God I can be as kind, as personable, as human, as Christian as you have been these many years.... The people of God have gained much from your fifty years of dedication and service."

In November 1966 Vizzard, while teaching English at Santa Clara University in 1940, described finding a colony of John Steinbeck's "Oakies" in ramshackle jalopies and shanties less than a mile from the campus. "I found more than poverty there. I discovered also that nobody was helping relieve the situation, not even the churches, not even my own." At Vizzard's retirement dinner on March 2, 1968, SAD's Higgins praised Vizzard for the "combination of scholarship, political know-how, great tenacity of purpose, and, above all, for genuine love for the poor." Vizzard was not slow to criticize public officials, such as President Kennedy, over a minimum wage for Florida farmworkers, but said, "I loved the man...but how can you be an honest friend if you don't criticize?"

Earlier, when Bishop Willinger scolded Vizzard and others for their intervention in his diocese during the Delano strike, Vizzard challenged Willinger's or any other ecclesiastical superior's right to forbid a presence, speeches, or writings in the case of "gross injustice and destruction of human dignity." Vizzard insisted that faithful Christians had to live out their commitments, whatever the costs.

He was convinced that the Church's honor and God's service would be better furthered if "churches, convents, rectories, and even schools, including seminaries, [were to] remain unbuilt or unfinished or even closed rather than that the Church should knuckle under to the threats of those who demand the Church 'keep its nose out of their business'."

CONCLUSION
& PREVIEW OF FUTURE VOLUMES

T his study, *Catholic Labor Priests: Five Giants in the U.S. Catholic Bishops' Social Action Department*, is Volume I of several projected volumes in a set titled *Labor Priests in the United States during the Twentieth Century*.

The research for this set of volumes, initiated in 1986, has been about almost one hundred members of the Catholic hierarchy, clergy, and religious congregations who were known as "labor priests" – from the late 1890s to the early 1970s. Most of the information about the priests and their work has come from archives of articles, letters, and reports of their activities, ideas, and sentiments. Researchers in the future will find this to be a veritable gold mine of data on these, heretofore almost unknown, vital actors in the U.S. labor–management scene for almost one hundred years.

References to labor priests in most labor history texts are rare, save for occasional allegations of "their role" in "driving communists out of Locals and/or Internationals" or "impeding progressive elements in the labor movement." Frequently, such exaggerated or unsubstantiated charges can be traced to confusing the labor priests with members of various chapters of a lay organization, the Association of Catholic Trade Unionists (ACTU). Both groups did aid in preventing a communist takeover of some of the U.S. labor movement in conjunction with some labor leaders, especially Philip Murray, when he was president of the struggling CIO. The labor priests were hardly responsible for a less "progressive labor movement," since Socialism was espoused by very few labor leaders and Communism, by even fewer. The assumption of many such critics is that only those ideologies are deemed "progressive."

Provided here is an abundance of detail for deeper analyses for many other individual studies of the labor priests' phenomenon, which future researchers are encouraged to pursue. There may have been few surprises, but certainly greater insights into the situation of the labor priests, as they championed or challenged several aspects of church, economic, political, and union life in the United States.

Vital to their social justice ministry was the role of the U.S. bishops' Social Action Department (SAD), directed by Msgr. John A. Ryan and assisted by Fr. Raymond McGowan, Msgr. John Hayes, Msgr. George Higgins, and Fr. John Cronin, S.S. These people provided labor priests with information, incentive, and inspiration "to go to the workers and the poor," as Leo XIII and his successors all proclaimed, as well as U.S. Catholic bishops from 1919 to 1986. Besides providing a variety of conferences, contacts, publications, speeches, and testimonies, the SAD staff carried on extensive correspondence with labor priests. All the while, Ryan formulated the policy directives that eventually germinated into Catholic Social Teaching on labor–management relations. As intelligent and diligent as Ryan, his staff, and labor priests were, they were also testimony to the late fifteenth and early sixteenth century Niccolo Machiavelli's dictum. "There is nothing more difficult to carry out, nor more doubtful of success, nor more dangerous to handle, than to initiate a new order of things." Almost as difficult to assess were the labor priests' overall contributions to the teaching and conducting of labor–management relations in the United States for approximately the first seventy-five years of the twentieth century. Others may eventually find better norms and data. They can only be encouraged. Yet, here's a contemporary try!

Parish and diocesan media outlets, lower and higher educational institutions, some Catholic organizations, and occasional secular sources communicated the teaching to a very limited audience, despite Ryan's astute policy formulations and the repeated articulations of others. Adapting to the U.S. church, union, economic, and political scenes Pope Leo XIII's seminal encyclical *Rerum Novarum*, Ryan contributed his Catholic University doctoral dissertation, the widely acclaimed "Living Wage," and a speech prepared for a Knights of Columbus Convention that eventuated in the U.S. bishops' *Pastoral Letter of 1919*. Despite its striking title, "Social Reconstruction" was more about social reform than revolution.

Yet, from these seedlings grew the mighty oak of Catholic social justice teaching in the United States, which to this day has few or no religious rivals or equals, save for better incorporation of sacred scriptural sources by some Jewish and Protestant thinkers—not a Catholic strongpoint until after the Second Vatican Council. Indeed, Ryan's seminal work influenced some policy formulations of the New Deal legislation, due to his close relations with influential persons in the executive, judicial, and legislative branches of the U.S. government.

To the dismay of some and disappointment of other commentators on the socio-economic-politico scene, however, the heritage of Ryan and his disciples failed to reach the level of a grand theoretical formulation. Actually, none of those men aspired even to a middle-range theoretical formulation. Driven by zeal to improve the lot of workers and their families, Ryan and his disciples relied on available information about very distressful conditions, insightful analysis, and Aristotelian-Thomist philosophical principles, to urge capital, government, and labor to advance adequate living wages, reasonable profits, decent employment hours, healthy and safe working conditions, limitations on child labor, provisions for illness and old age, and opportunities to better people's lot by exercising their constitutional rights to freedom of speech and assembly in forming and joining labor unions.

These priests rejected Communist and Nazi totalitarianism with their pronounced materialism, atheism, and collectivism. They also critiqued the selfish individualism of the laissez-faire capitalism of the time, as well as some forms of socialism, distributism, or corporatism fostered by Catholic social activists or literal exponents of Pius XI's 1931 encyclical *Quadragesimo Anno*. In the labor priests' earliest thinking, Socialism was tantamount to Communism, but in their later thinking there was greater nuance, especially under the influence of Pope John XXIII and the Second Vatican Council. Except for one or two labor priests, there was a willingness to cooperate with socialists and even communists in labor union campaigns, provided honesty and fairness toward workers was not clouded by some untenable aspects of Socialism and Communism.

The audience Ryan and disciples hoped to reach and influence was limited. Their largest potential audience was the weekly Sunday Catholic parish Mass. Attendance was compulsory "under pain of mortal sin," but many Catholics did not heed the dictum and time allotted during Mass for addressing Catholic social justice teaching was very scant—a very infrequent sermon on social justice, an announcement lost amid more local and immediate items, some bishops' preference for study groups, which were scarce and rarely attended, brief notices lost in weekly parish bulletins, or the seldom purchased and even more seldom read diocesan newspapers.

Outside of parish settings there were organizational settings, such as Knights of Columbus councils and Holy Name Society meetings, which very briefly or tepidly cooperated, unlike the more zealous and radical *Catholic Worker* movement. More highly organized and continuous assistance came from the Association of Catholic Trade Unionists, despite sporadic misunderstandings with some labor priests and bishops, especially over anticommunist tactics. Though approved by local bishops and guided by appointed chaplains, ACTU was not as widespread or long-lived as the Labor Schools. Sometimes there were misunderstandings with international or local unions, over perceived ACTU interference in internal or intra-union affairs or favoritism toward fledgling CIO unions, which initially had limited resources compared to AFL unions.

Other limitations for Ryan's disciples' outreach and influence was a lack of adequate training for priests in social justice, despite efforts of the SAD staff, Catholic Conference on Industrial Problems, local Summer Seminars for Priests, and diocesan or religious communities Labor Schools. Similar limitations were traceable to inadequate seminary training in Catholic social justice teaching, as well as occasional disputes with and among members of the hierarchy. These and other limitations were evident in labor priests' concerns about the Church and differences among some labor priests, save for much agreement about the Detroit radio orator Fr. Charles Coughlin and his followers, who misunderstood or misconstrued Catholic Social Teaching on labor–management relations and U.S. labor law.

A final area of limitations were the attempts to curb the work of Ryan and his disciples by bishops, religious superiors, and university officials, out of concern for ecclesiastical niceties, perceived excessive zeal, and fear of retaliations from wealthy donors. Such attempted restrictions often led to disappointments, fears, doubts, resentments, and identity crises among some labor priests. Such restrictions may also account for the relative paucity of archival material on labor priests. Such may also be due to labor priests not saving correspondence, underestimating their efforts, failing to record their activities, or the disfavor and suspicion in which some labor priests were held, inducing some pastors or archivists to discard or neglect the labor priests' belongings.

Volume II on Labor Priests' Role
within Unions

Volume II in this series will address the role of labor priests within the unions. As indicated throughout this research, labor priests did more than teach union members and attract management officials to the Catholic Church's insistence that the role of labor unions was indispensable to economic life, as Pope John Paul II later said so eloquently in his encyclical *Laborem Exercens* (Human Labor). For labor priests assisted and challenged local and international unions.

Examples abound and are the most popular references to labor priests over the years. The earliest were the struggles with anti-union public officials in San Francisco by Fr. Peter Yorke in the early years of the twentieth century. In 1902 Fr. John Curran of Wilkes-Barre, Pennsylvania, persuaded his friend President Theodore Roosevelt to bring obstinate "coal barons" to settle a long-standing strike with UMW president "Johnny Mitchell." Years later Curran assisted dissident locals striking UMW because of John L. Lewis's alleged favoritism toward the soft coal miners in other states, especially about health and pension payments. In 1910 Fr. Peter Dietz (Milwaukee and Cincinnati) formed the Militia of Christ, an earlier and more complicated version of ACTU, with AFL union presidents as officers and board members in an attempt to inculcate Catholic union members with the Church's Social Justice Teaching. Misunderstandings and controversies with some members of the hierarchy, as well as his own difficult actions, led to the demise of the militia. Yet he ultimately succeeded, after years of lobbying, in influencing the U.S. labor movement to resist communist attempts to control worldwide union movement. One author—but not without a challenge from SAD's McGowan—declared Dietz as "an agitator and organizer, and a journalist…[who] exerted a greater influence directly on the labor movement than any other priest." In 1911

Bishop Schrembs of Grand Rapids, Michigan, took part in an investigative-mediating effort to end a furniture strike. The efforts failed, but Schrembs supported the strike, which got rather ugly. In 1914 Chicago's Fr. John Maguire, O.S.V., began twenty-five years of service, holding the record for settling eighty-seven out of ninety strikes, largely through his arbitration skills. Notable were his settling of a long and bloody Kohler strike in Wisconsin and gaining an equitable closed shop agreement for workers at Colorado's Green Mountain and Power Plants, after five AFL unions had failed. Praise for his work came from many sources, especially from President Franklin Roosevelt and Labor Secretary Frances Perkins. In 1927 Bishop Lucey of Amarillo, Texas, supported the repeal of the Texas antistrike legislation, which foreshadowed his later work as archbishop of San Antonio, supporting the Railroad Brotherhood, Texas Federation of Labor, Texas Industrial Union Council, and his constant opposition to Public Law 78, which created the dreadful braceros programs for migrant workers.

In 1930 SAD's McGowan proposed a child labor amendment and later a wage-and-hours law, calling "the living wage a primordial right more ancient than any contract between man and man." He saw no reason why an unprofitable small business should go on forever at the expense of its employees. He defended the integrity of most union leaders, calling employee–management, union–management collaboration "a near guild." In 1931, as bishop in Cleveland, Ohio, Schrembs aided negotiations against the city's major hotels and urged each CIO SWOC and three corporations to settle. In 1935 Msgr. Francis Haas (Milwaukee and Washington) tried to reconcile AFL president William Green and John L. Lewis in the wake of the CIO split from the AFL. Despite the interventions by Haas, President Roosevelt, and Labor Secretary Perkins, the efforts failed. In 1935 Haas settled the Cigar strike in Tampa, Florida. In 1937 he settled the Silk Industry strike. In 1938 he settled the Chicago and

North Shore dispute. In 1939 he was an expert but nonvoting delegate at the ILO's American States Conference. In 1940 he settled the Marathon Rubber and the General Tire strike and in 1941 the Allis-Chalmers strike. Most notable was his influence on President Roosevelt in the transformation of the Fair Employees Practices Committee into the Fair Employees Practices Commission. Throughout World War II and afterwards, he served on assignments from Labor Secretary Perkins—enough in number to gain him the reputation as one of the most professional mediators and arbitrators in the nation! In 1934 San Francisco's Archbishop Mitty, in the midst of the Maritime Workers Pacific Coast strike, expressed appreciation for union opposition to the federal government's plans to extradite Harry Bridges for communist membership. As early as 1936 Fr. Jerome Drolet of New Orleans became involved in several struggles of the Transport Workers Union (TWU) and the National Agricultural Workers Union. In 1937 SAD's Hayes helped to settle a Bethlehem Steel strike. From 1938 to 1939, New York's Fr. William Dobson, S.J., tried to offset Transport Workers Union president Mike Quill's running of the New York Transit System and to eliminate communist influence in that union, as well as in the New York City teachers union.

In 1940 New York's Fr. Corridan, S.J., assisted Fr. Carey, S.J., fighting communist influence in the Transport Workers Union, United Electrical Workers Union, and Amalgamated Clothing Workers Union. In 1941 Fr. Cronin battled communist influence in Baltimore Local 43 of the Union of Marine and Shipbuilders, so essential later for the U.S. efforts in World War II. In 1942 SAD's Hayes aided the United Farm Equipment Workers Union, working in a Chicago McCormack plant, to obtain needed industrial equipment. Hayes was also concerned about the challenges of the International Harvester Company workers, the International Ladies Garment Workers Union, and the CIO Executive Committee under

President Philip Murray. In 1942 Hartford's Msgr. Donnelly challenged the leadership of the Mine, Mill, and Smelter Union, through a wearying and protracted battle that ultimately ended in success. Early in right-to-work legal battles, generated by the Taft-Hartley amendments to the Wagner Act, Donnelly was expert in uncovering hypocrisy in the advocacies by many in media and corporate circles. His greatest claim to fame was his expertise, along with SAD's Higgins, in negotiating settlements for César Chávez's United Farm Workers Union and skillful shepherding throughout the Church the unofficial Catholic bishops' support of the grape and lettuce boycotts. In 1944 SAD's Higgins was involved in some con versation about and with UAW's Walter Reuther concerning socialist influences in the union and some problems between the Utility Workers and Transport Workers. According to an organizing director of the AFL–CIO, Higgins was the most knowledgeable and accepted cleric in the nation, with respect to the trade unions. Yet "when those same leaders were doing things that [the Catholic concept of unions] would not support, Higgins very articulately let them know about it." Ultimately, Higgins and Donnelly were responsible for the grape and lettuce boycott. Higgins's columns and speeches effectively diminished opposition to the boycott from a small but boisterous group of Catholic priests. Higgins deemed the "raiding and "sweetheart contracts" between the Teamsters and California growers as "one of the darkest and most shameful days in American labor history." He called in all his IOUs to convince other unions to oppose the action by the Teamsters, including a strong personal reproach to AFL–CIO president George Meany. Until his death he relentlessly opposed all immigration proposals that smacked of a braceros program. In 1944 Fr. Masse, S.J., criticized the communist-infiltrated Communications Union, supported the CIO's Political Action Committee (PAC), and criticized CIO president Philip Murray's opposition to federal aid to religious education. Masse sought support for a paper on "Johnson and Johnson on Industrial Peace," but opposed blaming unions for inflation. In 1947 Fr. George Dunne, S.J., came to the rescue of the Conference of Studio Unions in their fight with the company union, the International Association of Theater and Stage Employees. From 1942 to 1978, St. Louis's Fr. Brown, S.J., mediated or arbitrated some four thousand 4, labor–management disputes. From 1943 to 1987, Philadelphia's Fr. Comey, S.J., was involved in countless mediation and arbitration cases, especially those involving firefighters and turnpike employees.

In 1950 Archbishop Lucey of San Antonio got seventeen dioceses to convert Spanish-Speaking Committees into farmworker-assistance organizations. In 1950 Fr. O'Connell, O.M.I., of New Orleans, signed a statement officially supporting a southern telephone workers' strike and urged the Bell Telephone system to negotiate. In 1951 Archbishop Lucey urged President Truman to veto Public Law 78 (which formalized the braceros program) without success, but he persisted in that effort for the rest of his life. In a 1951 report to the Catholic Committee of the South, O'Connell revealed that he had assisted about a dozen unions in a variety of ways. In 1951 Fr. Boss, S.J., warned union leaders in San Francisco that if they act for their own special and selfish interests they will eventually lose support of the membership. In 1952 SAD's Higgins wrote a column to let UAW's Walter Reuther know that he was being watched, lest he exhibit an extreme socialist approach to unionism. In 1952 New York's Fr. Carey, S.J., complained to CIO's Philip Murray that the Distributive Workers Union was rumored to be getting a CIO charter, despite its well-known flirtation with the Communist Party. In 1953 Carey reported that the XIIR had aided some twenty-five unions. In that same year Fr. Twomey, S.J., of New Orleans supported the strike of the National Agricultural Workers Union (NAWU) and urged the Teamsters to support the cause of the Louisiana sugarcane workers. In 1955 Detroit's Fr. Clancy told a union presidential candidate, Sam Fishman, to insist on a retraction from ACTU's *Wage Earner* for a smear about Fishman being a Trotskyite. In 1955 Higgins said that the German Steelworkers Union (DGB) leadership was not looking out enough for the benefit of the German people, but he didn't want his name published. In 1957 Jesuit Fr. Twomey noted in Chicago's Catholic labor alliance publication, *Work*, that the labor movement needed "a terrific shakeup," because Beck's Teamsters and Hall's International Longshoreman's Union were thoroughly regarded with disgust. In 1957 SAD's Cronin joined a rabbi and protestant minister to mediate the Kohler–UAW controversy in Wisconsin—again without success. In 1958 the San Francisco Spanish Mission Band, which had introduced César Chávez to Delores Huerta, began union organizing because appeals to the AFL–CIO were being ignored. The Band began the Agricultural Workers Association (AWA) and wrote its constitution with Delores Huerta, which prompted the AFL–CIO to send an organizer and establish AWOC.

In the 1960s *New York Post* columnist Westbrook Pegler wrote some articles totally smearing labor leaders as "bad." Strong and detailed rebuttals were published by SAD's McGowan, Fr. Shortell, S.J., of Worchester, Massachusetts, and New York's Fr. Smith, S.J. Throughout the 1960s, Fr. Vizzard, S.J., served as legislative aide to the National Catholic Rural Life Conference and César Chávez. In 1961 he wrote to AFL–CIO president George Meany, protesting Teamsters siding with growers against Chávez's UFW. His lobbying and public utterances aided the passage of several important pieces of federal legislation, including the 1962 Migrant Medical Help Law, the 1963 Farm Labor Contractors Law, the 1964 repeal of Public Law 78 (Bracero Law), and the 1974 amendments to the Child Labor Law. Also in the 1970s, in light of the U.S. bishops' failure to formally support Chávez's boycotts, San Francisco's Archbishop Mitty told people to let their conscience be their guide. In 1977 Pittsburgh's Fr. Rice decried the absence of a strong Left in the

U.S. trade unionism and wondered if the fault was communists or people like himself who fought them. In 1979 Higgins advised the southeast Catholic bishops in support for the Amalgamated Clothing Workers Union boycott of the J.P. Stevens Textile giant. Also in 1979 Higgins assisted in attempts to revive better collaboration between union leaders and interfaith social activists. In 1990 SAD's Higgins sternly, but privately, rebuked the AFL–CIO Executive Council for contemplating "a disastrous mistake" in supporting a "pro-choice" or "pro-abortion" resolution that some internationals had submitted. In 1995 Fr. Rice said his anticommunist campaign had been too intense and the decline of unions since the 1950s was causing them to lose the fight against "Capital." Yet in 2002 he relied on the publication of the *Vernona Papers*, saying that there was a real communist threat against the United States in the designs of the U.S. and Russian Communist parties on U.S. education and its defense and communications industries.

In addition to assisting or challenging labor unions, labor priests also revealed and decried corruption in the ranks of labor unions, however infrequently and mild. In the late 1940s, Fr. Carey, S.J., was alerted to the "bad situation" in the Portland, Oregon, labor movement, where the leadership was "dedicated to its own perpetuation." Carey said such situations "turned his hair grey," confessing that his New York XIIR spent more time "protecting men against racketeers and thugs." Also in the late 1940s, San Francisco's Fr. Donahoe told an AFL convention that the power of the National Association of Manufacturers (NAM) had to be resisted by purging corrupt union leaders and he warned against "a certain snobbishness and inordinate love of wealth."

In the 1950s, New York's Fr. Smith, S.J., said that, absent democracy in corporations, it was not "fair or feasible to expect the full ideal of democracy to be exercised by unions that must deal with giant corporations." He was convinced that corruption in unions was minimal and no more than in corporations. However, he expected no real corrective without strong enforcement by state and federal agencies and an AFL–CIO Code of Ethics. Smith also thought dictator-type union leaders were a small minority and more benign, save those in the Teamsters and the Building Trades. In 1953 Minnesota's Fr. Gilligan praised most of the more than two hundred national labor leaders, save for being timid about telling the membership about the limits of collective bargaining demands. He characterized most union failings as "moral faults because members did not apply their personal moral code and Ten Commandments to the actions of the Union." In 1955 SAD's Fr. Higgins said that, despite media overkill, the public had a right to expect labor leaders to be examples of greater honesty and integrity than any other group of people in public life, as professionals and self-proclaimed champions of social justice. In 1957 Connecticut's Fr. Donnelly called a few dishonest labor movement people "parasites" or "betrayers." In 1959 he wrote a stern letter to AFL–CIO president George Meany, reminding him of his tardy response to a bad leadership situation in Connecticut.

In 1973 California's Fr. Vizzard, S.J., bemoaned the sordid history of the treatment farmworkers as mere chattel by Teamsters and the Farm Bureau. In 1995 Pittsburgh's Fr. Rice said the media as big business was usually capitalist, antiunion, or indifferent. Like everyone else, unions had corrupt leaders—murderers of leaders, abandoning the rank-and-file, etc. He'd give labor leaders a "B-plus" and even an "A" as a force for justice, but added that "sometimes they should be bolder."

What about a grade for the labor priests, whether in their running of schools, writing, or speaking on behalf of U.S. workers over the years? In light of almost insurmountable opposition to unions from management and media, such an assessment will not be easy. Nevertheless, the abundant data on labor priests supplied here gives other scholars and researchers the wherewithal to proceed with the evaluation by comparing our information with studies already available. Let's get on with it!

Volume III on Labor Priests
& Labor Schools

While influential in government circles and successful in labor–management settlements and frequent speaking in labor–management gatherings, Haas mostly left development of the educational component to SAD and to labor priests at the diocesan and college-university levels. There have been various estimates of the number, nature, and influence of Labor Schools or Institutes of Industrial Relations. However, in 1947 the distinguished educator and arbitrator in labor–management relations, Fr. Leo Brown, S.J., calculated that there were ninety-eight Catholic-sponsored labor–management programs, of which sixty-four were operated by parishes or dioceses and twenty-four by Catholic colleges or universities.

Meetings were held on either Tuesday or Thursday evenings, for as few as eight weeks or as many as thirteen weeks. Nominal fees were charged for courses such as: public speaking and debate, collective bargaining, current labor problems, economics English composition, labor history, parliamentary procedures, psychology, and social ethics. Whatever the auspices, the purposes, curricula, faculties, and students were similar. Rarely was membership limited to Catholics, but most frequently the requirement was union membership. Brown rated the quality of the teaching by volunteer labor leaders and professors as equal to that of professional teachers in programs elsewhere. Results in the end were mixed, but the programs accomplished more than simply routing communists out of international or local unions. Indeed, Brown's conclusion carries a message even for today: "If every year 7,500 union and management officials...could be trained through such courses...one could reasonably hope for a pronounced improvement in the nation's industrial life."

There were many reasons why such hopes have not been realized, but one important reason was that soon after many management officials realized that Catholic Social Teaching stressed the essential role of labor unions in the economic life of a society, management enrollments regretfully declined. Nevertheless, if one takes account of many short-lived Labor Schools under parish, college, or ACTU auspices beyond 1947, they would probably numbered more than two hundred. Likewise, if one takes account of priests who showed more than passing interest and devoted limited time, the number of labor priests approaches three hundred. Hopefully, a project for others for another time!

Whatever the ultimate outcomes of Catholic educational programs in labor–management relations, initially the bulk of instruction and intensity of motivation was attributable to the personnel and service of SAD. Ryan and McGovern primarily gave direction, but Hayes, Higgins, and Cronin provided outreach. While Higgins has been most widely known and hailed, the groundwork in three short years was laid largely by the almost forgotten Hayes, whereas Cronin's effort was mostly consumed about Communism. Diocesan Labor Schools flourished in Chicago, Detroit, Hartford, Massachusetts, New Jersey, New Orleans, New York, Philadelphia, Pittsburgh, and San Francisco. Each had unique features, mirroring the personalities and interests of directors Carey, Clancy, Comey, Donahoe, Donnelly, Hillenbrand, Rice, and Twomey. Religious community programs, with exceptions earlier in Philadelphia and New York, and at Notre Dame, were mostly Jesuit Labor Schools later called Institutes of Industrial Relations, in Kansas City, New Orleans, New York, Philadelphia, San Francisco, and Scranton. Rationale for changed titles was to indicate the Catholic insistence on labor and management collaboration and a nod to industrial psychology or industrial sociology in academia.

Attempts to gauge differences of importance between the diocesans and the religious would be an exercise in futility, so different were the audiences, locales, and personnel. One might argue that the automotive industry was more crucial at the time than the shipping industry, or curbing Fr. Coughlin was more important than the coal miners. Yet, the problem is what are the criteria for importance and where is the data on the extent of influence. Perhaps the research of others might provide the marker.

Catholic labor–management education was not limited to the efforts of SAD, religious communities, or academic institutions, however. For quite influential—albeit at a later and for a shorter time— were the efforts of ACTU. Although subject to diocesan approval and guided by diocesan-appointed chaplains, ACTU ran similar type Labor Schools, which were fairly independent of Church control. For the most part, ACTU was recognized and respected, even though not an official Church organization. Sometimes it was mistaken for one, even by some poorly informed academics. Yet, while appreciated by the likes of Br. Justin Brennan, F.S.C., of Manhattan College and New York's Fr. John Monaghan, ACTU received criticism at times from St. Louis's Fr. Leo Brown, S.J., and New York's Fr. Phil Carey, S.J. The complaints were for intrusion in some Catholic institutional activity or internal union affairs. Carey, however, thought that ACTU did more good than harm and he distinguished the organization from other Catholic professional groups for doctors, lawyers, etc., which existed until the mid-twentieth century.

There was another very short-lived lay group, the Catholic Social Justice League, which had very little episcopal and clergy support, until it wanted to diminish the role of the National Council of Catholic Men (NCCM). While the evidence from labor priests' files is scant about the labor–management involvement of Dorothy Day and The Catholic Worker, there is evidence of the important encouragement she gave to Fr. Drolet of New Orleans and the unfortunate rejection of her assistance by Cincinnati's Archbishop McNicholas, which smacked of high-handed clericalism.

Volume IV on Labor Priests
in Relation to Economics &Politics

Whatever the limitations of their ministry in the estimation of the church, labor unions, or educators, labor priests became knowledgeable about economics and quite concerned about its impact on workers and the poor, and they were determined to improve their lot. Labor priests benefited from the writing and thinking of their colleagues about the competence and right of the Church to speak about—indeed, pass judgment on—the economy. Primacy of place and influence belonged to Ryan, for whom all free human action, even in the economy, came under the moral law and the Church's duty was to teach the moral law and help people save their souls by right conduct, by laying down moral principles, by declaring some actions morally lawful and others unlawful, and by advocating certain practices without binding force due to practical expediency involved. Social Gospellers, like Rauschenbusch, used faith and scriptures to take in the broad sweep, but Ryan used reason and natural law to analyze each problem in detail.

Bishop Karl Alter of Toledo and Cincinnati, Ohio, stressed that only judgments of officially approved theologians enjoyed authoritative Church teaching on economic matters. Convinced that complaints about encyclicals were due to superficial reading, Fr. Louis Twomey, S.J., of New Orleans, insisted that the surest foundation of human rights and responsibilities derived from people being created in God's image and that, while Catholic social justice teaching was authoritatively and publicly proclaimed by the Church, its acceptance really depended upon people of goodwill.

Many more labor priests commented on Capitalism as an economic system, with all accepting it over Communism and Socialism, but they were quite critical of various aspects of Capitalism. One of the challenging critiques was given by Detroit's archbishop Edward Mooney, because of his position in the Church as responder to Fr. Coughlin, the influential radio orator, and the site of Detroit's prestigious and powerful Economic Club. Wealthy business executives were told that the 1938 economy was in Capitalism's, rather than in people's, grip and "for decades the trend of economic development has been towards stifling widespread competition, concentration of wealth in the hands of a minority, and the creation of an increasingly large class of property-less wage earners."

The present economic life represented the climax of a period in Christian history "by an insistence on the principle of unrestrained competition and on the utterly private character of property." Such an economic philosophy postulated economic laws supposedly as immutable as the laws of physics or chemistry, a pursuit of self-interest creating the maximum good for all, and the law of supply and demand automatically regulating the scale of wages and prices of goods. Such an economic philosophy began in France as "physiocracy" and developed in the United States as laissez-faire capitalism, rejecting the intervention of labor unions and championing exemption from government oversight except for the maintenance of order. Such a system was "in flat contradiction with the ethics of historic Christianity and historic Judaism as well" and its advocates blatantly asserted or clearly implied that "the field of economics is quite distinct from the field of ethics."

Traditional Christian ethics, however, emphasized a twofold character of ownership—individual or private, social or public—as well as a right to property or use of property. Traditional Christian ethics treasured generosity that helps the needy, but the common outlook preferred rewarding remunerative jobs and production of needed goods—when the profit motive is an inadequate motivator. "The ethico-economic school of thought contends that both the individual and social character of labor [must] be taken into account."

For Mooney, a living wage that provided for the maintenance of the worker and his family, along with a large measure of security for the willing worker was "the least wage due in justice from the employer." He hoped economic life would be directed not by the contradictory principles lying undisturbed below the surface of economic life, but by principles that would be acceptable to "high-minded and humane citizens." Complaints about the ethical principles would be greatly weakened when economic life was judged in terms of religion. For, religion of historic Judaism and historic Christianity gave ethics of economic life the sanction of God's judgment and calls for charity as well as justice.

Cleveland's Fr. Robert Navin stated that there would be no quarrel about the use of wealth for production or investment purposes, but asked other questions about Capitalism. "[Why] is it that we hear so much of the evils of Capitalism? Are these evils inherent in the system or can the system be cleansed of them?" Does modern-day Capitalism really work a hardship on the majority of people or is it merely discontent on the part of the "have-nots," as they contemplate the position of the "haves"? After tracing the rise of Capitalism by culling the works of oft-cited writers, Navin said that whatever these authors' interpretations, the originators of Capitalism were "nothing more or less than law-breakers, who acted directly against the legislation of the Church, the State, and the Guilds. Some writers emphasized a "capitalistic spirit" or "individualistic selfish spirit of greed and covetousness...marked by an inordinate striving for wealth accompanied by a lack of consideration for others." Yet the Church had always taught "wealth has a social value and that it is absolutely immoral for a man to oppress his neighbor, either in the accumulation or in the use of his wealth."

Corporatism, as an alternative or *tertium quid* between Capitalism and various forms of socialism, was touched upon by Leo XIII and elaborated on by Pius XI. Early on, corporatism was espoused by some labor priests, but the concept was eventually discarded. Criticism focused on proposing that each occupational group should be accorded public status; failing to reckon the dangers associated with occupational groups (tendencies toward professional conservatism and restrictive monopoly practices); claiming that the occupational group order was essentially a "democratic" solution to the problem of securing for wage earners a share of control over the conditions of their work; and oversimplifying the manner in which the new social order would be established.

The central focus of supporters was a continued stress on Catholic principles and contrast with alternative theories, while ignoring any political implications of the Catholic reform program, not appealing to an adequate political theory in its appeal to an occupational group system without offering convincing grounds for supposing the problems of governmental intervention in economic life or of democratic control in industry would be solved. SAD would have had to discover the political impact of corporatism and revise it. SAD's insistence on government programs was said to be due to the existing pressing needs and the gigantic obstacles to union organization, wage increases, and labor–management cooperation. SAD's description of occupational groups was less significant than the conviction that the popes placed primary responsibility for the establishment of social justice on public authority.

Moreover, critics failed to place discussion of occupational groups in the context of Ryan's notion of "economic democracy," which involved a subsidiary and hierarchical order between the state and individual person or corporation. Both capitalists and workers in a particular industry would be empowered by law to fix all wages, interest, dividends, and prices; to determine working conditions; to adjust industrial disputes; to carry on economic plans. Local groups would be the federation of a national group for the whole industry and of all industries for the nation. Ryan never accepted all the ramifications of Pius XI's plan and never integrated the system into his thoughts. On the other hand, however, critics still failed to grasp that SAD and other labor priests were not, as noted above, intent on creating a complete political theoretical framework.

Labor priests, however, did comment on and become involved in labor–management relations, such as hopes for employee involvement in the profits and ownership of industry or business; the reconcilability of high wages and high profits; union organizing and contract negotiations; strikes and lockouts; denial of equating unions with violence; labor violations; right-to-work laws; obligation of unionized employees to pay union dues for the services and expenses of union representation; obligations and cautions in recognizing the right to organize; health care; education; burial; academic/business/clergy/legal/human resources; preference for timely face-to-face conciliations and arbitrations over lengthy sessions and voluminous transcripts; support and cautions for compulsory union membership and/or trade association membership; the necessity and permeability of labor unions for economic health; rights and cautions about doctors' strikes; necessity of detailed knowledge of employees' and employers' cultures; essential role of natural and moral virtues in labor–management relations in light of moral lapses among many employers and journalists; persistent employer opposition to unions despite evidence of great acceptance and cooperation during World War II; necessity of institutions like the NLRB and White House Labor–Management Conferences; pitfalls of "voluntary unions"; defense of John L. Lewis as neither a communist nor a fascist; complexities of health-care costs in negotiations; defense of real patriotism by labor and management; challenge for unions to be involved in community affairs and not just suitable contract resolutions; complexities of unemployment and negotiations; obligations of workers to join good unions; near-unanimous condemnation of the Taft-Hartley Act; reflections on industry councils plans; importance of Catholic principles in construction contracts for Catholic institutions; cautious support of a living wage when a business's survival might be at stake; defense of the integrity of most labor leaders at the same time criticizing "moss-back" business leaders; labeling the self-interest of labor unions and collective bargaining "industrial democracy"; insistence on removal of "anti-human" aspects of the Taft-Hartley Act; condemnation of Dixiecrats as antiunion and antidemocratic; challenge to owners of agricultural/sugarcane plants/farms; disapproval of machinery factories for misuse of workers' rights; foreseeing later "plant flight" phenomenon; qualified support of "closed shops" versus almost total rejection of "open shops"; concern about federal laws about expenditures in union elections; suggested procedures in "emergency strike" situations; passing reference to papal teaching about "codetermination"; "family living wage" theory versus prevailing/ change/equivalence/productive wage theories; union failings deemed insignificant compared to management failings.

Labor priests spoke about other economic issues, directly or indirectly distinct from labor–management issues. For example, pleas for a balanced approach of labor policy boards; a transition to a peace-time economy after World War II; full employment; national planning; a living and saving wage; controls on profits-wages-prices; illness and accident insurance; entrepreneurship; pathology in a capitalist system not legally protected to focus on the common good; industrial versus fiscal policy in causing the Great Depression; Reaganomics; just wage; arbitration; mediation; agricultural workers; and emergency strikes.

Some relations between labor priests and business leaders revealed opposition or agreement, misunderstanding or understanding, hostility or friendship. Sometimes, there was opportunity for dialogue or reconciliation, especially when business leaders had participated as students or professors in programs of the Labor Schools or Institutes of Industrial Relations. Given the tenor of labor relations from the 1890s to the 1970s, participation was rare or infrequent. Sometimes business leaders attended courses or lectures, only to stay away as Church support for the right to organize or to take other work action was taught consistently.

No labor priests embraced Communism, but some accepted a non-Marxist type of Socialism. No labor priests espoused Nazism or Fascism. Some were less critical of Franco's Spain due to perceived anti-Catholic bias in the media and academic circles. Most labor priests accepted Capitalism, but most also were critical of its shortcomings and injustices. Indeed, Capitalism was the framework or context for rejection of Communism, Nazism, and Fascism, although the overall context of criticism of any political and economic systems was Catholic Social Teaching, which insisted on freedom of religion and respect for human dignity.

As concerned and as vocal as labor priests were about labor–management relations and other economic issues in the capitalist system, they went further by recommending a variety of legislative changes to improve the lot of workers and others. Examples abounded: state and federal laws or amendments for an eight-hour day; accident and illness insurance; workers' compensation for occupational diseases; prohibition of "yellow dog" contracts; National Industrial Relations Act [NIRA]; child and family welfare; improved and affordable housing; adequate family living wages; family health; employment system; Civilian Conservation Corps [CCC]; unemployment insurance; job training; union organizing; strikes; family allowance; fair employment practices [FEPC]; National Labor Relations Act [NLRA]; closed shop; union shop; farm labor protections; civil rights; etc. However, there was also some opposition to "right-to-work" [RTW] laws; labor-racketeering; plant seizures; Taft-Hartley; military conscription; social security; and fair labor standards [FLSA].

Labor priests also focused on other political challenges, especially with regard to Hispanics and other minorities. After World War II, Communist Party efforts to infiltrate newly arrived Mexican families to Toledo, Ohio, were frustrated when Church officials realized that social justice activities would succeed only by collaboration with labor union, government, and cultural activities. Especially helpful to Puerto Ricans was insistence on recourse to fair employment practices by the National Conference of Catholic Charities to offset discriminatory behavior of employers. In Oklahoma and Texas, Hispanics were aided by mutual help agencies of the Southwest bishops. In several northern cities, efforts were made to train young priests to minister to Hispanics in formerly Irish, German, Italian, and Eastern European parishes.

Prominent were assistance from the U.S. Catholic Committee for the Spanish-Speaking and the establishment of the Catholic Committee on Migrant Farm Labor. Also contributing was the U.S. and Mexican bishops' Inter-American Religious Committee to highlight income disparity in Latin America by participation in the 1959 "Conference on Migratory Labor." Priests in California and Texas offered early assistance to the Agricultural Workers Organizing Committee (AWOC), which eventually led to the successes of César Chávez's strikes, pilgrimages, and boycotts, as well as the National Council of Churches Farm Labor Committee, the successful mediation work of Bishop Joseph Donnelly and Msgr. George Higgins, and AFL–CIO president George Meany's curb on Hoffa's Teamsters' raiding and sweetheart contacts with growers in California. Yeoman's work was done by the legislative lobbying of Fr. James Vizzard, S.J., and the National Catholic Rural Life Conference in attempting to undo Public Law 78 and labor contractors' interference in California and elsewhere, a battle still not thoroughly completed, as Central and South American immigrants flee for a better life up north.

Besides aiding the mostly Catholic Hispanics, labor priests came to the aid of largely Protestant African-Americans. In early 1956, there were efforts to have Michigan develop its own FEPC, in collaboration with the state's Commission on Civil Rights, the NAACP, the Jewish Community Services, and the League of Catholic Women. In Buffalo and New York City, opposition to job discrimination against African-Americans and other minorities in construction, long-shore, housing, railroads was strong.

In 1958, the U.S. bishops, after undue delay, issued a pastoral on racism. Unjust attacks on the National Association for the Advancement of Colored People (NAACP) and Congress of Racial Equality (CORE) for leniency toward communists were sharply repelled by SAD's Fr. Cronin. There was vocal and institutional support for the Peace Corps and scholarships in Africa, Asia, and Latin America. Scorn was poured on the hypocritical Johnny-come-lately cries for minority jobs during debates about right-to-work legislation, especially in Connecticut. The message of papal encyclicals, especially those about justice and labor unions, was attractive to African-American leaders.

In the South, priests and bishops were vocal in their opposition to the White Citizens Councils and the KKK. Among several Jesuits, there was advocacy for social integration of Catholic campuses and outspoken condemnation of racism—personal and institutional. New Orleans's archbishop Rummel endured much maligning from opponents of Catholic parish and school integration. Continued challenges were issued to southern union leaders about racism, especially by Archbishop Lucey, Jesuit Frs. Twomey and Ficther, Fr. Jerome Drolet, and Fr. Vincent O'Connell, O.M.I.

In Chicago opposition to the racism in urban renewal projects and contract-buyers schemes was strong. Minnesotan monsignors Ryan and Gilligan often wrote and spoke about the immorality of the "color line." Outstanding work on behalf of FEPC was performed by Msgr. Haas, not only in persuading FDR to give it some longevity but in chairing the commission for several years. From the late 1960s to the early 1980s, much was done to sustain the efforts of inner city priests, especially by Chicago's Msgr. John Egan's Catholic Committee on Urban Ministry and New Jersey's Msgr. Al Welch's National Conference on Interracial Justice.

When speaking of labor priests' dealings with politicians, it must be said that, with the exception of SAD's Cronin, who temporarily served as Richard Nixon's speechwriter and advisor on "Catholic questions," the trend was encomiums and appointments. The former surfaced during banquets or eulogies, when the significant contributions of the labor priests to the betterment of labor–management relations were extolled. The latter, advisory or investigative, followed upon or led to such contributions and were virtually innumerable: state or federal labor boards, mediation boards, investigative commissions, boards of inquiry, employment relations boards, international commissions esp. after World War II, mediation and conciliation commissions, emergency boards, labor standards committees, immigration committees, housing boards, judiciary committees, and committees on grants and contracts.

Labor priests also had other dealings with politicians: testifying before federal, state, county, and municipal legislative bodies. Yet, probably the most influential labor priest with politicians of every stripe was Msgr. Francis Haas, of Milwaukee and Washington. Haas served on the Wisconsin Labor Board, NRA, NLRA, Works Progress Administration (WPA), Department of Commerce Waterways, National Resources Planning Board, ILO, Federal Industry Committees, U.S. Conciliation Services, National Defense Mediation Board, Emergency Railroad Labor Panel, U.S., Michigan FEPC, and Truman's Civil Rights Commission. Frances Perkins, Roosevelt's secretary of labor, called Haas, "one of the nation's best arbitrators."

APPENDICES

Appendix A. Theological Sources

Leo XIII's Rerum Novarum

Rerum Novarum captured most of Pope Leo's later concerns about the Church and its relations to society, the economy, and State. His encyclical branded "the condition of the working classes…the question of the hour."[1] Published in 1891, the encyclical rejected socialist solutions to the evils of the Industrial Revolution by a defense of private property and condemnation of excessive State intervention. Leo's remedy was a mixture of Church teaching and action, proper State intervention, and appropriate associations of workers and employers.

Without distinguishing the varieties of socialists or mentioning communists, Leo dismissed their goals of doing away with private property, so that all property becomes common to all and is administered by the State or municipal bodies. While insisting that private property was necessary for personal maintenance and development, indeed was a natural right, Leo stressed that private property had to be used responsibly for the benefit of the needy. Such was a duty not enforced by human law, but by Christian charity and even justice in cases of extreme need. State interference would deprive persons and families of their rights, giving rise to instability and bondage, envy and invective, discord and disinterest in exerting one's talents and industry.

The Church had an irreplaceable role of teaching and charitable works. Leo recognized that within Capitalism there had "to be acceptance of human inequalities and sufferings as well as class collaboration," but warned against the tendency to maintain the status quo and deny the need for reforms based on the proper understanding of the duties and rights of employers and workers. In God's eyes poverty was no disgrace, for true human worth and nobility lies in moral qualities, "virtues...equally within the reach of high and low, rich and poor and ... followed by the rewards of everlasting happiness." Employers and workers "should dwell in harmony and agreement, to maintain the balance of the body politic." To prevent and uproot social strife, "there is no intermediary more powerful than Religion...by reminding each of its duties...and especially of the obligations of justice." Religion demanded reforms: insisting that workers are not chattel whose only reason for being is to provide their physical strength and monetary value to employers, but have dignity and worth as humans and Christians. Besides teaching morality, the Church had to intervene through relief associations and special funds for the needy.

The State must "make sure the laws and institutions, the general character and administration of the commonwealth shall be such as of themselves to realize public well-being and private prosperity." Every class should benefit, especially the poor and wage earners who make up the mass of the needy and should be especially cared for and protected by the State. Individuals and families should be safeguarded, not absorbed, by the State. "[Whenever] the general interests or any particular class suffers or is threatened with harm, which in no other way can be met or prevented, the public authority must step in to deal with it." The State must defend the spiritual and moral interests of workers, so they can have proper leisure to worship and rest; safeguard "private property by legal enactment and protection"; remove by public remedial measures "causes which lead to conflicts between employers and employed"; prevent strikes, which harm the common good and trade and threaten public peace; protect workers from the cruelty of greed as instruments for money-making, by regulating working hours and conditions, especially for children and women.

Striking was Leo's call for a living and just wage to enable a worker "comfortably to support himself, his wife and his children...to put by some little savings and thus secure a modest source of income." Thus, the "gulf between vast wealth and sheer poverty would be bridged over and respective classes will be brought nearer to one another." "If through necessity or fear of a worse evil a worker accepts harder conditions because an employer or contractor will afford him no better, he is made the victim of force and injustice." The state has the duty "to induce as many as possible of the people to become owners," but not to deprive, by excessive taxation, "the private owner of more than is fair."

Important for the present research was Leo's insistence on associations or organizations that "afford opportune aid to those who are in distress" and "draw the two classes more closely together." He spoke of workingmen's unions that consisted of workers alone or workers and employers together, because it was the natural right of every person to enter into private societies that pursue the advantages of their associates. It was the State's duty to protect this right. Although the State may prohibit such associations, if the common good is at stake, the State should not impose unreasonable regulations. Forbidden were associations, controlled by secret leaders, who would expose religion to peril and "do their utmost to get within their grasp the whole field of labor, and force workers either to join them or to starve." Recommended was the formation of Christian associations to help workers to "unite their forces and shake off courageously the yoke of so unrighteous and intolerable oppression." Besides promoting religious and moral instruction, the Christian associations should, whenever possible, appoint a committee to settle disputes between owners and workers, provide regular employment, and create a relief fund for workers. Catholic scholars largely agree that Leo did not think in terms of full-scale trade unions and was influenced by the "corporatism" and "paternalism" prevalent in the *Semaines Sociale*, which he regularly attended while papal legate to Brussels, before becoming pope. The encyclical ended with strong exhortations to government and employers, especially with an insistence on the Church's right to speak on the evils of the day and the obligation of "[every] minister of holy religion to bring to the struggle the full energy of his mind and his power of endurance."

Labor priests displayed energy of mind and heart, but often had to contend with periodic criticisms of *Rerum Novarum*, understandable in some cases because scholars interpreted the encyclical in different ways. For some, the encyclical lacked any deep analysis of Capitalism, Socialism, and the role of history.[1] While Socialism was condemned as totally evil, capitalists were judged from an individualist not a systemic perspective. While the flagrant inequalities between different social classes and problems of economic distribution were underplayed, recognition of more modern equalitarian aspirations and the social function of property were virtually missing. Though the encyclical's ideas were new to most Catholics at the turn of the century, in light of the tepid teachings of earlier popes, Leo's ideas were considerably behind the advances of the worker movement. Twenty-five years earlier the First International was established and several decades earlier unions had been established in Europe and England. Indeed, between the fear of Socialism and confusion about the understanding of ownership of personal property and the exact idea of ownership of the means of production, the impression among Catholic employers that the encyclical was quite progressive. Such was not warranted, due to abstract arguments rather than adequate analysis. It was taken up with ethical considerations and remained vague on most of the practical problems of the day. *Rerum Novarum*, while more cautious and moderate than the few Catholic U.S. activists of the time, was far ahead of most Church members, which was clearly evident in their indifference or negative reaction. Nonetheless, there was enough interest, one way or the other, to prepare a more attentive audience forty years later for Pope Pius XI's *Quadragesimo Anno.*

Pius XI's Quadragesimo Anno

Published in 1931, *Quadragesimo Anno* (On Reconstructing the Social Order) began with a very enthusiastic endorsement and account of the impact of *Rerum Novarum.*[1] Leo's writings were said to be a bold attack and overthrow of "the idols of Liberalism" (laissez-faire economics), an ignoring of long-standing prejudices, and an advance of its time beyond all expectation, "so that the slow of heart disdained to study this new social philosophy, and the timid feared to scale so lofty a height." Such encomiums of predecessors' writings thereafter became the usual manner of introductions to later papal encyclicals. The praise of Leo continued: "Catholic principles on the social question have...passed little by little into the patrimony of all human society." Quite a tribute, but too much credit for one man's work and too wide a scope for its impact. Coupled with the amplifications and clarifications found in *Quadragesimo Anno,* however, Leo's primal text of modern Catholic Social Teaching did have an impact on Catholics later, especially through the labor priests. Restated were the principles of the right of property, harmony of classes, just wages, moral and spiritual rather than economic roots of the problem, a limited but very necessary role of the State and the value of voluntary associations, as well as an appeal to natural law and the Church's authority in social and economic matters. Emphasized was that for reconstruction of the social order, "two things are especially necessary: reform of social institutions and correction of morals." The modern economic order was said to be built not on true moral laws, but on "completely free rein...given to human passions," especially the "unquenchable thirst for riches and temporal goods." Yet there were also new developments concerning modern Capitalism, private property, capital and labor, just wages, role of the State, role of associations, Communism, and Socialism.

Modern Capitalism and modern industry had advanced so that human society was clearly divided into two classes. One was very small but enjoyed almost all the advantages that modern society inventions created. The other included the large numbers of workers, oppressed by poverty and unsuccessfully trying to escape their everyday plight at work and elsewhere. So-called inevitable economic laws were said to be responsible for this state of society. Overlooked were attempts to hide violations of justice that lawmakers not only tolerated but often sanctioned: they want the "whole care of supporting of the poor committed to charity alone." Catholics were advised not to believe that such an enormous and unjust inequality in the distribution of this world's goods truly "conformed to the designs of the all-wise Creator." This dominant economic system is the result of a competition in which the strong survived thanks to "an immense power and despotic economic dictatorship concentrated in the hands of the few." Such accumulation generated three kinds of conflict: the struggle for supremacy itself; the struggle for supremacy over the State; and the struggle for supremacy among States. Pius XI said, "free competition has destroyed itself; dictatorship has supplanted the free market; unbridled ambition for power has likewise succeeded greed for gain; all economic life has become tragically hard, inexorable and cruel." Even the State had become "a slave, surrendered to [the] passions and greed of men." On the international level, there was economic nationalism or economic imperialism, internationalism finance or international imperialism. In appealing to Leo's authority, Pius XI would not condemn Capitalism, as long as it adjusted to the norms of right order. In Pius XI's mind, the social character of economic activity, social justice, and the common good were polar opposites of scorn for the dignity of workers. He moved to a discussion of private property, capital and labor, just wages, the role of the State, and the role of various intermediary associations.

In defending private property Pius XI spoke of its twofold character: individual persons and common good. Repeating Leo XIII, he stated, "The right of property is distinct from its use" and "cannot be destroyed or lost by reason of abuse or non-use." Yet "the duty of owners to use their property only in the right way" comes under the heading of virtues, "the obligations of which cannot be enforced by legal action." In terms of requirements of the common good, the State "can determine more accurately what is permitted and what is not permitted to owners in the use of their property." A person's superfluous income is not left wholly to the owner's free choice, for "the rich are bound by a very grave precept to practice almsgiving and munificence." More than Leo XIII, Pius XI stressed the right and duty of the State to specify the limits of private property and its use.

Pius XI said that neither capital nor labor could claim the products of combined efforts. In social justice one class cannot exclude the other from sharing in the benefits of the productive process. "Each one...must receive his due share, and the distribution of created goods must be brought into conformity with the demands of the common good or social justice." He was convinced that the distribution of wealth was gravely defective, especially in light of the poor (proletarians) in developing countries and a "huge army of rural wage workers, pushed to the lowest level of existence and deprived of hope of acquiring some property in land" and opportunity of accumulating a just share of the fruits of production.

Pius XI's discussion of just wages went beyond Leo's, stressing industry and thrift for gaining some property to a distinction about the wage contract. It was not deemed "essentially unjust," but more advisable that, in the present conditions of society, it could be modified somewhat by a "partnership contract." Thus, employees "become sharers in ownership or management or participate in some fashion in the profits received." Since labor enjoyed an individual and social character, Pius XI laid out three factors in fixing wages. First, workers must be paid a wage sufficient to support themselves and their families, but it is grossly wrong "to abuse the years of childhood and the limited strength of women" and to force mothers of families "to engage in gainful occupations outside the home to the neglect of their proper cares and duties, especially in the training of children." Second, it would be unjust to demand excessive wages that a business could not pay without "its ruin and consequent calamity to the workers." Third, "the amount of pay must be adjusted to the public economic good," which requires abundant employment facilities, a right proportion between various wages and prices—including a balance between agricultural, manufacturing, and other sectors of the economy—and wages sufficient to enable workers "to attain gradually to the possession of a moderate amount of wealth."

In discussing the role of the State, Pius XI reiterated Leo's injunction that just freedom of action must be left to individuals and families, only on condition that the common good is served and harm to any individual is avoided. However, Pius XI rejoiced that there was a "new branch of law" to protect the sacred rights of workers; these rights flow from the human and Christian dignity of workers and they protect life, health, strength, family homes, workshops, wages, and labor hazards. States also have a major role to play in promoting the proper distribution of wealth, because "the right ordering of economic life cannot be left to a free competition of forces." Those forces, especially any forms of economic dictatorship, must be kept within just and definite limits and brought under effective control by the State.

Again, praising the success of Leo's ideas on voluntary associations, which were still fewer in number than socialist and communist associations, Pius XI cautioned about Catholics joining "secular unions." Such unions, he believed, should always profess justice and equity and Catholics members should have full freedom to follow their consciences and Church laws. Bishops had the right to approve of Catholic workers joining secular unions. Secular unions must always be complemented by Catholic associations for the moral and religious training of the workers. Then, Pius XI introduced the concept of subsidiarity: let subordinate groups handle matters and concerns of lesser importance. The State would handle more freely, powerfully, and effectively what belongs to it alone: directing, watching, urging, and restraining, as occasions require and necessity demands. Respect for subsidiarity makes social authority stronger and more effective and the condition of the State will be happier and more prosperous. Thus, Pius XI did not attempt to denigrate or dismiss the necessity of intermediary associations in reducing or restraining class conflicts, in order to promote harmony and cooperation in various industries and professions. In fact, he evaluated "a special system of syndicates and corporations" that arose at that time. Advantages, probably in Italy, were noted. "The various classes work together peacefully; socialist organizations and their activities are repressed; and a special magistracy exercises a governing authority." On the other hand, there was a fear that the syndical and corporative order savored too much of an involved and political system of administration, which served particular ends rather than leading to reconstruction and the promotion of a better social order. Also, there was a danger that the State, instead of confining itself to furnishing necessary and adequate assistance, might substitute itself for the free activity of individuals and other groups in society.

Unlike Leo, Pius XI distinguished two types of Socialism, which were often bitterly hostile to one another but without abandoning their fundamental opposition to Catholic teaching. One type had sunk into Communism with two objectives: unrelenting class warfare and absolute extermination of private ownership. This type, which was said to be and had proven to be openly hostile to the Church and God, had laid waste to vast regions of Eastern Europe and Asia. "By violence and slaughter, the pope said, "this type of socialism seeks] to destroy society altogether." The other type of Socialism, which kept the name and was more moderate, "inclines toward and in a certain measure approaches the truths that Christian tradition has always held sacred." Socialism's demands at times came very close to those of Christian reformers. Furthermore, if recourse to violence and opposition to private ownership continued to recede, Socialism would no longer differ from the desires and demands of those striving to remold society on Christian principles. Also, a degree of nationalization or socialization of some means of production would be indirectly legitimized. Pius XI argued, however, that even granting such points of agreement between Catholic Social Teaching and the milder form of Socialism, the socialist concept of society remained "utterly foreign to Christian truth" because Socialism was based on an entirely atheistic and materialistic concept of humans and society. "Religious Socialism, Christian Socialism, are contradictory terms; no one can be at the same time a good Catholic and a true Socialist." Catholics then were urged not to "profess socialist doctrines" or "join associations which are socialist by profession or in fact." Even further, Pius XI said, "Let us remember that Liberalism is the father of this Socialism that is pervading morality and culture and that Bolshevism will be its Heir."

Authors have commented on the seeming contradictions in *Quadragesimo Anno*, which still stir debate in some more conservative Catholic circles. According to Desrochers, some authors thought Pius XI was referring to the "State-controlled corporations that Mussolini was trying to build up."[1] Desrochers said Calvez and Perrin thought Pius XII was influenced by the example of Salazar in

Portugal. Yet, Desrochers himself was not sure whether Pius XI was referring to Spain's Republican Party with Socialist support, Norman Thomas's small U.S. Socialist Party, England's more humane and moral Labor Party, or the socialist parties in German and France, which were well organized, strongly anticlerical, tended toward Communism, and held many seats in their respective assemblies. Whatever the ultimate outcome of such a debate the seeming inconsistencies, if not contradictions, in Pius XI's encyclical, the activities and writings of many labor priests in the United States were more moderate, especially after the release in 1919 of the U.S. bishops' *Pastoral Letter*.

U.S. Catholic Bishops' Pastorals

The influence of the U.S. bishops' *Pastoral Letter of 1919* was commented on above: its foreshadowing several New Deal programs, its basic authorship by Msgr. John A. Ryan, and its utilization by many labor priests. Yet, what is not generally known about this document is that it was approved only by the NCWC Administrative Committee of four bishops, not the full body of cardinals, archbishops, and bishops at that time. Its Foreword succinctly stated its need (to remind all that the only safeguard of peace is social justice and a contented people) and its purpose (to raise hope in facing multiple national and world problems by offering some guidelines).[1] Despite the aversion of many to the term social reconstruction, the inability to determine precisely what parts of the social system needed reconstruction and an uncertainty about the specific methods and measures suited to bringing about the necessary reconstruction, the bishops reviewed important proposals from various individuals and groups.

Examples of statements—the inclusion of which revealed Ryan's acumen—came from English Cardinal Bourne (his pastoral letter); the British Labor Party (authored by the Fabian socialist Sidney

Webb); the AFL Committee on Reconstruction; British Quaker Employers; the U.S. Chamber of Commerce; and the Inter-denominational Conference of Social Service Unions, which comprised nine Protestant bodies and the Catholic Church. The tone of all those statements varied from the radical—the policies of the British Labor Party—to the conservative—the U.S. Chamber of Commerce's 1918 statement, which contained nothing of importance regarding the labor phase of reconstruction.

The bishops did not expect any great social changes in the United States, however, in light of the diminished ravages of war, fewer disruptions of industrial relations, and fewer government interventions than in Europe. Thus, they proposed a more practical and moderate program of reconstruction, one likely to be attainable within a reasonable amount of time, in order to provoke Catholics into expressing their faith in good deeds and to spur on all sectors and levels of society to constructive action.

Benefits derived from the wartime experience of prestigious governmental agencies and from legislative measures enacted during that period had to be continued and expanded.

- Top priority ought to be given to returning service men, returning them to their former jobs or even more attractive employment, including giving them land and loans to become farmers.

- Retain and strengthen the highly successful U.S. Employment Service.

- No female worker should remain in any occupation harmful to health and morals, despite the many contributions of women to the war effort. The proportion of women in industry should be kept to the smallest practical limits and they should find suitable employment, especially in domestic occupations.

- Provided a goodly number of returning servicemen were available, wages and demand for goods ought to be kept at attainable levels *and* women engaged in the same tasks as men should receive equal pay for equal amounts and qualities of work.

- The National War Labor Board should continue in operation and be endowed with all the power for effective action under the U.S. Constitution, because its principles, methods, machinery, and results constituted a definite and far-reaching gain for social justice.

- Save for the exception of skilled workers, wages should not be reduced from wartime levels, even when the cost of living dropped from earlier high level. For in Catholic teaching a living wage is only the *minimum* due in justice. And, in fact, a living wage is the most effective instrument for both labor and capital.

- The example and precedent, experience and knowledge developed in housing projects during the war should not be forgotten or lost.

- The worst features of social conditions that menace industrial efficiency, civic health, good morals, and religion should be eliminated.

- If adequate laws and enforcement do away with the extortionate practices of monopoly, prices will automatically be kept at as low a level as possible, lower even than what they might be as a result of direct government determination.

- Even more effective than any government regulation of prices would be the establishment of cooperative stores, which would also train working people in habits of saving, careful expenditures, business methods, and capacity for cooperation.

- In addition to better utilization of existing agencies and laws, the bishops focused on labor problems and legislation. States, they said, should enact laws to keep wages high enough to make possible the amount of savings necessary to protect the worker and family against sickness, accidents, invalidity, and old age.

- Until levels of legal minimum wages are reached, workers need comprehensive provisions for insurance against illness, invalidity, unemployment, and old age.

- Funds for such insurance should be levied on the industry in which the worker is employed. Any government contribution should be only slight and temporary. No contribution should be exacted from workers whose wages do not meet the needs of the worker and family.

- Individual freedom of the workers and family should not be interfered with by the administration of the fund, for such interference would separate workers into a distinct and dependent class, offend their domestic privacy, or threaten their individual self-reliance and self-respect.

- Thus, all forms of state insurance should be regarded as merely a lesser evil and be so organized and administered as to hasten the coming of normal conditions.

- While the establishment and maintenance of municipal health inspection in all schools—public and private—is of great importance and benefit, every effort should be exerted to supply wager-earners with specialized medical care through the development of group medicine.

- The right of workers to organize and bargain collectively through their own spokespersons should never again be questioned.

- Also, there should be "shop committees," cooperating with trade unions, to give workers the proper share of industrial management, to promote the general welfare of the workers, to improve relations between employers and employees, and to increase the efficiency and productiveness of each workplace.

- Legislation concerning safety and sanitation in the workplace needed to be extended, strengthened, administered, and enforced.

- Vocational training should ensure industrial and cultural education for children of the entire society, including those attending parochial and other private schools. "We want neither class divisions in education nor a state monopoly of education."

- Public opinion must be further educated on the abolition of child labor. This, the bishops explained, remained the domain of state legislatures. Since attempts at federal legislation had been declared unconstitutional, a proposed amendment to a Federal Reserve Bill that would impose a 10 percent tax on profits on all goods produced by children was a step to take.

Given all the proposals pertaining to the past and looking to the future, the bishops were firm in stating the need for focusing on ultimate aims, a systematic program, and a philosophical foundation. The retention of Capitalism and objection to Socialism were "givens." Socialism was deemed to generate more bureaucracy, political tyranny, helpless individuals, social inefficiency, and decadence. However, three defects of Capitalism were also cited. First, an enormous inefficiency and waste in the production and distribution of commodities. Second, insufficient incomes for the majority of wage earners. Third, unnecessarily large incomes for a small minority of the privileged capitalists.

To the bishops, the reforms they proposed would greatly reduce the insufficiency in production. The waste of commodity distribution could be practically eliminated by cooperative mercantile establishments and cooperative selling and marketing associations. To achieve such goals, however, workers had to be more than wage earners and become in some way owners and instruments of production. The bishops thought this could become a reality, in gradual stages, through cooperative productive societies (owning and managing the industries) and co-partnership arrangements (partial ownership of stock and a share in management). Finally, to remedy excessive gains by an already wealthy minority there had to be an end to monopolistic control of commodities; adequate government regulation of public service monopolies; and heavy taxation of incomes, excess profits, and inheritances.

The U.S. bishops' *Pastoral Letter of 1919* concluded with a quote from Pope Leo XIII in 1891: "Society can be healed in no other way than by a return to Christian life and Christian institutions." Whatever the programs, policies, or legislation, the bishops were insistent on the need for a renewal of the spirit of labor and management. "This is the human and Christian [way], in contrast to the purely commercial and pagan, ethics of industry."

Later, there were other U.S. bishops' pastorals, especially during the depths of the Depression in 1933 and 1940, as well as statements on farm labor and race relations. Many, like the 1984 peace pastoral and the 1986 economic pastoral, aimed to apply to the United States Vatican documents, especially those from the Vatican Council II and popes John XXIII, Paul VI, and John Paul II. More recent U.S. bishops' teaching contains much more material from Sacred Scripture, lending a more interfaith relevance to otherwise perceived "Catholic" and "Church" analysis and prospects on cultural, economic, political, and social issues of the day.

Appendix B.

Labor Priests, with Details

Last Name	First Name	Location
Alter	Archbishop Karl	Toledo-Cincinnati, Ohio
Benecke, S.J.	Karl	San Francisco, California
Boland	John P.	Buffalo, New York
Bolger, C.S.C.	William A.	Notre Dame, Indiana
Boss, S.J.	Andrew C.	San Francisco, California
Boyle, S.J.	Edward F.	Boston, Massachusetts
Brennan, F.S.C.	Cornelius J.	New York, New York
Brown, S.J.	Leo C.	St. Louis, Missouri
Callaghan, S.J.	Hubert C.	Worcester, Massachusetts
Cantwell	Daniel	Chicago, Illinois
Carey, S.J.	Philip A.	New York, New York
Carney	Francis W.	Cleveland, Ohio
Carroll, S.J.	Clifford A.	Spokane, Washington
Clancy	Raymond S.	Detroit, Michigan
Comey, S.J.	Dennis J.	Philadelphia, Pennsylvania
Coogan	Thomas F.	Los Angeles, California
Corridan, S.J.	John M.	New York, New York
Cox	James R.	Pittsburg, Pennsylvania
Cronin, S.S.	John F.	Baltimore, Maryland
Curran	John J.	Wilkes-Barre, Pennsylvania
Darby	Thomas J.	New York, New York
Dempsey, S.J.	Bernard W.	Milwaukee, Wisconsin
Devine, S.J.	Thomas F.	Milwaukee, Wisconsin

Dietz	Peter E.	Milwaukee, Wisconsin
Dobson, S.J.	Philip E.	Jersey City, New Jersey
Donnelly	Bishop Joseph F.	Hartford, Connecticut
Donohoe	Bishop Hugh A.	San Francisco, California
Donovan	Leo B.	Detroit, Michigan
Dore, O.P.	Vincent C.	Providence, Rhode Island
Doyle, S.S.J.	John	Galveston, Texas
Drolet	Jerome	New Orleans, Louisiana
Dunne, S.J.	George H.	Los Gatos, California
Egan	Jack J.	Chicago, Illinois
Erbacker, O.F.M.	Sebastian	Detroit, Michigan
Eschweiler	Francis L.	Milwaukee, Wisconsin
Fitzgerald, C.S.C.	Mark J.	Notre Dame, Indiana
Fitzpatrick, S.J.	Joseph P.	New York, New York
Flynn	Patrick J.	Rochester, New York
Friedl, S.J.	John C.	Kansas City, Missouri
Gallagher	Cornelius	Steubenville, Ohio
Gallagher, S.J.	Ralph A.	Chicago, Illinois
Gallery, S.J.	J. Eugene	Scranton, Pennsylvania
Gavin, S.J.	Mortimer H.	Boston, Massachusetts
Gibbons	Bishop Edmund F.	Albany, New York
Gilligan	Francis J.	St. Paul, Minnesota
Haas	Bishop Francis A.	Grand Rapids, Michigan
Hanna	Archbishop Edward J.	San Francisco, California
Hayes	Msgr. John M.	Chicago, Illinois
Healy	James A.	Buffalo, New York
Higgins	George F.	Washington, D.C.
Hillenbrand	Reynold	Chicago, Illinois

Hoffman	Mathias M.	Dubuque, Iowa
Hubble	Karl D.	Detroit, Michigan
Husselein, S.J.	Joseph C.	Milwaukee, Wisconsin
Kearney	Bishop James E.	Rochester, New York
Kelly, F.S.C.	Brother Bernard	Philadelphia, Pennsylvania
Kelly	George A.	New York, New York
Kelley	William J.	Buffalo, New York
Kerby	William J.	Washington, D.C.
Kern	Clement H.	Detroit, Michigan
Kilcoyne	George R.	Manchester, New Hampshire
Kulpinski	Msgr. Stanley A.	Buffalo, New York
Kurth	Edmund A.	Dubuque, Iowa
Lamanna	Joseph P.	Albany, New York
Land, S.J.	Philip S.	Washington, D.C.
Lavelle	Richard B.	Brooklyn, New York
Lucey	Archbishop Robert E.	San Antonio, Texas
Maguire, O.S.V.	John W.	Arlington Heights, Illinois
Masse, S.J.	Benjamin L.	New York, New York
McGowan	Raymond A.	Washington, D.C.
McKeon, S.J.	Richard M.	Syracuse, New York
McNicholas	Archbishop Nicholas T.	Cincinnati, Ohio
Mitty	Archbishop John J.	San Francisco, California
Monaghan	John P.	New York, New York
Mooney	Cardinal Edward	Detroit, Michigan
Muldoon	Bishop Peter J.	Rockford, Illinois
Mullaly, S.J.	Edward J.	Philadelphia, Pennsylvania
Mulvey, S.J.	Daniel P.	Kingston, Jamaica
Munier	Joseph D.	San Francisco, California

Navin	Robert B.	Cleveland, Ohio
O'Connell, O.M.I	Vincent J.	New Orleans, Louisiana
O'Connor	William T.	Davenport, Iowa
Parsons, S.J.	Wilfred	Washington, D.C.
Phillips	Charles	San Francisco, California
Purcell, S.J.	Theodore C.	Chicago, Illinois
Quirk, O.P.	Charles B.	Providence, Rhode Island
Rice	Msgr. Charles O.	Pittsburg, Pennsylvania
Rummel, Arch.	Joseph	New Orleans, Louisiana
Ryan	Msgr. John A.	Washington, D.C.
Salandini	V. P.	San Diego, California
Schrembs	Archbishop Joseph	Cleveland, Ohio
Shiel, Bp.	Bernard J.	Chicago, Illinois
Shortell, S.J.	Thomas E.	Worcester, Massachusetts
Siedenburg, S.J.	Fredric J.	Chicago, Illinois
Smith	Sherill	San Antonio, Texas
Smith, S.J.	William J.	Brooklyn, New York
Stein	Anthony	Paterson, New Jersey
Swanstrom	Bishop Edward E.	Brooklyn, New York
Tobin	Thomas J.	Portland, Oregon
Tranchese, S.J.	Carmello A.	San Antonio, Texas
Twomey, S.J.	Louis J.	New Orleans, Louisiana
Vizzard, S.J.	James L.	Washington, D.C.
Yorke	Peter C.	San Francisco, California

Appendix III

Labor Priests, without Details

Last Name	First Name	Location
Adama		Albany, New York
Alvarez	Augustine	San Francisco, California
Andryaskiewirz		
Arzuba	Bishop Juan	
Darrett, S.J.		St. Louis, Missouri
Bauer	Donald	Syracuse, New York
Bausehlanrl	Raymond	Columbus, Ohio
Beix		Milwaukee Wisconsin
Blatz	Albert B.	St. Paul-Minneapolis, Minnesota
Boland	James	Philadelphia, Pennsylvania
Boldt	William	Albany, New York
Bona	Thomas	Chicago, Illinois
Boyd		Chicago, Illinois
Boyer	J. Edward	Buffalo, New York
Boyle	John B.	Cincinnati, Ohio
Breer	Vincent I.	San Francisco, California
Brennan	Cornelius	Philadelphia, Pennsylvania
Brock		Providence, Rhode Island
Brady	Lawrence A.	Akron, Ohio
Brady	Bishop Matthew	Burlington, Vermont
Brosk	Edmund J.	Providence, Rhode Island
Buckley	Joseph	Brooklyn, New York
Burke	Ronald	San Francisco, California
Burno	Frank	Rochester, New York

Bums, S.J.	B.	Scranton University
Burns	Bernard	Chicago, Illinois
Byrne	Francis E.	Philadelphia, Pennsylvania
Byrne	James	Albany, New York
Byme	John	New York
Cahill	John	Brooklyn, New York
Cantillo		Buffalo, New York
Cardin	Victor	Red Lake, Minnesota
Carney	Thomas A.	Dickerson, Texas
Carrabine	Martin	New York
Carroll	John	Cleveland, Ohio
Casey	Joseph	Indianapolis, Indiana
Casey	William	Brooklyn, New York
Chapman, S.J.	Charles	Loyola
Chodocki, O.M.I.		Pass Christian, Texas
Chutio, O.S.B.	Gervase	Latrobe, Pennsylvania
Cihala,	John J.	Tonington, Connecticut
Clancy	Matthew	Toledo, Ohio
Clarke		Chicago, Illinois
Clougherty		Pittsburgh, Pennsylvania
Coady	Leo	Washington, D.C.
Coffield,	John	Los Angeles, California
Colburn	Frank	Los Angeles, California
Coir	Michael	Paterson, New Jersey
Collins	John	Albany, New York
Collins	Thomas J.	Detroit Michigan
Conarty	Thomas	Brooklyn, New York
Corbett, S.J.		Philadelphia, Pennsylvania
Cordov	C.A.	Binghamton, New York
Craig, M.M.	Hugh	Korea

Critis, O.S.B.	Gervase	Latrobe, Pennsylvania
Cronin	Daniel J.	Worcester, Massachusetts
Cronin	John F.	Brooklyn, New York
Cunningham	Lawrence	Austin, Minnesota
Cunningham	Lawrence	Detroit, Michigan
D'Agostino	Lorenzo	St. Michael, Vermont
Daly	Mark	California
Dawson	William	Philadelphia, Pennsylvania
Day, O.F.M.	Mark	Fresno, California
Deane	Joseph	San Antonio, Texas
Decker, O.M.I.	Paul	San Antonio, Texas
Deegan		San Francisco, California
Delaney, S.J.	John	New York
Devlin		Los Angeles, California
Donne	Joseph	San Antonio, Texas
Deters, S.J.	Richard T.	
Devine	Thomas	Holyoke, Massachusetts
Doherty	Bishop Joseph	Yakima
Donahue, O.S.V.	Joseph	Chicago, Illinois
Donovan	Leo	Albany, New York
Dougherty		Pittsburgh, Pennsylvania
Dougherty, S.J.		Scranton University
Dowin, , S.J.	William	
Dowling	Edward	
Downey	John	Lynn, Massachusetts
Drier		Plymouth, Pennsylvania
Duffy	John	Buffalo, New York
Dunne	Lanihert	Newark, New Jersey
Dynievicz	Daniel	Chicago, Illinois
Ebner	Mark S.	St. Louis, Missouri

Edison	Thomas	Detroit Michigan
Ellinger	Paul	San Antonio, Texas
Fagan	Girard	Newark, New Jersey
Faidel	Michael	Pittsburgh, Pennsylvania
Faistl	Clement F.	Columbus, Ohio
Fay	Thomas	Boston, Massachusetts
Feeley, S.J.	Raymond	San Francisco, California
Finn	John A.	Springfield, Massachusetts
Finn	John J.	Albany, New York
Finrican	James	LaCrosse, Wisconsin
Fitchler, S.J.	Joe	New Orleans, Louisiana
Flanagan	Joseph F.	New Canaan, Connecticut
Flanagan	Frank	Cincinnati, Ohio
Flanagan	W.J.	Lansing, Michigan
Flynn	Patrick J.	Buffalo, New York
Forton	Gerald	Buffalo, New York
Fox	John P.	Alaska
Fox, S.J.	Richard	LeMoyne College
Francis, O.F.M.	John	Cap Vitoria, Kansas
Freking	Msgr.	Cincinnati, Ohio
Fufford	Michael	Albany, New York
Galik	George	Duluth, Minnesota
Gallery, S.J.	Eugene	Scranton, Pennsylvania
Gallik	Msgr. George A.	Duluth, Minnesota
Gallilo	George	Chicago, Illinois
Garcia	John	San Francisco, California
Garvin	John L.	Oklahoma City, Oklahoma
Gavin	John, C.M.	Brooklyn, New York
Gefell	Joseph	Buffalo, New York
Geisler	Joy	Albany, New York

Gerber		Peoria, Illinois
Giay	James	San Francisco, California
Giblin	Charles L.	New York, New York
Gilmore	Bishop Joseph M.	Helena, Montana
Glenn	Lawrence	Chicago, Illinois
Glenn	Lawrence	Duluth, Minnesota
Gobig	G.N.	Ohio
Goney	Maximiliano	San Francisco, California
Gordon	Michael	Buffalo, New York
Grenier	Stephen	Providence, Rhode Island
Griffin	Joseph	New Britain, Connecticut
Griffins		Altoona, Pennsylvania
Griffins	Joseph	Butte, Montana
Grode	Joseph	Erie, Pennsylvania
Grody	Phillip	Albany, New York
Habig	G.N.	Canton, Ohio
Haffey, S.J.	Henry	St. Peters, Jersey City
Hagerty	T.J.	
Hamel, S.S.E.	Edmund	St. Michael College, Vermont
Hammond	Joseph	Brooklyn, New York
Harbrecht, S.J.		Georgetown University
Harcy	Paschal	Costa Mesa, California
Harkin		Oklahoma City, Oklahoma
Hart, S.J.	Dan	St. Peters, Jersey City
Harvel, S.S.E.	Edmund J.	St. Michael College, Vermont
Hauley	Richard H.J.	Brooklyn, New York
Head	Bishop Edward	Buffalo, New York
Helling, , S.J.	Frederick	Brooklyn, New York
Hennessy, S.J.	James	Brooklyn, New York
Hensler	Carl P.	Pittsburgh, Pennsylvania

Herk, J.F.M.	D.	St. Michael, Arizona
Hickey	Bishop Dennis	Buffalo, New York
Hicknov		Richmond, Virginia
Higgins, S.J.	Thomas	St. Joe, Philadelphia
Hinds	Harold	Albany, New York
Hiti	Matthias	Chicago, Illinois
Hogan	Charles	Cleveland, Ohio
Holleman	Henry	New Orleans, Louisiana
Hughes	Joseph	Duluth, Minnesota
Johnson, S.J.	Jeff	El Paso, Texas
Jones	Bishop William	Puerto Rico
Jordan	R.D.	Pittston, Pennsylvania
Josklin, S.J.		Scranton, Pennsylvania
Joyce, S.S. Sp.		Norwalk, Connecticut
Kanally		Boston, Massachusetts
Kane		Scranton, Pennsylvania
Kay	Thomas	Albany, New York
Kazinsky	Adelbert	Braddock, Pennsylvania
Kearney	Bishop James	Rochester, New York
Keenan, S.J.		Seattle, Washington
Kelly	William	Denver, Colorado
Kelly	Martin F.	Cleveland, Ohio
Kennedy	Robert	Brooklyn, New York
Kenny	Keith	California
Killion	William	
Kiorelly		
Kirby	Edward	Cleveland, Ohio
Kirv, O.F.M.	Brian	Quincy College, Illinois
Kunkle		Chicago
Kum, O.F.M.	Brian	Quincy College, Illinois

Kusiak	John P.	Cavlor, Ohio
Lanelle	Richard	New York
Lappan	Thomas	Pittsburgh, Pennsylvania
LaReau		Albany, New York
Larkin	Martin P.	Duluth, Minnesota
Larkin	Mark	Chicago, Illinois
Larkin	Martin	Duluth, Minnesota
Larkin	William	Chicago, Illinois
Larkin	William	Duluth, Minnesota
Lavelle	Richard B.	Brooklyn, New York
Lee	John	Buffalo, New York
Lehrinan	John	Buffalo, New York
Lickens. S .J.		West Boden, Hawai'i
Lickling, C.S.S.R.	Bernard	
Liebroatz. O.F.M.	Arthur	San Francisco
Lockwood	Msgr. James T.	
Lopez	John	San Antonio, Texas
Lopez	John	New Orleans, Louisiana
Lappor	Thomas	Pittsburgh, Pennsylvania
Lofus		Oklahoma City, Oklahoma
Marren	John	Chicago, Illinois
Marshall	Eugene	Pittsfield
Masteison	Donald	Chicago, Illinois
Mattingly	H.E.	Columbus, Ohio
Maxwell		Buffalo, New York
McCarron, S.J.		Baltimore, Maryland
McCulloly	Thomas	San Francisco, California
McDonald, C.S.S.R.	Maurice	Brooklyn, New York
McDonell	Donald	San Francisco, California
McGill	Henry	Mobile, Alabama

McGovem	Edward	
McGrady	Thomas	Boston and Kentucky
McIntosh, S.J.	William	Los Angeles, California
McLaughlin	Gerald L.	Lennox, Massachusetts
McLaughlin	J .F.M. Emmitt	Phoenix, Arizona
McLaughlin	Michael	Brooklyn, New York
McManus	Edward	Albany, New York
McNamee		Oklahoma City, Oklahoma
McNamara		Savannah-Atlanta, Georgia
McNay	Peter	New York, New York
McNelis	Francis A.	Altoona, Pennsylvania
McNulty	James M.	Paterson, New Jersey
McSorley. S.J.	Richard	Scranton and Georgetown University
Meagher	Arnold	
Mechoi	Thomas	Chicago, Illinois
Michael	Chester	Richmond, Virginia
Mies	Thomas	Detroit, Michigan
Millett	Gerald	Albany, New York
Miltner, C.S.C.	Charles	Portland, Oregon
Mock	F.G.	Beatrice, Michigan
Mohony	Archbishop Roger	Fresno, California
Mollory	Joseph	El Paso, Texas
Moody	Joseph	New York
Mooney	Robert	Providence, Rhode Island
Mravak, S.J.	Joseph	Fordham University, New York
Mulcaire, C.S.C.	Michael	Portland, Oregon
Murphy	Leon P.	San Antonio, Texas
Murphy, S.J.	Paul	Boston, Massachusetts
Murray, C.S.C	Raymond	Notre Dame, Indiana
Murtagh	Lawrence	San Antonio, Texas

Nugent, S.J.	Francis	
Nugent, O.P.		Chicago, Illinois
O'Brien, S.J.	Thomas	Portland, Oregon
O'Brien	Bishop Henry J.	Hanford, Connecticut
O' Connor	John J.	Albany, New York
O' Connor	Maurice	Chicago, Illinois
O'Connor	Maurice	Duluth, Minnesota
O'Connor	Neil	Saginaw, Michigan
O'Connor	Paul P.	Alaska
O'Keefe	Joseph	Cleveland, Ohio
O'Keele	Msgr. Joseph	Akron, Ohio
O'Leary	Bishop Thomas	
O'Neil	Augustine	
O'Neil	Emmett J.	Anaconda, Montana
O'Reilly	Arthur	Albany, New York
O'Rourke, S.J.	John,	San Francisco, California
O'Toole	Msgr. Barry	Pittsburgh, Pennsylvania
Oberle, C.S.S.R.	Joseph	
Olivarez	Luis, Claretian	
Oochesey	E.J.	St. Louis, Missouri
Orlemanski		Pittsburgh, Pennsylvania
Ostheriver	Anthony	Philadelphia, Pennsylvania
Palmer	Harold	Brooklyn, New York
Pascek, O.S.B.	Bonaventure	Latrobe, Pennsylvania
Pena, S.J.	Jose	San Francisco, California
Petro	Joseph	Chicago, Illinois
Powers	John	New York, New York
Quinn	Michael	Brooklyn, New York
Randall	John	
Reintjies, C.S.S.R.	William	New Orleans, Louisiana

Roach	John	
Rooney, C.P.	Gerard,	Union City, New Jersey
Rooney, S.J.	Joseph	Philadelphia, Pennsylvania
Sawkins	A.J.	Toledo, Ohio
Schaughnessy		Peoria, Illinois
Schnepp, S.M.	Brother Gerard	San Antonio, Texas
Sebastian, O.F.M.		Detroit, Michigan
Sharkey	George	Camden, New Jersey
Shea	Edmund J.	Butte, Montana
Shea	Edward J.	New Haven, Connecticut
Shealy, S.J.	Terence	New York
Shirber		
Shokely	George	Camden, New Jersey
Showley	John J.	Paterson, New Jersey
Silvius	C.P.	Des Moines, Iowa
Sirok, C.S.S.R.	Paul	
Smith	Joseph	Cleveland, Ohio
Sokolowski	Bronislaus	Chicago, Illinois
Splaine	Michael	Boston, Massachusetts
Stroh		
Sullivan	Maurice	New York, New York
Sysina	Anthony	
Thomas	S.A. Ralph	Peekskill
Thompson		Portland, Oregon
Torpey	Eugene	Canaan, Connecticut
Trese, S.J.	Thomas	Colombiere College
Vogel	Cyril J .	Pittsburgh, Pennsylvania
Vogt	George	Rochester. New York
Wallner, S.J.	Francis	Scranton University
Veig	Edmund	Davenport, IA

Wholei	Joseph	Chicago, Illinois
Wilken	Robert	Detroit. Michigan
Wilson, S.J.	George	Scranton University
Wolf		Detroit, Michigan
Woll, O.F.M. Cap.	Martinez	Crocon, Point, Illinois
Wolomsky	John	Wilkes-Barre, Pennsylvania
Yordon	Frank	Racine, Wisconsin
Zeiser, O.S.A.	R.	New York

BIBLIOGRAPHY

No author. 1962. *Catholic Weekly* (Kansas City, Mo.), November 17.

No author. 1974. "Rebel Priests Tell Why They Stay." *Milwaukee Herald Sentinel*, April 13.

No author. 1949. NCWC News Service, August.

No author. 1954. NCWC New Service, November 22.

No author. 1998. *Pittsburgh Gazette*, November 21.

No author. 2000. "Chicago's 'labor priest' gets top civilian award," *Catholic New World* (Chicago), August 20–September 2.

Abell, Aaron I. 1946. "Monsignor John A. Ryan: An Historical Appreciation," *The Review of Politics* 8 (1): 128-34.

Abell, Aaron I. 1963. *American Catholicism and Social Action: A Search for Social Justice, 1865-1950*. Notre Dame, Ind.: Notre Dame University Press.

Avella, Steven M. 1994. "Reynold Hillenbrand and Chicago Catholicism," in Ellen Skerrett, Edward R. Kantowicz and Steven M. Avella, eds. *Catholicism Chicago Style*. Chicago: Wild Onion Books.

Becnel, Thomas. 1980. *Labor, Church, and the Sugar Establishment, 1877–1976*. Baton Rouge: Louisiana State University Press.

Bergman, Gregory M. 1970. "Father Yorke: The Strike and the Pope," *Way*, 35–40.

Bergman, Gregory M. 1978. "Warrior Bold: Father Yorke of San Francisco," *Way* (November): 37–52.

Betten, Neil B. 1969. *Catholicism and the Industrial Workers during the Great Depression*. Ann Arbor: University of Michigan.

Blantz, Thomas E. 1982. *A Priest in Public Service: Francis J. Haas and the New Deal*. (Notre Dame Studies in American Catholicism). Notre Dame, Ind.: Notre Dame University Press.

Boyle, Edward F. 2000. "At Work in the Vineyard: The Jesuit Labor Apostolate," *In All Things: A Jesuit Journal of the Social Apostolate*, March.

Broderick, Francis. 1963. *Right Reverend New Dealer John A. Ryan*. New York, N.Y.: Macmillan.

Bronder, Saul E. 1982. *Social Justice and Church Authority: The Public Life of Archbishop Robert E. Lucey*. Philadephia: Temple University Press.

Brusher, Joseph S. 1971. *Consecrated Thunderbolt: Father Yorke of San Francisco*, Hawthorne, N.J.: Joseph F. Wagner.

Cerny, Karl. 1955. *Monsignor John A. Ryan and the Social Action Department: An Analysis of a Leading School of American Catholic Social Thought*. PhD diss., Yale University, Political Science. Ann Arbor, Mich.: University Microfilms.

Costello, Gerald M. 1980. "Profile of a Priest: George Higgins, One of a Kind," *America* 143 (12): 42–46. October 25.

Costello, Gerald M. 1984. *Without Fear or Favor*. Mystic, Conn.: Twenty-Third Publications.

Cronin, Bernard C. 1943. *Father Yorke and the Labor Movement in San Francisco, 1900–1910*. PhD diss., Catholic University of America.

Cronin, John. 1939. "Money: Master or Servant," *Sign*, April.

Curran, Charles E. 1982. *American Catholic Social Ethics: Twentieth-Century Approaches*. Notre Dame, Ind.: Notre Dame University Press.

Dolan, Jay, and Gilberto M. Hinojosa. 1994. *Mexican-Americans and the Catholic Church, 1900–1965*. Notre Dame, Ind.: Notre Dame University Press.

Donovan, John. 2000. *Crusader in the Cold War*. PhD diss., Marquette University.

Dunne, George. 1990. *King's Pawn: The Memoirs of George H. Dunne, S.J.* Chicago: Loyola University Press.

Editorial. 1962. *America* 107 (35): 1167. December 1.

Ellis, John Tracy. 1952. *The Life of James Cardinal Gibbons: Archbishop of Baltimore, 1834-1921*. Vol. 2. Milwaukee, Wisc.: Bruce Publishing Co.

Ellis, John Tracy. 1987. *Documents of American Catholic History*. Vol. 2. Wilmington, Del.: Michael Glazier.

Feister, John. 1955. "Msgr. Charles O. Rice," *St. Anthony Messenger*, September 23–27.

Fisher, James. 1999. "Covering the Waterfront Culture and Ideology in the Catholic Metropolis, 1936–1960. A Preliminary Paper." In Corridan File, New York Jesuit Province Archives.

Fitzgerald, Mark J., 1954. "Catholic Labor Schools in the United States," an unpublished paper delivered on April 12, 1954, to the Monthly Conference of Holy Cross Priests, at Notre Dame, Ind., University of Notre Dame Archives.

Fox, Harrita. 1953. *Peter E. Dietz: Labor Priest*, Notre Dame, Ind.: Notre Dame University Press.

Frisbie, Margerie. 1991. *An Alley in Chicago: The Life and Legacy of Monsignor John Egan*. Kansas City, Mo.: Sheed and Ward.

Gearty, Patrick. 1953. *The Economic Thought of Monsignor John A. Ryan*. Washington, D.C.: Catholic University Press.

Gribble, Richard. 1993. *Catholicism and the San Francisco Labor, 1896–1921*. Edwin Mellen Press.

Harrington, Michael. 1960. "Catholics in the Labor Movement: A Case Study," in *Labor History* 1 (3): 231–63.

Heineman, Kenneth J. 1994. "A Catholic New Deal: Religion and Labor in the 1930s Pittsburgh," *Pennsylvania Magazine of History and Biography* 118 (4): 364–94.

Higgins, George G. 1981. Book review of Douglas P. Seaton, *Catholics and Radicals: The Association of Catholic Trade Unionists and the American Labor Movement from Depression to Cold War*. Lewisburg, Penn.: Bucknell University Press.

Higgins, George G. 1979. Born Again Coalition? *Commonweal* (June 22): 356–57.

Ignatius, Br. Eugene, F.S.C., and Br. Erminus Joseph, F.S.C. Date unknown. *Good Soul: A Biography of Brother Elzear Alfred, F.S.C, LL.D*. Philadelphia: La Salle University.

Jones, Arthur. 1978. "NCCB-USCC Retires Higgins," *National Catholic Reporter* 15 (1): 1 ff.

Kelly, George A. 1948. "The ACTU and Its Critics," *Commonweal* 49 (December): 298–302.

Kelly, George A. 1989. *Inside My Father's House.* New York: Doubleday.

Lynch, Thomas A. 1997. "Father John P. Monaghan," in Michael Glazier and Thomas J. Shelley, eds. *Encyclopedia of American Catholic History.* Wilmington, Del.: Michael Glazier.

Lyons, Mary E. 1987. "Peter C. Yorke: Advocate of the Irish from the Pulpit to the Podium," in Carl Guarneri and David Alvarez, eds. *Religion and Society in the American West.* New York: University Press of America.

McCarthy, John R. 2003. "Corridan's Corner: New York's Waterfront and Fr. John Corrridan, S.J.," *Dunwoodie Review* 26.

McDonnell, Claudia. 2003. "Priests on the Docks," *Catholic New York,* September.

McKeever, Patrick J. 1994. *Rev. Charles Owen Rice: Apostle of Contradiction.* Pittsburgh: Duquesne University Press.

McKenna, Norman. 1949. "The Story of ACTU," *The Catholic World* 118 (March): 453–45.

McNaspy, C. 1978. *At Face Value.* New Orleans: New Orleans Institute of Human Relations at Loyola University of the South.

Miller, John H., ed. 1966. *Vatican II: Interfaith Appraisal.* Notre Dame, Ind.: Notre Dame University, Press.

O'Brien, David J. 1965. *American Catholic Social Thought in the 1930's.* PhD diss., University of Rochester. Ann Arbor, Mich.: University Microfilms.

Payne, John R. 1976. *A Jesuit Search for Social Justice: The public career of Louis J. Twomey, S.J., 1947-1969.* Austin: University of Texas at Austin.

Poluse, Martin. 1991. *Archbishop Joseph Schrembs and the Twentieth-Century Church in Cleveland: 1921–1945.* Kent State, Ohio: Ohio University Press.

Riesel, Victor, and Aaron Levenstein. 1949. *New York Times,* January.

Ryan, John A. 1941. *Social Doctrine in Action: A Personal History.* New York: Harper.

Sarbaugh, Timothy J. 1981. "Father Yorke and the San Francisco Waterfront, 1901-1919," *Pacific Historian* 25 (Fall).

Seaton, Douglas. 1975. *The Catholic Church and the Congress of Industrial Organizations: The Case of the Association of Catholic Trade Unionists, 1937–1950.* PhD diss. Rutgers University.

Smith, Sherrill. 1966. "Speck of Hope," *Labor Reporter*, November 28.

Smith, William. 1944. "A Degree in Industrial Relations," *Jesuit Educational Quarterly*, January.

Sorvillo, Mark B. 1990. *Bishop Bernard J. Sheil: Hero for the Catholic Left.* PhD diss., University of Chicago.

Steinfels, Peter. 2003. "Beliefs," *New York Times*, May 3.

Stocker, Joseph. 1951. "Father Dunne: A Study in Faith," *Nation* (September 22): 236-39.

Taft, Philip. 1949. "The Association of Catholic Trade Unionists," *Industrial and Labor Relations Review* 2 (2): 210–18.

Tentler, Leslie, W. 1990. *Seasons of Grace: A History of the Catholic Archdiocese of Detroit.* Detroit: Wayne State University Press.

Walsh, James P. 1973. "Father Peter Yorke of San Francisco: From Politics and the Church to Education and Intellectual Life: an Irish-American Travail," *Studies*, Spring. Dublin, Ireland.

Walsh, James P. 1975. "Peter Yorke and Progressivism in California in 1908," *Eire* 10, 73–81. Dublin, Ireland.

Ward, Richard. 1958. *The Role of the Association of Catholic Trade Unionists in the American Labor Movement.* PhD diss., University of Michigan. Ann Arbor.: University of Michigan.

Wilkes, Paul. Date unknown. *Fire in the Heart: Reflections by Father Frank Eschweiler.* Milwaukee: Hi-Publishing Corp.

Wilkes, Paul. 1973. *These Priests Stay.* New York: Simon and Schuster.

OTHER BOOKS FROM PACEM IN TERRIS PRESS

Toward a Regenerative Postmodern World Church and
a Regenerative Postmodern Global Civilization

REMEMBERING THE PROPHETIC VISION OF ST. JOHN XXIII
Radical Traditional Founder of Postmodern Global Catholic Social Teaching
Joe Holland, Forthcoming in 2014

CATHOLIC SOCIAL TEACHING & UNIONS
IN CATHOLIC PRIMARY & SECONDARY SCHOOLS
The Clash between Theory & Practice within the United States
Walter "Bob" Baker, 2014

SPIRITUAL PATHS TO A GLOBAL & ECOLOGICAL CIVILIZATION
Reading the Signs of the Times with Buddhists, Christians, & Muslims
John Raymaker & Gerald Grudzen, with Joe Holland, 2013

PACEM IN TERRIS
Its Continuing Relevance for the Twenty-First Century
Josef Klee & Francis Dubois, Editors, 2013

PACEM IN TERRIS
Summary & Commentary for the Famous Encyclical Letter
of Pope John XXIII on World Peace
Joe Holland, 2012

100 YEARS OF CATHOLIC SOCIAL TEACHING
DEFENDING WORKERS & THEIR UNIONS
Summaries & Commentaries for Five Landmark Papal Encyclicals
Joe Holland, 2012

HUMANITY'S AFRICAN ROOTS
Remembering the Ancestors' Wisdom
Joe Holland, 2012

THE "POISONED SPRING" OF ECONOMIC LIBERTARIANISM
Menger, Mises, Hayek, Rothbard: A Critique from
Catholic Social Teaching of the Austrian School of Economics
Angus Sibley, 2011